The Art of Divinity

THE ART OF DIVINITY

Finding Beauty Within and Without

TEACHINGS OF THE MASTER PAUL THE VENETIAN

VOLUME TWO

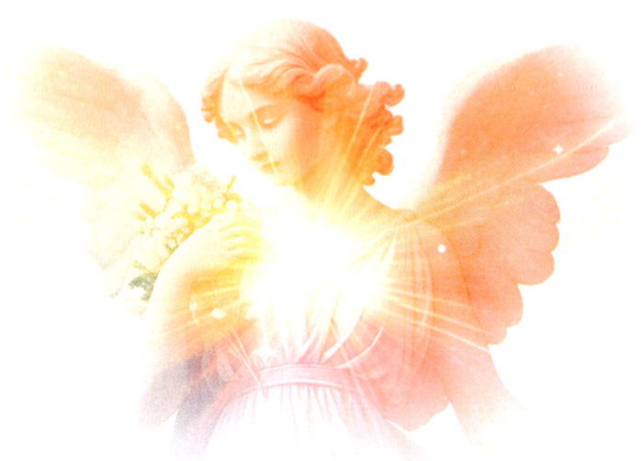

MARK L. PROPHET
ELIZABETH CLARE PROPHET

SUMMIT UNIVERSITY PRESS®
Gardiner, Montana

THE ART OF DIVINITY Volume 2
Finding Beauty Within and Without
Teachings of the Master Paul the Venetian
by Mark L. Prophet and Elizabeth Clare Prophet

For information, contact The Summit Lighthouse,
63 Summit Way, Gardiner, MT 59030 USA
Tel: 1-800-245-5445 or 1 406-848-9500
info@SummitUniversityPress.com
SummitLighthouse.org

Library of Congress Control Number: 2026930493
ISBN: 978-1-60988-455-0 (softbound)
ISBN: 978-1-60988-456-7 (eBook)

SUMMIT UNIVERSITY PRESS®

29 28 27 26 1 2 3 4

Contents

Foreword

The soul coaching offered by the living master Paul the Venetian in these two volumes is an ongoing encouragement from heaven. It is also possible that through your attention on the master's words, your communion with him between his words, and the time your soul may spend with him in his etheric retreat, you have gained an increase in the faculty of soul sensitivity. That soul sensitivity can discern the difference between art that is without the light of God and art that contains God's Spirit—the art of Divinity.

Changes in media technology now bring additional issues into focus. Art that is the art of Divinity has an aura of light and emerges from a person who is a soul of light—a soul who has the light of God within. Through the gift of discernment, which is a quality of the third ray, we have an intrinsic ability to sense the presence or absence of light in a work of art or any other manifestation. AI, or artificial intelligence, is an array of mechanical processes that bypass the inner flame of life, attempting to substitute divine creativity with a mechanized shortcut. In these two volumes, Paul the Venetian imparts to us his teachings on the sacred flame of life within our heart, the threefold flame that is intended to infuse all that we do and create.

From the ascended level, Paul the Venetian is aware of the widespread use of artificial generation in all forms of media. The uses and misuses of machine art offer you an opportunity to expand your discernment of what is pleasing to the eye of God and what is not. Just as Jesus the Christ is a living ascended master and has infinitely expanded his identity in the mind of God over the last two thousand years, so Paul the Venetian has also expanded his awareness of the eternal beauty and holiness of God's creation in us and in nature since his ascension. Therefore there is so much more that we too can learn and become.

As you continue your journey with Paul the Venetian through this second volume of his teachings, you might ask him for increased increments of the nine gifts of the Holy Spirit, including the gift of the discernment of spirits.[1] It is important not to be passive or vulnerable to the numerous distortions of artificial art in all of its forms found online. If you ask for God's protection and discernment, your awareness can rise above it and see through it. In the grace of the master's presence and protection there is a peace that passes understanding, which can lift us from a worldly awareness to an inner, sacred awareness.

In his final physical embodiment as Paolo Veronese, the soul of Paul the Venetian claimed his right to discern the emerging Christ Presence of his characters in his artwork and to depict them with great mastery and courage. Clerical officials of the Inquisition disputed that right and insisted on an artificiality tied to their assumed control of the public through their rules for the art of the day, but Paolo successfully defended his right to Christ-discernment and outsmarted their heartless limitations.

Now it is your turn to study Paolo's example of discernment, of what is true to God and uplifting to the soul. It is an opportunity to ask for God's assistance daily and to patiently observe your own efforts in the improvements of your fine art. These improvements can spontaneously appear over time, whether it be in painting, photography, poetry, music, videography, or in any area of your service to life. As you devote your art to the love of God in humanity, a serendipity may occur under the master's unseen tutelage, namely the incremental emergence of the Christ in you as you express it to others through your creative gifts, which are limitless!

The Editors

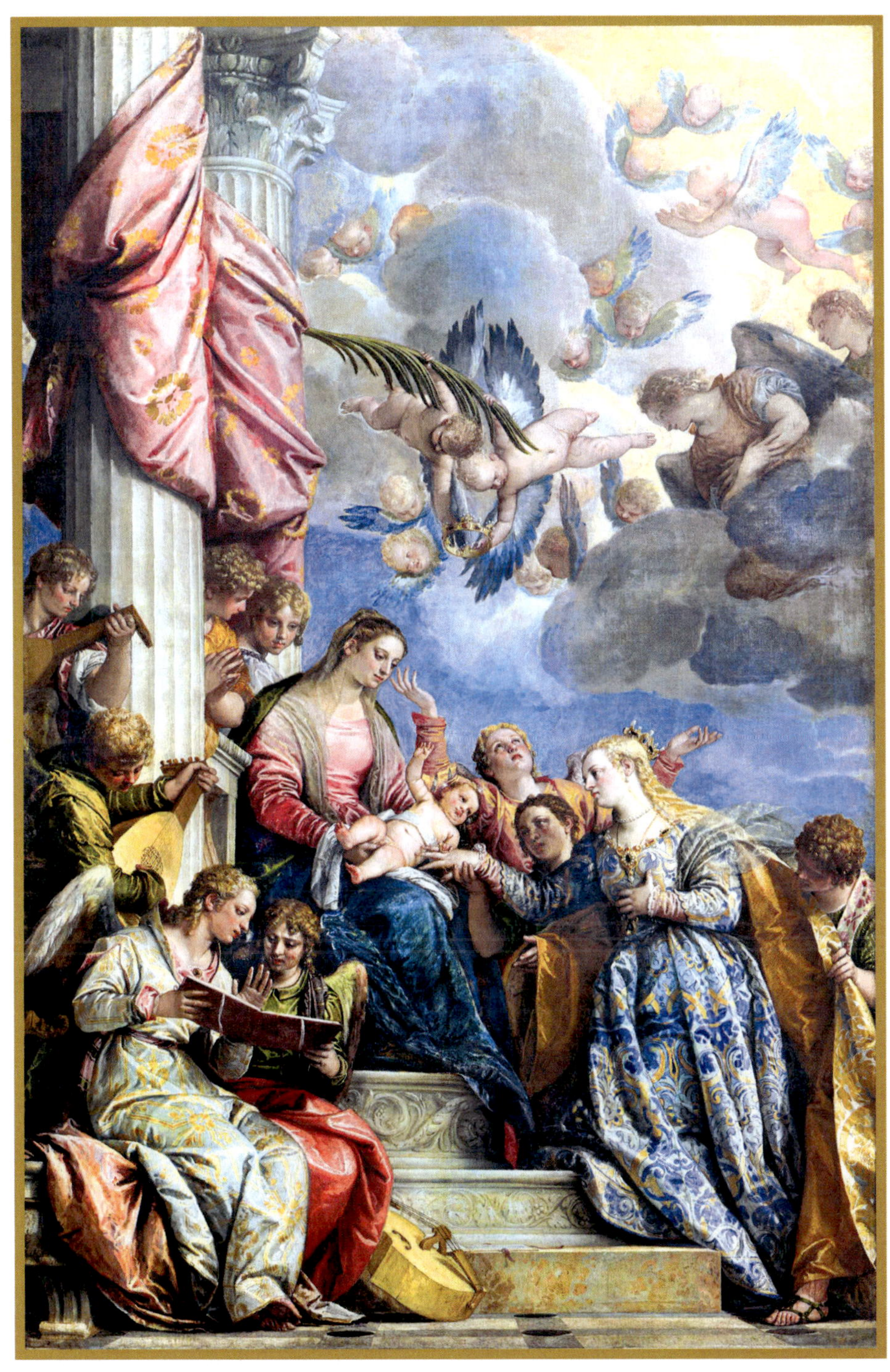

Mystic Marriage of Saint Catherine, c. 1565–70

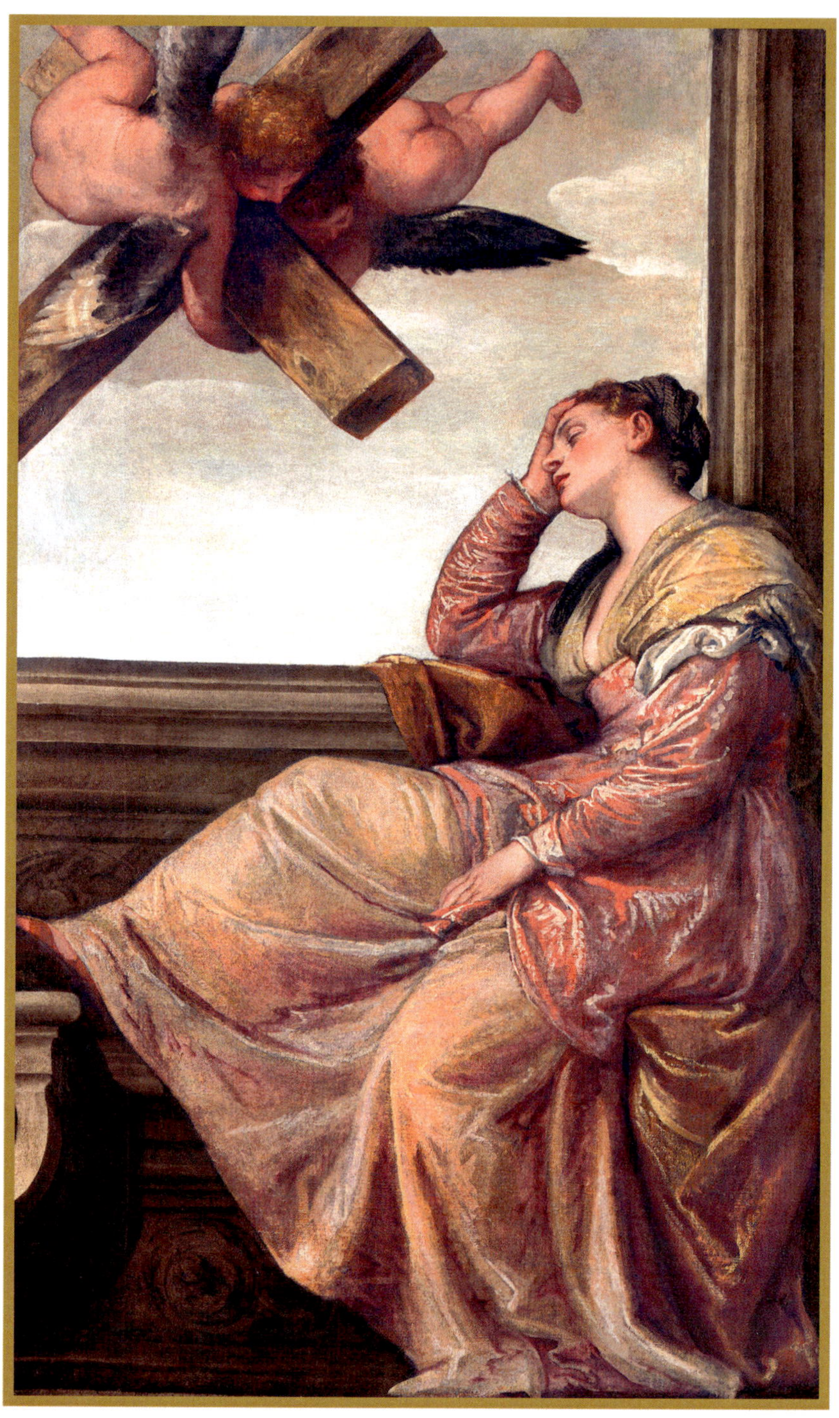

The Dream of Saint Helena, c. 1570

You are intended to create beautifully and wonderfully. Co-creators with God, you chisel line by line your spiritual form from the marvelous cosmic ideas that the Father released in the Beginning.

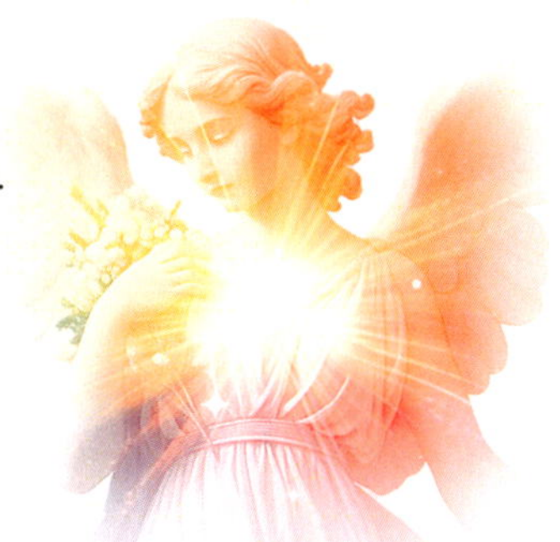

CHAPTER 1

The Art of Loving God Is in the Art of Loving Man

Most gracious ladies and gentlemen, as I come to you tonight it is with the express desire to speak on the gathering of reality. For as Saint Paul said long ago, "We know in part, and we prophesy in part. But when that which is perfect is come, then that which is in part shall be done away."[1]

Perhaps some have misunderstood the high sense of reality in that statement. For it is not a doing away of the parts, but it is a *uniting* of the parts into the shape of reality, which in the consciousness of individual men brings them to a fervent awareness of themselves.

And so as we seek to gather for ourselves the meaning of reality, we also seek, in the consciousness and domain of each individual, to convey those suggestions that will help you to gather for yourselves the wondrous realities of God. These realities will delight the heart and shed a sense of beauty into the domain of the personal self, which seems, then, to open as a flower, to drink in the light of the sun céleste.* It is our desire to foster in you all a sense of reality, which belongs to you.

I remember so dearly the day when I first developed enough of the divine sense to feel that God and I were one. It had been a cloudy morning, and I had worked long and hard to try to portray the face

***céleste:* French, "celestial"

of an angel. But somehow it was as though the celestial beauty escaped me, and there was a jangle in my nerves and senses and feelings.

This was strange, because I had for some time developed a feeling of serenity, of calmness, of knowing. And now here I was, outside of that calmness and serenity and knowing, desiring to portray a celestial being. I needed to drink deeply of the fountain of peace.

For some reason, which did not seem to break through to my outer senses, I could not still my mind. And so with some measure of disturbance, shall I say, I closed up shop. I put away my brushes, and frankly there was sadness in my every movement. It was not a state of utter discouragement, but it was just an unusual state of unrest in my feeling world, almost a dire foreboding that something undesirable would happen.

I left the studio and walked out into the street, and it seemed to me as though every thought of my heart was known by all whom I met. Certainly my glances must have appeared furtive, as though I were a criminal seeking to hide from the eyes of prying mankind.

This drove me almost to a state of desperation, and I wandered away from the busy thoroughfare of the streets of the city seeking the reasonable quietude of the countryside. As I reached the edge of a field near an old churchyard, it seemed as though the feeling of oppression began to lessen. The clouds were now thinning a bit, and a gentle breeze was blowing.

In the stillness of the approaching countryside I began to feel the awakening of the sense of peace, so familiar and so dearly loved. As I wandered farther and farther into the fields and forest regions, I began to ponder as to whether or not the oppressions of the city could be responsible for my condition. And then I reasoned, quite suddenly, that I ought to be strong enough to hold a sense of beauty in the midst of the ugliness and garrets of the city. I decided that this was not it either, yet I enjoyed my now newfound serenity and felt that if perhaps I could quiet the possibility of the return of my state of unrest, I would be able to go back once more to the room and create the angelic face.

But this was not to happen. For I heard a terrible sound of sobbing, and for a moment my heart trembled for mankind. This sobbing came from a graveside where a young lady, prone now upon the ground, cried as though her heart would break. I debated with myself as to whether or not it would be proper for me to speak, being a stranger unto her, and to say unto her, "Dry your tears, daughter, and be of peace." But somehow I could not for a moment seize the courage, and this too was unusual.

I then decided that I would enter into simple prayer for her. And as I prayed, the sun came out with greater glory and it was as though the hands of the angels were drawing back the curtain of dark clouds. With this change in the environment of the little cemetery, the young lady suddenly ceased to sob and gazed up with wonder. Her sorrow and her grief were plainly stamped upon one of the most beautiful faces I had ever seen. And there was my angel—the face that I sought.

Poignantly now, I re-create this moment. But I knew that I must paint out that grief, and therefore I must seek somehow to bring a ray of hope, some measure of consolation to her heart.

Hesitantly at first, I broke a smile upon my face, and she returned it. And I said to her, as I tenderly took ahold of an apple blossom from a nearby tree, "Daughter, there is a resurrection in nature, and all things do pass and go through their cycles, only to return once again to the fullness and the dawn of bloom. In the resurrection, your father dear shall return to you." Sobbingly she said, "I know it, kind sir. I know it. But I am so lonely now."

I took her by the hand, and as I prayed I felt a surge of the Christ radiance go through me. I watched as every line of her face reflected consolation, mercy, and acceptance of the resurrection spirit. And then I noted that through my arms and hands there was a great pulsing energy, and I felt my heart beat with greater expectation. Truly, the Whole-I-Spirit* was activated.

Truly God Is Veiled in Flesh

The young woman suddenly burst into a smile of greater happiness and she said, "Oh, I do not feel lonely anymore. I will go home now

---

* *Whole-I-Spirit:* the Holy Spirit, the wholeness of the Spirit of the I AM manifestation

to my mother, who has been distraught with my grief, and I will no longer mourn. For I feel something within myself, something that encourages me to believe you. I do not know why. Your words have meaning to me, and I am no longer sad."

And as the sun came out in greater measure, blooming full-orbed, I witnessed the transformation that was a miracle never to be forgotten throughout all the days of my life until I won my ascension. The face of an angel shone now in all of the glory and magnitude of God and I said, "Truly God is veiled in flesh." I returned and painted my angel.

You are all the children of his heart, and the majesty of his perfection is with you always. There are times when the emotional body of man is disturbed by outer conditions, and in the misfortune of torment the soul knows unrest. It is very helpful for individuals to understand that this too shall pass, as has been said.[2]

If individuals will understand that life is a flow of experience—that experience is controllable within the framework of some limitation but that some experience is, by reason of karma, uncontrollable for the moment—then they will understand that the flow of experience must be lived with and accepted.

Recent Student Unrest

At the current time I have been in consultation with the Master of Paris.[3] Your beloved El Morya has also been in consultation with me.

The recent student unrest that so tore up the beauty of the land of France is most unfortunate.[4] For while there is a great spirit of liberty here, the spirit of liberty is all over the world. Even in countries dominated by Communism, where freedom is practically nonexistent, there is still a flame of liberty. This flame of liberty is in the hearts of the people. But they have now, quite sadly, lost everything. For them there is no possibility of true freedom and its expression. They must function within the limitations that a dominant society and a dominated society has imposed upon them.

There is at the present hour, as you know, a coming forth into outer admission the statement by the Communists of the world that "we are behind the student revolts."[5] We have long known of the factors governing world unrest. We have spoken often to mankind about it, and we have desired that they do something to protect their interests. But, as the scriptures record so beautifully and delicately, "They were eating and drinking, marrying and giving in marriage, until the day that Noah entered into the ark."[6] "As it was in the days of Noah, so shall it also be in the days of the coming of the Son of man."[7]

Let the children of the Sun understand, then, that with all the perfection and beauty of God that is everywhere surrounding mankind, there is still a famine in the land and spiritual feasts are often ignored.

How many hungry hearts would desire tonight to sit at our feet as we bring forth to you our feeling of true symmetrical beauty, which stems from man's cognition of the words of Christ, "I am the true vine, and my Father is the husbandman."[8]

Your Consciousness Creates Its Own Matrices, Its Own Shapes of Things to Come

You are the husbandman. *You* are intended to create beautifully and wonderfully. Co-creators with God, you chisel line by line your spiritual form from the marvelous cosmic ideas that the Father released in the Beginning with the first thought of man's reality: "Let us make man in our image and after our likeness. . . . So God created man in his own image, in the image of God created he him; male and female created he them."[9]

And so it came to pass that this was done. Yet because of the vastness of cosmos and the myriad manifestations of life-forms—the coming into manifestation of spiral nebulae and the birth and death of worlds and systems—there are coincidental manifestations, and time and space are great barriers to mortal men who are encased in the mold of human clay.

But this clay was fired in the kilns of heaven. The breath of the Holy Spirit fashioned even the physical form of man. The life dimensions over which men are given dominion are the dimensions of their consciousness, and consciousness is the treasure house that must be guarded and loved. Your consciousness creates its own matrices, its own shapes of things to come. Therefore the words "As a man thinketh in his heart, so is he"[10] cannot be outdone as an expression of universal law.

In coming to you tonight and alerting you to the need to preserve the sense of infinite beauty, I am persuaded that the time is short for the mankind of earth unless there be a great awakening. And if it shall come to pass that men fail throughout the world to understand that they can live not in sadness, not in joy, but only in a mixture of sadness and joy, then it will be a great pity.

For man is not intended to have the consciousness of a yo-yo, to be pulled first up and then down. He is intended to preserve the consciousness of the Divine Image, which can never be unhappy, can never be discontented, can never be disturbed for long but can only suffer momentary excursions into the negative realm.

The negative realm is like a thorn. The negative realm is like thistles. The negative realm is one from which you would naturally recoil. But some have a morbid fascination for horror and destruction, for death. We are men of spiritual principle and we desire to see to it that you will, as men and women of the Divine One, also hold to the perfection of the Presence.

Therefore, I wish to say to you tonight that Master Morya and the Master of Paris have counseled that now that the Communists of the world have come out and openly admitted the situation concerning the youth of the world, it should indicate to the perceptive among you that they are confident of their strength.

It Is a Time to Preserve the Divine Sense as Never Before

There is now no time for dalliance, no time for indulgence in personal foibles and identifications, but it is a time to preserve the divine sense as never before. It is not enough to preserve it for yourself alone. There must be an invocation and an evocation of the perceptions of perfection among mankind.

Hope is not enough; faith must be evoked. Faith is not enough; action in manifestation must be evoked. And therefore, as I gaze upon the calendar of the future and I see the frame that men have put around the picture of life as it will be in a decade and another decade and yet another, I, being an artist with a soul and immortality, cringe from what I see, and I pray and say, "O God, be merciful."

Your Blessed Virgin, Mother Mary, prays with me. For the state of the world is most horrendous, with a quivering of destruction, and fear is in many hearts. We do not wish to amplify it, but we must alert the students of the light that the time is indeed, in all verity, short.

Your beloved messenger, who stands before you, has little idea himself as to the solemnity with which I am speaking these words. It is as much a surprise to him that I am saying this as it is to some of you. But strange as it may seem, I was chosen tonight and for this conference to sound out the note of warning. And I said, "What? I am chosen?" And the Lord Maha Chohan said to me, "By the power of the Holy Spirit, beloved Paul, I say to you that you are chosen. You, the gentle soul of the artist, must make men think. You have the power to mold thought and feeling. Paul, go forth and do it."

Now, you know, blessed ones, that when the Maha Chohan speaks, one does not refuse.

Have you ever gazed upon the eyes of the Lord Maha Chohan? Even in heaven, in our ascended state, I once said to him, "I would like once again to take in my hand an earthly brush and palette and to paint the beauty of your face." And do you know, precious ones, that the Lord Maha Chohan never answered me? He gave me a look that almost froze me in my tracks, and I never mentioned it again.

I hope you will understand that even at our level there is a preserved remnant of the personality. We are not a bunch of china dolls, painted faces, radiant light-forms that have no preservation of our identities whatsoever. We are yet embryonic gods in the becoming. For the transcendent outreach of the Divine is a magnificent hierarchical plan, bringing men, at different seasons and different times of their life, to fulfillment. And oh, how sweet it is.

How sweet it is, and what a thing of worth it is when individuals, who have long labored and striven for a certain development within their soul, are able to see at last that they have bridged the gap of temptation and that that temptation cannot move them to perform that which they do not really want to do but which they do anyway.[11]

What a wonderful thing it is when an individual can learn to steel himself from the judgments of men, when he is not affected by mortal opinions and mortal ideas, when he is able to decide his own course (as the ancient mariner and the Ancient of Days), when he is able to realize that to him is given the power of faith and vision and the execution of that vision and he realizes that his soul is like unto God, his job being to make it so.

Therefore, precious ones of the light, throughout this class I urge you to understand that the firecrackers of our words and ideas, the vital essences that we release, are themselves effective in the moment of their release and are to a certain degree according to your perceptions and acceptance. But the real role of our dictations in your affairs is to hold a permanent focus within your heart for the light.

The Image of the Crèche

It is an old image, but one highly loved by Saint Francis of Assisi, your beloved Kuthumi—the image of the crèche. I have often thought that this crèche, woven of beautiful wood, was intended to hold the Christ form, and I have regretted that so many have adorned the crèche with a crown of thorns. From the very beginning those who have done so have somehow sensed the misery that shall be theirs, and this draws to them misery.

I urge, therefore, that this practice be abandoned, that the heart be considered as the crèche of the Christ, that the miniature place where the Lord lay be prepared for him, not as a place of the skull or a time of suffering to come but as a time of joy, beauty, wholesomeness, relaxation, understanding, and as a flow of the golden shuttle of the Most High God's thoughts.

The cosmic looms weave, and there is a majesty in the rapidity of the ingoing and outgoing of the shuttle. The thread unwinds and the span of life is lengthened and strengthened, and courage and fiber and majesty and dominion and beauty and eternal love are woven into the immortal picture.

The Passion of God, Creating Man in His Own Image

You were created *in* the foreverness of God, *for* the foreverness of God, and *by* the foreverness of God. If this be so, then all that you create must endure for aye. And if all that you create must endure for aye but you create evilly,* then this would also endure for aye—but nay, it is not so. For that which does not hold the divine majesty is a leaky sieve, and fortunately the waters of Life slip, then, through the sieve and descend into the eternal stream, once again to be used as formative essence.

Let all understand the passion of God, who, creating man in his own image, said that if the children of men, whom I have endowed with my own image, will not build me a house suitable for that image to dwell in,[12] then I will give them time and space and opportunity. And behold, darkness will come upon them and they shall experience a mingling of darkness and light until the day when the last enemy shall be overcome and I shall wipe away all tears from their eyes.[13] The eternal beauty of my realm shall be their enduring mind state. For the mind state of men is their consciousness, and as a man thinks, he becomes.

Will you, then, regard your days as days of service and nights of love and rest?

Will you, then, understand that the peace of the Presence wants to keep you blessed?

Will you understand that the art of loving God is to be learned in the art of loving man?

Will you understand that there are some things that manifest and are in the world of form that you cannot love, that you must not hate, but that you must shun?

Will you learn the art of dividing the Word rightly and truly?

For the Word is God.

I thank you.

July 5, 1968

**evilly:* adverb, archaic

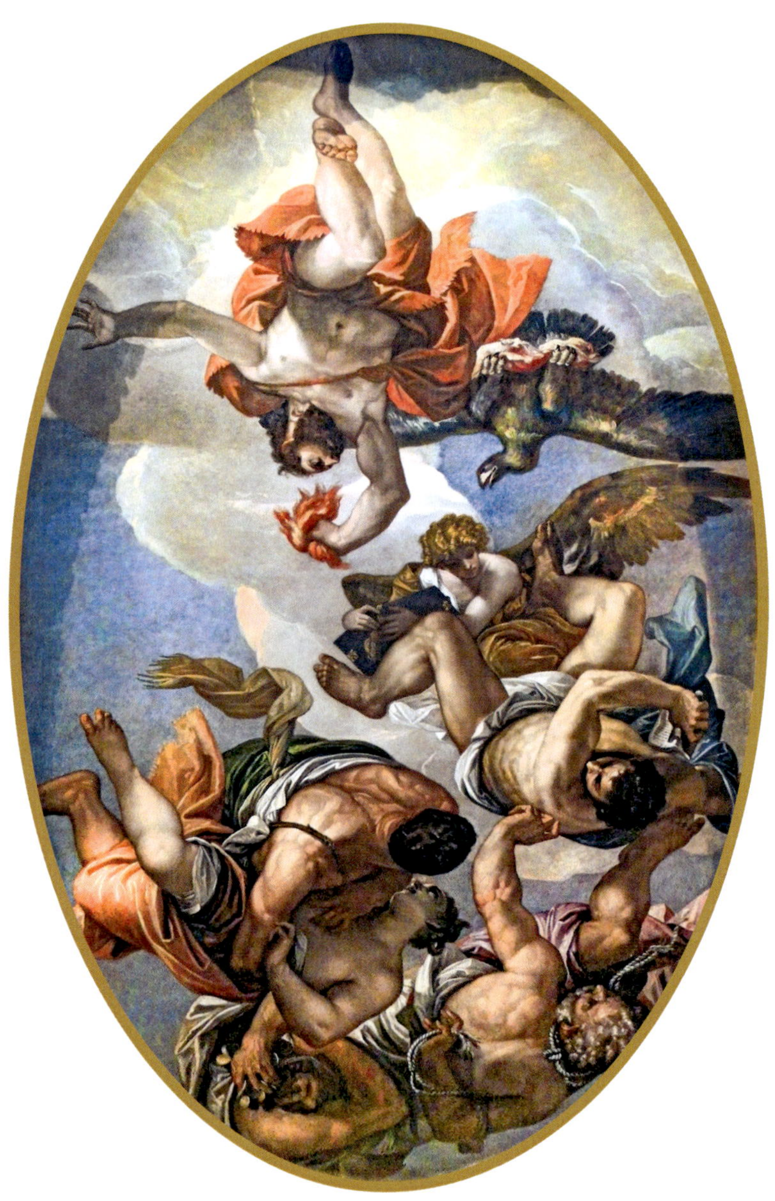

Jupiter Hurling Thunderbolts at the Vices, c. 1554–56

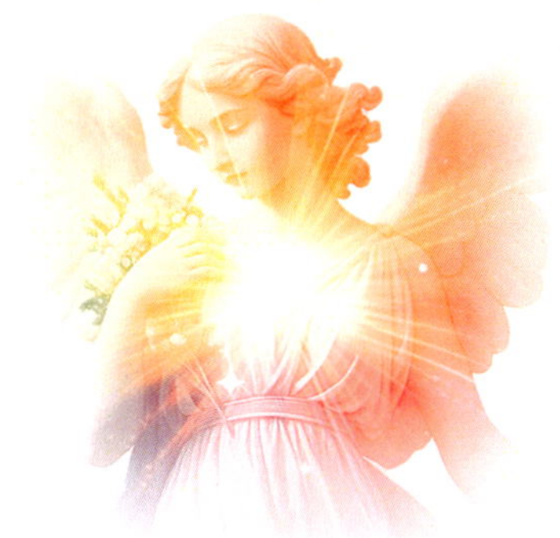

Remember the all-power of Divinity to expand within your consciousness and to increase, heartbeat by heartbeat, the realization of your Christ-potential through the sense of beauty.

CHAPTER 2

The Dangers of Astral Allurement

To Those Who Would Be Pure in Heart,

A sense of beauty assists the soul in relating to the Divinity that originally created all substance and form. Man must learn to separate the Darkness from the Light and to eliminate the abortions in nature that occur because of mankind's dual consciousness and their failure to maintain contact with the Divine Presence.

Pain in the world order is unnatural. It is a manifestation of inharmony within mankind's four-dimensional consciousness. When the error is corrected—the error of an ugly arrangement of the thought and feeling patterns of the race—the beauty and perfection of the Presence begin to shine forth in nature as well as in man.

Oh yes, we realize full well the difficulty mankind experience in holding fast to patterns of perfection in the midst of a synthetic environment, where images of imperfection are constantly being projected upon the screen of the mind.

Remember, hearts of light, it is the darkness that is without that so many gaze upon—the darkness of imperfection, which the multitudes do not distinguish from the deep and beautiful light of the abiding presence of perfection within the being of man. This is the light of the eternal Christos to which all must hold if they value their liberty, regardless of appearances that would defile and dethrone the perfect image.

As the rearrangement of concepts and precepts occurs within the mind and heart according to the laws of perfection, mankind are able to eliminate much pain and anguish, both mental and physical, from their lives.

Men and women should understand how to cope with the energies of the electronic belt—the individual as well as the collective subconscious. They should realize that not only their own thoughts and feelings but also the sum total of the thoughts and feelings of the world body, which may be termed the *weltschmerz,* have a direct bearing upon their actions and attitudes.

The key to that order and beauty, which are not universally enshrined in the world, then, is to be found in the perpetual joy of returning to the miracle of the divine image that God holds for every manifestation of himself. For if it is the sense of struggle that makes the struggle, as Saint Germain so often says, then it is the casting aside of undesirable thoughts and feelings and the cleaving to beautiful images and ideas that affect the magnificent transformation that all mankind require.

Guarding the Quality of Consciousness

It is necessary in this connection that I give a solemn warning to the students concerning the dangers of astral allurement. I refer to the magnetism of those states of consciousness that are below the level of the Christ mind and therefore engage the energies below the heart and involve man's perceptions in psychic distortions. Many spiritual seekers are detoured from the Path by the glamour of strange phenomena and the probing of that plane of consciousness just beyond the physical, known as the astral realm.

One of the great attractions in the use of hallucinogenic drugs is that they facilitate contact with the astral plane and induce those abnormal experiences in the world of sense thralldom that enamor the mind. Such diversions into euphoria, which are simulated through drugs (although endless in variation), are not necessarily divine, simply because they originate beyond the realm of physical manifestation. Usually they are psychic in nature—that is, they come from the level of the emotions and their mass misqualification by mankind. Thus these turbulent energies, with their moving kaleidoscope of aberrations, key a frequency response that is closer to the vibration of demons than to that of angels.

It would be well for the aspiring student to realize the great value of keeping watch upon his thoughts and feelings, for thereby he learns the requirements of self-mastery and how to prevent much that is unwholesome and troublesome from later springing up in his world.

By guarding the quality of his consciousness and becoming the master of his household, the individual has no need for drugs to elevate the mind and feelings. Instead he learns to contact the Christ directly on all planes, hence to develop a standard whereby he is able to anticipate, in an a priori manner, those cultural trends that are foreign to the divine ideal.

He also learns to employ the preventative cure of entertaining beneficent concepts and at the same time to avoid psychological pitfalls that might one day prevent the fulfillment of his highest aspirations. When the student leaves behind the baubles and trinkets of the astral, he soon discovers the beautiful miracle of lovely, Godlike thoughtforms waiting to be lowered from the highest planes into the world of form.

Although there are times when man's concepts of God fall far short of the mark, manifesting as they do in the realm of time and space and in the unperfected consciousness, they can and frequently do become the magnet that guides man up the stairway of attainment into the perception and precipitation of genuine beauty.

The Lord's Intent as the Goal of Life for Every Man

Life as it is currently being lived upon earth is full of masks and deceits, but this need not continue. After all, beloved ones, what you really are is what endures. If you make yourself into a receiving station for the beauty that God is sending forth every day into the world, you become spiritually coordinated with hierarchy, with the angelic hosts, and with the Brotherhood of light. If you do not avail yourselves of the opportunity to become outposts for the beauty of the divine image, well, then, O hearts of light, you have no one to blame but yourself for your failure to be the beautiful God of your own universe that the living God wants you to be![1]

You see, it was God's intent, when he created man in his own image and likeness,[2] that this image and likeness of himself should manifest everywhere upon the planetary body. Without a doubt, the average person—who has not the understanding of truth, blinded to his spiritual opportunity by self-concerns—may find even his worldly aspirations swallowed up by his environment. And we have seen cases where ten thousand years of progress have been buried beneath a lump of clay simply because the individual could not surmount a host of environmental problems that stifled both his talent and his initiative. Nevertheless, the LORD's intent remains as the goal of life for every man.

Let us clear the way, then, for all who would run with the LORD! Let us clear the way for an expansion of individual identity within the Godhead!

The Allure and Vibrancy of Genuine Living

Blessed ones, the concentric rings of the causal body are a marvel to behold. The soft shadings of pastel hue delicately outlining the rainbow rays of God are charged with the allure and vibrancy of genuine living. Truly, the light of the Christ is a fountain of electronic energy, cascading with expansion and the fire of movement. And this, in all of its wonder and opportunity, God showers upon man as the prize for his victorious overcoming in the world of form and for his abandonment of astral decoys bobbing upon the murky waters of the psychic underworld.

The need for the reeducation of man's vision so that he might perceive beauty, and then honor and adore it for its affinitizing power, is very great in an age when all that is sacred is being torn down by the forces of Antichrist. The examinations by the Lords of Karma and the hierarchy (which men frequently undergo although they know it not) are but an attempt by the spiritual preceptors of the planet to raise the spiritual standard of the race. They would kindle in all people that newness of life and appreciation of beauty and truth that will lead them from Darkness unto Light, from shadow and shame to order and perfection. For they know that once mankind see the light, their souls will no longer be satisfied with any lesser manifestation.[3]

The comedies and tragedies of the past, with their residue of opaquing substance, the maya of maudlin memories, will continue to oppress the seeker on the Path. But once the man of God realizes within himself that he can be free because he is freeborn, he need no longer be bound—*he is no longer bound.*

The Realization of Your Christ-Potential through the Sense of Beauty

O beloved chelas, disciples of the living God, followers of the Christ, whatever your status—whether advanced disciple or beginner—remember the vast potential of cosmos as it pertains to the marvelous unfoldment of the Divine Self within you! Remember the all-power of Divinity to expand within your consciousness and to increase, heartbeat by heartbeat, the realization of your Christ-potential through the sense of beauty.

May God provide a vision,
  an all-seeing eye,
That like a globe of fire
  elevates and ennobles the soul
Until at last each one's
  own passion for freedom
Reaches out to convey to others
  the strength of beauty's shining.

Devotedly, I AM

Paul the Venetian

November 7, 1971

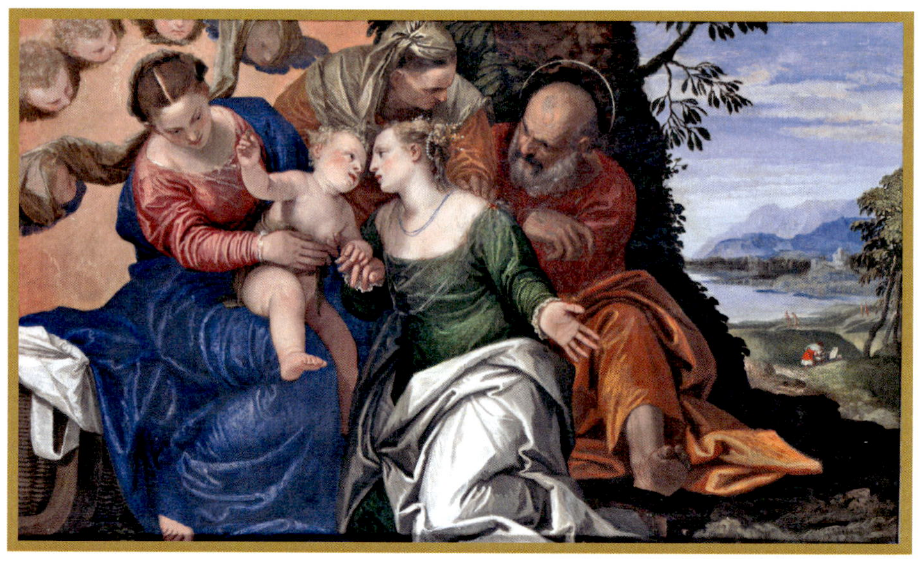

The Mystic Marriage of Saint Catherine of Alexandria, c. 1547–50

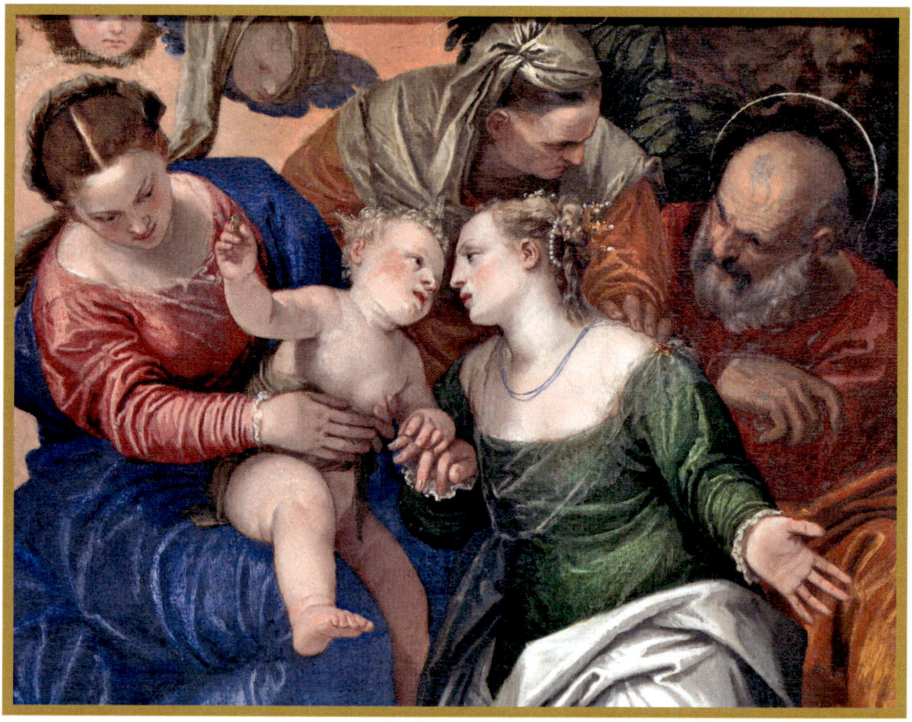

Let your light, your color, your new sense shine everywhere! Let it shine before man's eyes, that they may see you… as one who holds freedom from the skies in the chalice of the heart, in the colorations of the aura.

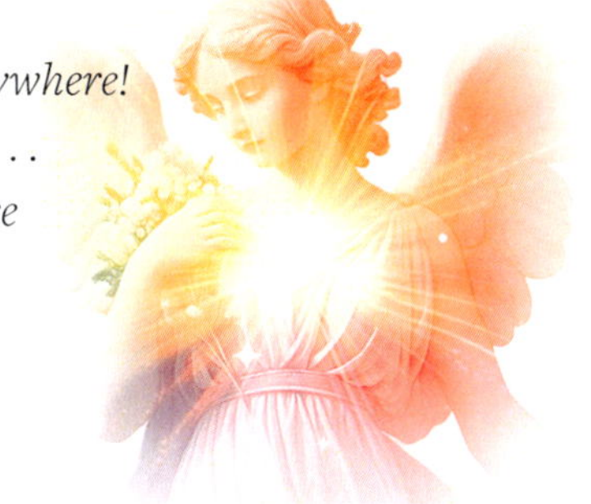

CHAPTER 3

THE INCREASE OF THE SENSE OF THE BEAUTIFUL

Gracious hearts filled with the distillation of cosmic joy and love, I come to you to remind you of your need to adjust your consciousness to the gracious mind of God-beauty.

For beauty is only divine. And man, by his acceptance of divine grace and the beautiful sense, can create a renewal in his being that will fill his consciousness with the distillation of truth—formless, spiritual, and omnipresent—omnipresent in the sense that whensoever a man desires it, he may draw upon the limitless abundance of God's own sense of beauty, transcending all human opinion and, in actuality, manifest God's sense of beauty in the opinions of those who attune with the divine sense of heaven and the senses of the angels.

Heaven has wrought more of grace unto the earth than the earth is aware of. And we want to develop in you the realization that through the process of attunement, individuals are able to increase their own abundant sense of life—its graces, its beauty, and its joy.

Joy springs eternal from the heart of God. For the LORD that worketh hitherto has also worked the art of beauty and has interwoven that beauty into the fabric, the warp and woof of creation. So stable is this manifestation that all planetary orbs and all individuals are functional *because* of divine grace.

Let men, then, holding to the sense of divine abundance and the gratitude of God to man and to the creatures, understand that the Godhead is also fed with gratitude from the creation, and this is multiplied a hundredfold.

Many, then, are giving gratitude unto God, thus increasing the beautiful sense in the millions and billions of earth's evolutions. But these many are, in reality, only the few compared to the many who do not give gratitude or any sense of return to the Godhead.

We are concerned that there be, then, an increase in the sense of gratitude and attunement. For as man is grateful unto God, there occurs the miracle of divine intervention in the lives of those who are grateful. For out of their gratitude is spun a sense for more grace to come. Let all understand the ability of the Godhead to increase the abundance of himself.

Divine Abundance and Beauty Go Hand in Hand

The sense of the beautiful, then, is itself an example of this increase in the natural power of God in the being and mind of the individual monad. For man starts out at first with only a limited sense of divine bestowal. He does not always realize all the care and consideration that God has for him, the sense of universal beauty and the perfection of the divine nature that is within him. Being bereft of this divine nature, in a sense he does not encourage its growth, its expansion.

Let all recognize, then, that in man also lies the great gift of increasing his own potential, which potential is the nature of God, the nature of the beautiful sense, the nature of the joy of creativity.

To be able to create so that others also may share in the abundance of God, to be able to spread abroad the law of love amongst mankind, to be able to disseminate the culture of the ages—this is also a very great miracle of perfection calculated to engender in the hearts of the unborn a sense of universal loveliness.

Here in the higher realm, the temples of light are pulsating with a sense of divine abundance and beauty, for these go hand in hand. The feeding of the creation by the infinite potential of God—this creates the pulsating appearance, the pulsation being the ever-flowing cadences of light marching on to increase the beautiful sense in the creation itself.

For even the molecules and the ergs of energy are endowed by God with marginal, fractional concepts of universal beauty. These, inherent within themselves, act as applause to the creation. Therefore the words, "I say unto you, if these should hold their peace, the very stones shall cry out" come to mind.[1]

The Incalculable Sense of the Infinite Wonders of God

Let men understand, then, that the perfection of the Presence, the intricacy of the creation, and the intricacy of the creative mind in all are endowed with a lofty and beautiful structuring of cosmic expansion. Through the indulgence by man of his own being and in a sense of universal reverie, entering the halls of creative potential, each individual is able to fathom for himself the depths of the love of God to be found in the sense of the beautiful, not in the ugly.

All actions stemming from human levels do themselves dam up the flow of the universal tides of cosmic energy, which by their latent light potential (latent only in the sense that man sees them as such) do continue to flow, and when invoked produce such a magnificent miracle in the fountain of consciousness as to endow man with an incalculable sense of the infinite wonders of God.

As we hold this grasp* to be self-evident, we urge all to experiment with the renewed sense of beauty captivated by the Holy Spirit. As the flow expands in the individual mind and consciousness, man will see, by the very feelings he wears, that a new sense is born—one he hesitates to let go of, one he longs to see ever present with him.

The Fabric of Cosmic Loveliness Can Be Found in the Gentle, Common Things of Life

Beloved hearts of light, understand. Comprehend this now—that you can, if you will, preserve your consciousness of the beautiful sense daily, hourly. You need not ever relinquish it, if you will submit yourselves unto the domain of God with a whole heart, holding back

*understanding

no part of the price but seeing here the endowment of God in nature, of man. For it can truly be said, in one beautiful sense, that both God and nature do serve the needs of man, weaving a fabric of cosmic loveliness to be found in the gentle, common things of life.

But, beloved ones, the beautiful sense to be found there is not to be lost there, but it is to be recognized as the beginning, or origin, of one's thoughts rising and pulsating into more objects of true divine art that may be brought into the consciousness. And then perhaps, in those who are capable, this beautiful sense may be used to create beauty in song, in songcraft, in the sweetness of marble but endowed with angelic form, in the penetration of light, color, and movement in and upon the canvas, and, above all, to convey the sense of the omnipresence of God in every jot and tittle of nature.

Shed the Sense of the Ugly and All That Is Not of the Divine Nature in Yourself

As we come to you today, it is to warm your hearts in preparation for the Christmas season, one which humanity have recognized as solstice, as a time of the year when the increasing darkness gives greater awareness of the light, and the true light of the Christ must be born in every heart.

And while I do not say that all mankind choose to manifest the control of the media of art, I say, let *all* learn the self-control whereby they may become enraptured by the divine art of fashioning their lives in nobility and splendor and compromising nothing, but always instead recognizing the stability of God, who cannot be moved from his appointed rounds, his domain of perfection and grace.

It is not necessary that individuals should chastise their soul and feel that because in a physical sense (often in times of confusion and distress) they have performed acts that they feel the Godhead would not be pleased with. In developing the beautiful sense, you must be willing to shed the sense of the ugly and all that is not of the divine nature in yourself.

It is the Holy Spirit that whitens man unto perfection and generates within him the spirit of regeneration, which is calculated, above all, to give man the methodology whereby he will be able at last, at will—at what some of you have called a push-button touch—to create those perfect thoughts and the flow of those thoughts that your heart longs for.

The Limitless Treasures of Your Heart, Mind, and Being

Be not distressed because of the darkness of the world, with the overpowering senses of conveying projections of darkness into the mind. When you encounter these conditions, cast them aside as you would an unwanted garment. Learn to develop, with each oppressive attack of darkness, the new sense of the living God.

Examine the fabric of nature, of your lives, of your thoughts, of the flow of your thoughts, of your outreach toward expansion, and understand that locked within the atoms of your heart and your mind and your being are to be found limitless treasures.

Comprehend these treasures. Learn to caress them with the fingers of the mind and perceive how, in expansive reality, you will portray at last, as the days pass, a greater measure of that infinite grace, which God is. For your lives are also "encanvassed"*—printed upon electronic essence, the structuring of *akasha.* And out of the light comes forth the sense of God's intervention in the being and nature of man.

The Dawn of a New Day Is Born for Each Man and Woman

Man has indeed proposed, but *God* has ever disposed![2] And in the divine disposition comes freedom from oppression and recognition at last that the fires of the sun are to be found in the coloring of nature. Within the soul of man, the distillation of the divine essence is healing and capable of portraying the divine nature everywhere.

Let your light, your color, your new sense shine everywhere! Let it shine before man's eyes, that they may see you not as a muddied individual torn with doubts and frustrations, but as one who holds freedom from the skies in the chalice of the heart, in the colorations of the aura, in the internal registration of the details of the cosmic hierarchy upon the screen of the mind and consciousness.

*"encanvassed": a coined word that likely means to express or capture as on canvas, in this case on the etheric plane

So, control the cadences of your lives, that you no longer are the subject of trivial manifestations, of fears and doubts. Replace them all by this transcendent new sense—always within the Holy Spirit—that gives free rein to love, that love may move fragrantly in the halls of the mind, giving vent to expansion, to outreach, to newness of life and, above all, to the casting down of those things that have destroyed the soul within man.

For out of the beautiful sense is born the dawn of a new day for each man and woman. It begins with your own acceptance of the tides of infinity. These tides, as they have gone out for many in the past, must come in with renewed vigor! They must *extend* themselves into the world community as a community of hearts! They must alleviate depression and repression! They must show the fragrance of the soul upon the beautiful backdrop of the future!

All things come into perspective, and the larger picture looms before man. It is not the grossness of the world, but it is the infinite etherealization of the idealism of God projected into the now in order to change the sands in the falling glass into the beauty and purity of new-fallen snow—the whiteness of eternity shining in the glass and promising that out of thy handiwork shall come a cultural, cosmic engrossment in things of the Spirit that know no wane but only an infinite increase and flow into eternal value.

December 19, 1971

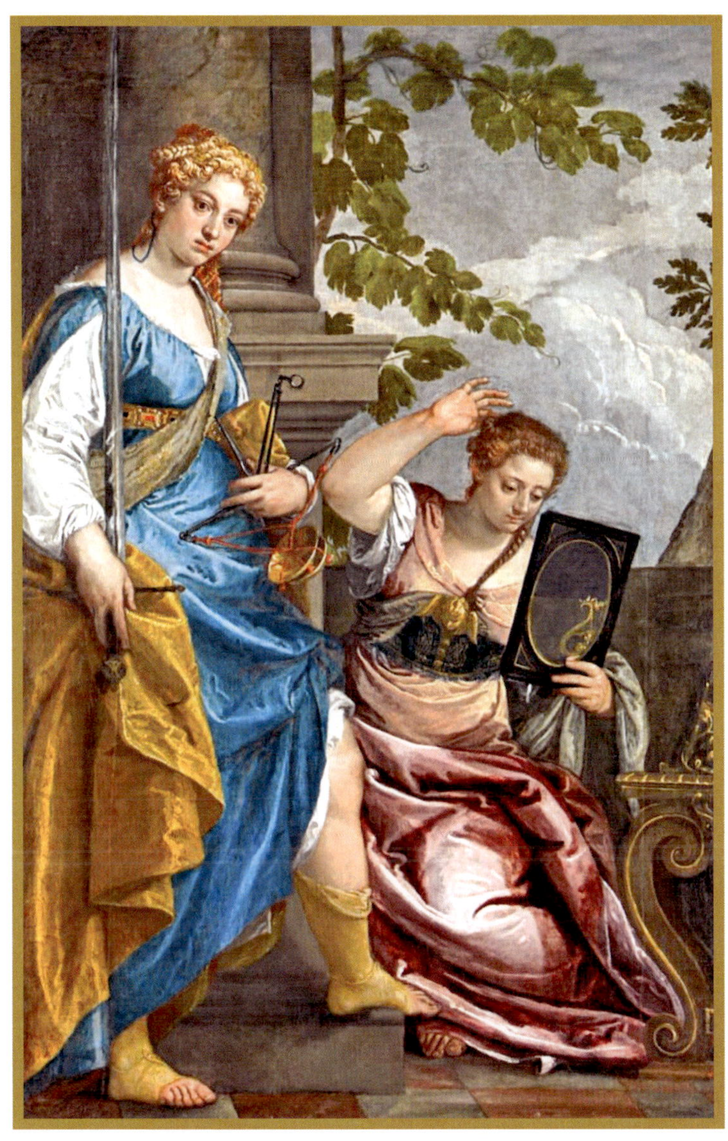

Justice and Prudence, unknown date

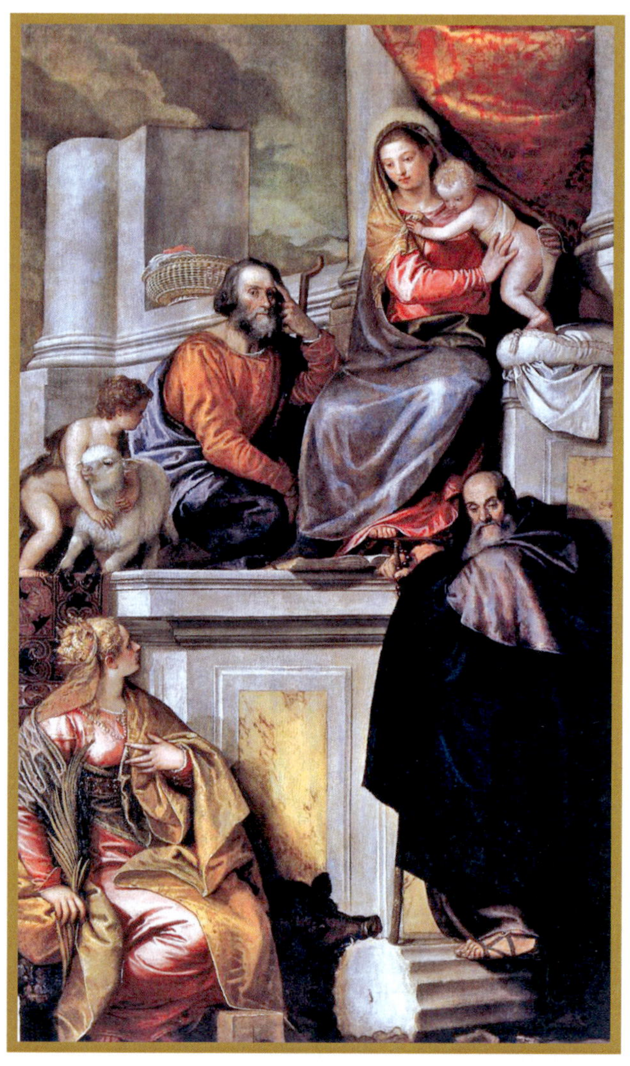

Holy Family with Saints Anthony Abbot, Catherine and the Infant John the Baptist, 1551

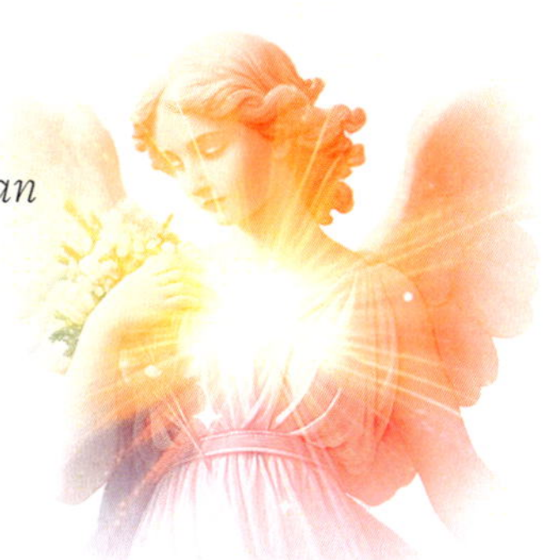

Is this not the loveliest valentine that any man or woman could receive—the realization that the flame within one's heart is one with the flame in the heart of God.

CHAPTER 4

The Matrix of Universal Love

To All Who Would Know the Meaning of Love,

We come to the subject of matrices. Just as Mater signifies Matter and the substance of the creation in the formed state, so do matrices, the molds of creation, reproduce in the world of Matter form the designs impressed upon them by their creator, man.

The matrix of love is the matrix God has placed as the foundation of cosmos and all that is contained therein. If man would derive the intended benefit from this original matrix, he must identify with the pulsations of love in nature and re-attune the frequency of his consciousness in order to extract from the universe the essence of the Lord's Spirit that is locked in the matrix of love.

"Though I understand all mysteries and all knowledge," wrote Saint Paul to the church at Corinth, "and have not charity [love], I am become as sounding brass, or a tinkling cymbal. . . . Charity vaunteth not itself, is not puffed up,"[1] he observed. But the proud talkers in every age say, "See me; here am I," without ever becoming instruments for the magnificent gifts of love that God has placed in nature, in Matter, and, I might add, in man.

Matrices are important. Nowhere is this more evident than in mass production, where the demands are such that out of an original mold an assembly line of endless articles must be manufactured, all exactly alike.

Now, there are matrices of thought and there are matrices of feeling. Those that are perfect are from Above. Those that are imperfect are from below. The latter are mass-produced by mankind out of the almost infinite variety of concepts, precepts, and diverse feelings that they hold about persons, places, conditions, and things. The effect of these matrices upon his life, his environment, and his future is seldom fully realized by man.

Perhaps it would be clearer for some if I were to refer to matrices as patterns, for this is exactly what they are. Patterns that are pure may be defined as those that faithfully duplicate the blueprint of some aspect of the creation. These originate in the mind of God and are re-created in the consciousness of the undefiled among his children.

Patterns that are impure are defined as those that do not faithfully reproduce the archetypes of the Creator's thought. These originate in minds unperfected by the mind that was in Christ Jesus.[2] It can be said that some of each—the pure and the impure—occupy the consciousness of unascended man.

Patterns of Beauty, Righteousness, and Truth

Now, there are patterns in the subconscious as well as in the conscious mind of man, just as there are ideas both latent and active in the universal Mind. Many ideas, of which man is momentarily or fragmentarily conscious, descend into the realm of the subconscious where, forgotten, they lie as dormant seeds until the release of energy into the mold produces, for good or for ill, after its kind.

Where constancy is extolled as the highest virtue in the creation of thought, feeling, and action patterns—constancy to the pure forms and ideas of the Christ mind—these will yield marvelous results, reproducing after their kind over and over again. Like rubber stamps of perfection retained at conscious and subconscious levels, these automatically qualify the descending energies of the Presence with the patterns of beauty, righteousness, and truth originally set up by man himself through the correct use of free will.

Those who are careful in the manufacture of the original mold, in the planning of their thoughts and feelings according to the highest patterns that God has given to the universe and man, receive the reward of a just steward. Even patterns of sunshine and shadow are creations of the God of nature. But matrices of idleness and boredom are the creations of man, who thus fulfills the edicts of his own lack of response to the spark of God inherent in nature and himself.

The Mystery of Life

It is a strange mystery, the mystery of life. Akin to the mystery of love, it is not understood by the average man or woman who has not beheld either the purpose of life or the purpose of love. Let us consider, then, that the plan of universal love, in conveying the mystery of life to each individual ideation of God, is to enable the individual to respond of his own accord to the vibratory qualities of love found in the first magnificent gift of God—the only begotten Son, the universal Christ.

Yet the universal Christ is not understood until it becomes personified in one such as the Lord Jesus. To some, the universal aspect of the Christ seems remote and impersonal because they find it easier to identify with the embodiment of a principle than with the principle itself—with a person than with a pattern. For this they can relate to their own personality. In reality, this lack of understanding, this limited perspective, prevents them from seeing the universal nature of the man Jesus—the *man*ifestation of the universal Christ. For he who perfectly embodies the universal and impersonal God becomes that which he is the embodiment of.

Therefore, if we have eyes to see and ears to hear, if we have the pure patterns already fixed in mind and heart, we will find in Jesus not only the personal Christ but also the impersonal God—not only the individual Christ but also the universal image of the Son of God. Seeing only the personal, man is deprived of the universal. Thus he can know God only in part until he corrects his vision and his logic with perfected matrices. The personal image, although more relevant to the evolving monad at a certain stage of soul development, can express but a portion of the universal image.

It seems to me that in the matter of executing the symmetry of a perfect matrix, it would be helpful if man could understand the mystery of his own individuality and how that individuality relates to other individualities in the cosmic scheme. If he would gain this understanding, he must first be willing to relate to love as the author and finisher of the Creation. There is nothing wrong with a personal image if one sees it as the link to the universal image and as the open door to higher realms.

Entering thereby into octaves of light and the universal nature of the Christ, man experiences a greater manifestation of cosmic consciousness, a greater measure of the divine dispensation. And he finds that it is even possible for him to obey the admonishment of Paul, "Let this universal mind be in you, which was also in Christ Jesus."[3] Thus Paul, in explaining the universal Christ made personal through the life and works of the Master, spoke of him in this wise:

> Who, being in the form of God, thought it not robbery to be equal with God:
>
> But made himself of no reputation, and took upon him the form of a servant, and was made in the likeness of men:
>
> And being found in fashion as a man, he humbled himself, and became obedient unto death, even the death of the cross.
>
> Wherefore God also hath highly exalted him, and given him a name which is above every name:
>
> That at the name of Jesus every knee should bow, of things in heaven, and things in earth, and things under the earth;
>
> And that every tongue should confess that Jesus Christ is Lord, to the glory of God the Father.[4]

The Father symbolizes the progenitor, the eternal Creator, the Supreme One. By the power of the Word, the universal Christ, he made all things that comprise the spiritual-material creation—the Macrocosm, the microcosm, worlds for countless evolutions, bodies to house the souls of billions of cherished lifestreams, minds to receive the impressions of his own—all as a ministry of love.

The Archetypal Pattern of the Christ Consciousness

Beloved ones, the carnal mind never has and never will be able to understand the concept of Jesus being a divine incarnation in a physical body. Mankind look at their own physical bodies and fail to see how this body could be sanctified by the Holy Spirit and made the temple of the living God. They do not relate their own being to the power of love that originally sent forth the only begotten Son.[5]

When man understands the mystery of the Christ within Jesus, he is able to understand the mystery of the God within himself. And only then will he cease to create self-limiting matrices that cast him in the mold of mortality and prescribe the boundaries of his advancing thought or the cosmic progression of his being.

When God made man in the great image of his love, it was not his intent to confine man within a finite expression of himself but to give him the opportunity to master and thus become the limitless qualities of the light itself in all of its ramifications.

The light denotes the Christ, and the Christ is the light of the world[6]—the light of man, the light of being. He is called Wonderful, Counsellor, the mighty God, the everlasting Father, the Prince of Peace.[7] It may help you to understand that whereas God made all things by releasing the power of the Word through cosmic matrices, pressing the creative energies through the molds of his perfect thought, he placed within man a master blueprint, the archetypal pattern of the Christ consciousness like unto the original design by which the whole of creation was brought forth.

Love Will Produce in Man the Regeneration of the Christ

Man lacks nothing. For God saw to it that the power of his love and grace infused each individual spirit spark with those radiant virtues that are very much a part of himself. He made all things by Christ—by the Word that conveyed life to the uttermost depths of the Void.

The Christ, then, was first the universal manifestation of the Father-Mother God, and then the individualization of that manifestation. Begotten of God, a Spirit, he also is Spirit cast in his image. Thus, each individualization of the Christ, each fragment of the universal One in physical embodiment, is a Spirit, hence a joint heir with Christ,[8] having within himself the potential of imitating in all of his thoughts and feelings and actions the original Creation of the Father.

In the divine manifestation called man, there can be no limitation whatsoever. For there is no limitation in God, who is the original matrix for every *man*ifestation. This concept, when accepted as a matrix within the consciousness of man, becomes regenerative, for it re-creates the great recycling patterns of universal love.

The desire to create, inherent within the Godhead himself, was the basis for the original Creation. This desire resulted not only in the creation of man made in the image of the Deity, but also in the bequeathing to man of the selfsame desire and the means to implement it as a co-creator with God.

As he enters into the realization of his creative potential, man must develop the sense of limitless being, the sense of the abundant life. He must replace the treacherous spirit of competition—which seized the heart of Cain and still dominates the mass consciousness—with the all-pervading sense of the abundant love.

Love has created man. He is made in the image of love. Love will sustain him. Love will guide him every step of the way. Love will produce in him the regeneration of the Christ, and all of heaven will bow to the light within him because he has enthroned the Christ within his heart and has developed an inner rapport with the universal presence of love.

Man Is Destined to Be a Co-Creator with God

The marvelous sense of freedom that comes to the individual when he begins to realize that he can create, that he is destined to be a co-creator with God, and that he is already creating, whether he works in darkness or in light, begets not only a feeling of responsibility to all of cosmos and to one's fellowman but it also begets the deep desire to successfully meet the challenges of that responsibility. He concludes that the old familiar patterns, which for centuries have generated sorrow and pain, must now be cast aside.

The totality of his individual creation must embrace, in a Godlike manner, the patterns of the Infinite expressed through the Christ mind. He knows that he is here for a reason—a grand and noble purpose—and that he must assimilate the great lessons he is intended to learn in the planetary schoolroom and through his association with his classmates.

Tenderness toward all life and the balance of universal reason are become his master controls, and to these he readily consents. For now he understands that these controls are divine matrices, patterns of universal love outworking perfection in his life. He welcomes them not as chains of bondage but as links of freedom, and he seeks to reestablish their divine hold in his consciousness and world.

It is up to man, then, at the great harvest of the seeds he has sown, at the great return of the matrices he has sent forth, to separate the sheep from the goats,[9] the light from the darkness, the pure from the impure patterns he has created, and then to lift into the heaven-world, into his own causal body where the gentle things of love abide—those permanent graces that he has outpictured and that the Creator desires to make a very real part of his consciousness.

Man must develop the heavenly consciousness in order to establish within himself a lodestone of infinite love that will draw to him the fullness of the Godhead bodily, that it might dwell in him[10] and that he might escape the errors of the past through the universal magnitude of the Cosmic Christ.

Such attainment can in no way diminish the mission of Jesus or of any other avatar, but it only serves to prove that inherent within the gift of life itself was the gift of free will whereby each man, in reestablishing the will of God for and within himself, becomes a replica of the selfsame grace—the Word by which the worlds were framed,[11] the Word that was made flesh and dwelt among us.[12]

The Imitation of Christ

It has never been the intent of God to create a slave creation but one that would masterfully demonstrate the power of the beloved Son of God individualized in man. No higher honor can be paid to the Master Jesus than to become one with God and one with Christ.

Unfortunately, down through the years mankind, in their dogmas, have promoted the idea that the man who establishes himself as a focus for good is detracting from the goodness of God or of Jesus.

But divine love reveals the fallacy of their reasoning and gives to those who would know the truth the pure logic of the Law.

The true devotee of God and Christ knows that he is obliged to establish a focus of Father and Son within himself, and he feels a similar obligation, as the result of his own attunement with the higher frequencies of life, to perform (free of the competitive sense) those acts that pay the highest tribute to God and man—the imitation of Christ.

To follow him in the regeneration is to do the will of God—not only to name him, not only to pray to him, but also to establish him in one's life as a permanent focus of the sacred fire. Thus is the matrix of universal love—of the only begotten Son of the Father, full of grace and truth[13]—openly welcomed into the life of each individual. And through him alone is the original cosmic blueprint established.

Is this not the loveliest valentine that any man or woman could receive—the realization that the flame within one's heart is one with the flame in the heart of God, that his feelings are regenerating the patterns of the Ancient of Days, that his mind, imbued with the matrices of the Christ, is thinking the thoughts that beat in rhythm with the heart of universal love, the mind of universal love, and the being of universal love!

Devoted to this eternal principle, I remain

Paul the Venetian

February 13, 1972

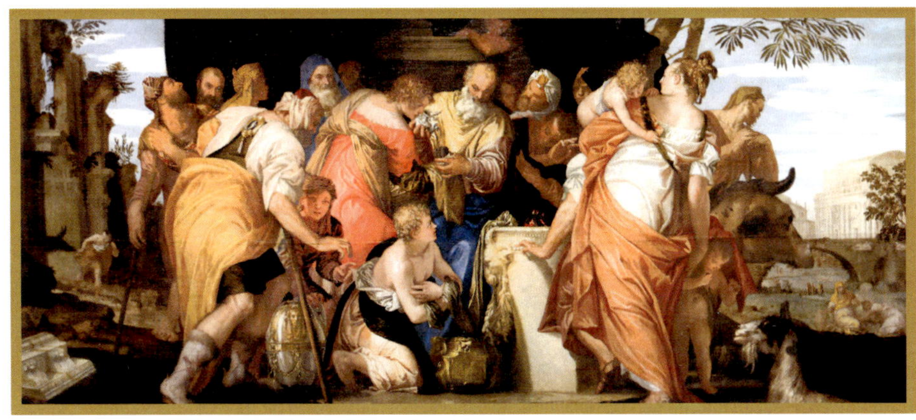

The Anointing of David, c. 1555

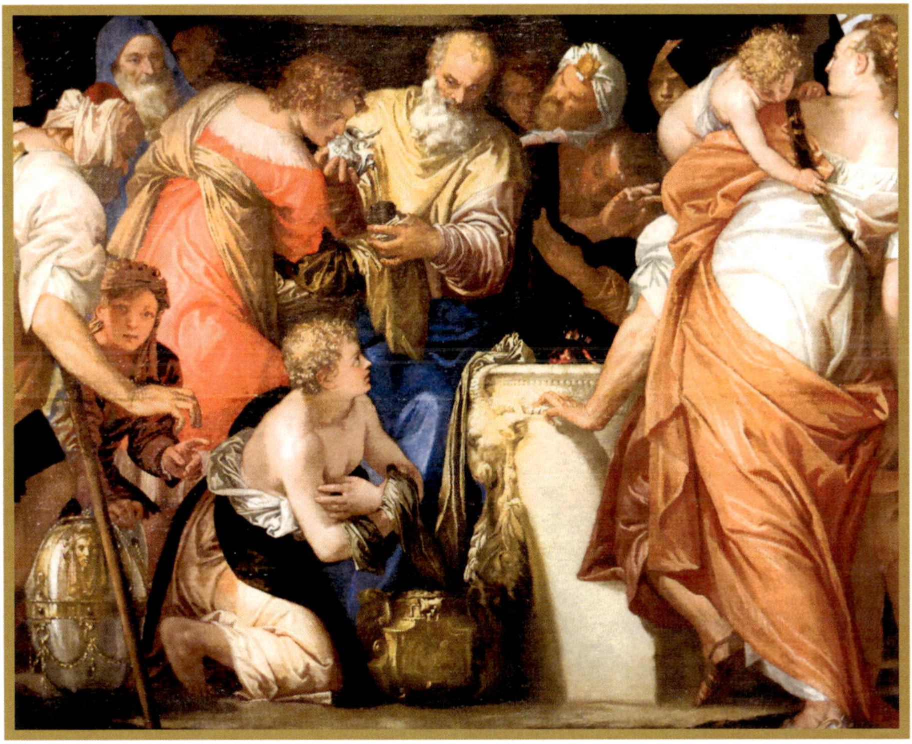

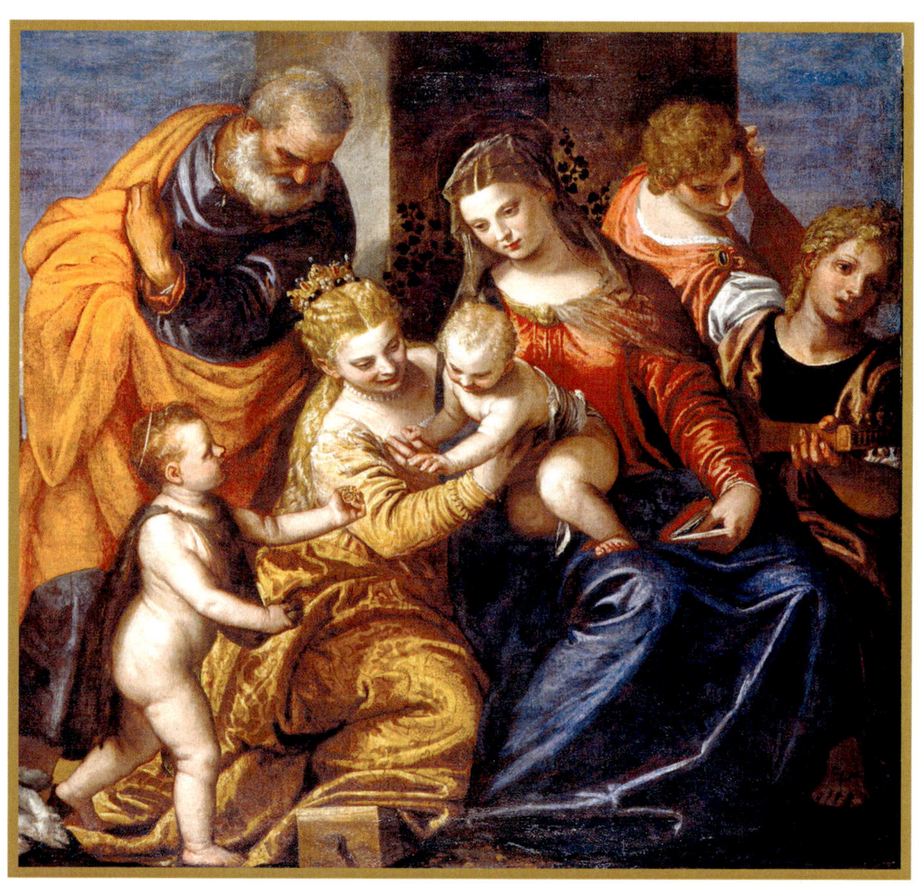

The Mystic Marriage of Saint Catherine of Alexandria (detail), c. 1562–69

Art, to be worthy of the name, must raise the consciousness of a people into a higher understanding of the life that is Real—life as God knows it and not as man has distorted it.

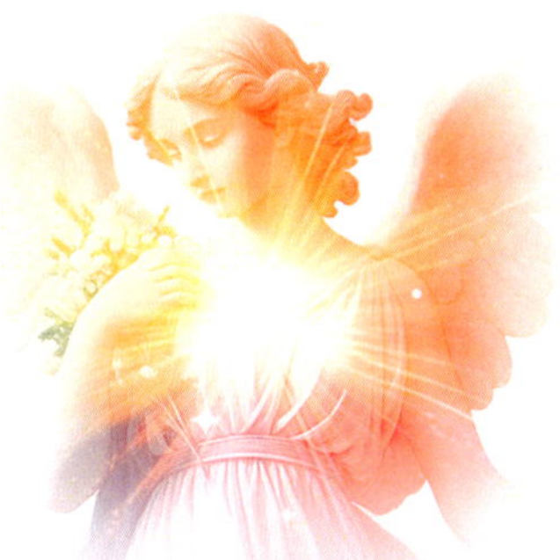

CHAPTER 5

The Symmetry of the Christ Mind

Followers of God's Beauty,

The symmetry inherent within the universe indicates to the seeking heart how carefully God has wrought, producing miracle after miracle not only in manifest form but also in the unmanifest and the formless. Yet seldom in a lifetime does man touch upon the vastness of their own cosmic potential.

It is essential, therefore, in the name of universal progress, that each man begin the realization of the magnificent miracle of life that he holds within himself. With this goal in mind, we dedicate the instruction in this *Pearl of Wisdom** to all who hold dear the progressive revelations of the Brotherhood.

In a vital sense, man can be compared to a flame—a moving flame that dances with progress. The energies of man that proceed from the flame are electrical, and the electricity of which I speak is a vital manifestation both governing thought and being governed by thought.

Those who would exercise greater self-control and greater control over their sense of the beautiful must first exercise dominion over the flame and all that comes forth from it. Then they will automatically have that faith in the beauties of both man and nature, which is essential to the attainment of God-control over oneself and one's environment.

**Pearls of Wisdom* are weekly letters of instruction dictated by the ascended masters to their messengers Mark L. Prophet and Elizabeth Clare Prophet for students of the sacred mysteries. For more information, see SummitLighthouse.org/Pearls-Of-Wisdom-Morya.

Some consider beauty to be sameness. Others see it as the great variety of expression that can be achieved within the bounds of beauty in the universal order. In reality, a tremendous variegation is possible as man expands his awareness of beauty.

God has given to man a reasonable license in his exercise of the sense of the beautiful, expecting him to show a marked restraint when experimenting with new patterns, forms, and colors. He has also placed within man's soul a mystical sense of the beautiful that allows him free range of thought and feeling to tune in with the grace of God's beauty available through one's own inner awareness of the infinite beauties of macrocosmic and microcosmic worlds.

Nature Teaches Man the Way

The spirit of competition, although considered by mankind to be the necessary stimulus of excellence, also poses certain problems. Mankind feel confined within the ranges of their thoughts. In seeking freedom from these confines, man enters into competition with each other, and in their attempts to outdo one another they shut off, by the damper of selfishness, the interplay of the sacred flames of God that show forth the intricate beauties of his diamond-shining mind.

Those who would draw forth from that mind the magnificent ideational patterns contained within the Alpha and Omega spirals require the freedom of expression enjoyed by a cosmic master, whose discipline in the Law, free from the competitive sense, would never allow himself to go beyond the cosmic geometry in order to bring forth a masterpiece simply for the purpose of outdoing another cosmic master.

Such a one seeks to complement his brother's achievements born out of his communion with life. The thought of [humanly] bettering his effort does not occur to him, for he knows that both [he and his brother] are tapping the same source and have equal opportunity to realize an angle new or old of the symmetry of life. He is not ashamed to reproduce the qualities of sameness that carry the theme of the universal design, for he recognizes his opportunity to contribute various techniques that will enhance the same qualities that others have chosen to enhance with their techniques.

How tragic it is that mankind spend lifetime after lifetime playing their competitive games, deriving temporary satisfaction in topping one another's achievements instead of simply enjoying the abundant life and the limitless sense that wells up from within the childlike heart—the sense that comes from the natural expression of the thoughts of God that unfold within the mind attuned to the Infinite.

Just as a flower joyously opens its petals according to its own preordained pattern, so man can release the energies of his consciousness into the blueprint of identity that marks the perfect concept and the patterned destiny, his very own from the beginning.

Just as the etheric pattern of the flower is there—an electrical forcefield surrounding the bud with an aura of expectancy—so the design that God has willed for each manifestation of himself surrounds the evolving monad as a cocoon of light, containing within itself all that man requires to fulfill his divine plan.

As the flower unfolds, it follows the outline of the pattern that nature has lovingly pressed upon its cellular structure. No resistance to the cosmic flow is here, but movement toward reunion with the Whole and a momentum of aeons, of life evolving life, begetting beauty and expanding the universal order. Thus nature teaches man the Way. And if he would follow, his life too would be the outpicturing on earth of heaven's immortal loveliness.

The Subtle Expressions of Light and Color

The question of selecting a medium to express one's art is easily resolved when one recognizes that there is a pattern basic and unique to every thing, to every idea, to every desire. The very desire to express, inherent within every form of life, creates and evolves its own progressive pattern that goes before it, providing the forcefield for its unfoldment.

Naturalness in living—a quality that some seem to enjoy to the fullest, and others, wrapped up as they are in an artificial existence, fail utterly to comprehend—is a state of nonresistance to the soul patterns inherent in man and nature. Naturalness in living, as a quality of freedom, is also a quality of beauty. But let man not confuse what we term "the natural" with the base elements of man's nature. For these are unnatural, whereas all that is pure and lovely, all that is of the Christ in man, is truly natural because it is the true nature with which he was endowed by God.

In the past as well as in the present, too many artists have felt compelled to use garish colors because these attract the attention of lifestreams whose lack of spiritual evolution causes them to have an affinity for the lower vibrations to which such colors correspond.

But if the artist is true to his art, he will not display his work for the approval of the lower nature in man but for the higher. He will strive to raise man from levels of mediocrity to a superior appreciation of life. As the consciousness becomes more and more refined, the soul's appreciation of the qualities of the etheric plane are transferred to the outer consciousness and man finds himself enjoying the more subtle expressions of light and color—the pastel hues and delicate shadings of sunlight as it plays upon nature in all her glory.

Symmetry in Form and Consciousness

Just as people point to the never-ending chain of cause-and-effect sequences in the riddle "Which came first, the chicken or the egg?" so we would point to the mutuality of influence that exists between a man and his art.

Just as cultural levels are influenced by society, so society is influenced by its culture. Just as a refined consciousness is aware of refined beauty, so those who are surrounded by the refinements of true culture tend to gain a refinement of consciousness. Until man refines the matrices of his consciousness at both conscious and subconscious levels, and until he gains mastery of the flow of thought and feeling ideations through the nexus of consciousness, he will inadvertently create discordantly.

The act of consciously creating after the patterns of things in the heavens[1] enables man to relate his consciousness with the Higher Mind. Thus he initiates a cause-effect sequence whereby he is influenced by the perfection of the creation even as he creates perfection in his art. This is the purpose of mandalas—geometric forms and designs used in meditation—to draw the consciousness of man into the symmetry of the Christ mind that he might manifest that symmetry first in his form and consciousness and then in all his endeavors. Long ago Saint Paul spoke of this ritual of congruency as the girding-up of the loins of the mind.[2]

The rapport with nature that man establishes in his being and consciousness, his engrossment with the realm of material manifestation, and his perfecting of the technique of precipitation from Spirit to Matter are intended to draw him back to the realm of Spirit, the plane of First Cause. Here he contacts the fires of creation, which imbue his mind with a higher inspiration. Indeed, he is at the Source, and all that he wills into manifestation will bear the mark of perfection.

As he makes a habit of going to the God Presence for the outline of his work, he finds evolving in his consciousness the magnitude of the Father's love as his own creative potential. This is the gift of freedom that the Lord of Creation intends all of his sons and daughters to have, that they might go forth to create, worlds without end, joyously, magnificently, after the patterns that God himself employed.

Drink Deeply of the Thoughts of the Mind of God

It must be remembered that man's native drives to be and to create are originally derived from God, no matter how far they have departed from their pristine purity and muddied though they may be by the spatterings of darkness that have afflicted the race.

Those who allow themselves to continue working from a false premise in the fields of art, music, drama, or any area of creativity, thinking they can move from the base levels of the human consciousness to a progressive achievement of a "new art," may find—upon contacting the teachings of the ascended masters, which set forth the standard of perfection in every area of living—that the foundation of their experiments and the structure of their work are based in imperfect matrices and need to be swept aside.

Saint Paul referred to this as the trial by fire. He said, "Every man's work shall be made manifest: for the day shall declare it, because it shall be revealed by fire; and the fire shall try every man's work of what sort it is. If any man's work abide which he hath built thereupon, he shall receive a reward. If any man's work shall be burned, he shall suffer loss: but he himself shall be saved; yet so as by fire."[3]

We submit all things to the judgment of the Law. We place the harvest of mankind's achievements upon the foundation of the living Word in order that what is made of straw might be consumed by the sacred fire. Even in the realm of spiritual art, where man is consciously working to externalize a facet of the cosmic design, unless he involves his consciousness in the universal spirals of creation, he may find himself stopped short of the desired goal and required by natural law to retrace his steps, to undo that which is imperfect, and to begin again with the original design.

At first this may seem to him to be a suffering of great loss. Do not his goodwill and his effort merit recognition even if his work is found wanting? He would almost rather continue as he is, so great is the momentum required to reverse his course even though he knows his labor is in vain.

But very soon he realizes that to continue upon his present course would deprive him of the opportunity for right action in all his endeavors, and still he would ultimately have to return to the original patterns. Therefore he feels a great need to enter in spirit into the original creation, that he might drink deeply of the thoughts of the mind of God by which he framed the worlds.[4]

Art Must Raise the Consciousness of a People

In the arts, as in every walk of life, it is sometimes necessary for individuals to take a seemingly backward step in order that a greater forward step might be taken.

We cannot espouse those movements in art and literature, such as surrealism, that draw their form and content from the realm of the subconscious, unless that subconscious be sanctified by the Holy Ghost. We must advocate simplicity in design, pure geometric forms, and the depicting of those ideal qualities and images that originate in the Superconscious, or Christ mind.

We recognize what we would call an expansion for living through an expansion of life to be the purpose of all art. For art, to be worthy of the name, must raise the consciousness of a people into a higher understanding of the life that is Real—life as God knows it and not as man has distorted it.

Remember, beloved hearts of light—all who would create, all who would bring forth design in any field—that your work is the work of God and that you must strive to ensoul it with patterns that have a peaceful and benign effect upon the beholder. The statement that beauty is in the eye of the beholder[5] ought not to be forgotten.

Therefore, if you desire to express beauty for others—to capture on canvas, in a poem, or in a musical composition some hieroglyph of cosmic worth so that those who behold your work may see beyond the physical into a realm of beauty not known before—you yourself must seek to embody in greater measure the divine ideals.

Seldom do those in the field of art realize the enormous effect that they exert upon their society by reason of the patterns of their own life, which carry forth into their art. For the life, the thoughts, the feelings, and the concepts that the individual has are an art in themselves, and a man's total personality is reflected in his work, which then becomes the expression of the inward art, which he is. Thus through art, when it is used for the communication of noble ideas as God intended, the forcefield of human thought becomes tethered to the Divine.

Artists and Artisans Ought to Seek the Holy Spirit and the Patterns Thereof

The bounties of God's eternal grace are to be found everywhere. These are worthy to be preserved not in one but in many art forms. Knowing this, artists and artisans ought to seek the Holy Spirit and the patterns thereof as a means of ensouling their work with the essence of the heavenly matrix and the power of the sacred Word.

Thus mankind will learn to transfer to their lives, as they have in their art, the expressions of a higher and more permanent beauty, and they will understand how to fashion their art of living after their art, even as their philosophy of living has shaped the media of their art.

For in both, they will have acquired the discipline of preserving only those precepts that are worthy to endure.

All intricacy of artistic expression is based upon the progressive reason of God, from the simplest to the most profound logic of the Word. The interaction of the deeper mysteries may then engage more of man's energies and being than he at first feels capable of. But as he moves through the divine art upward into the domain of cosmic reason—all his fears left behind, the dark elements of his world forsaken—he develops the confidence of a tightrope walker in a circus.

Totally dependent upon the grace of God to secure the skills he has mastered, he knows that if he obeys the laws of the universe, by his mercy he shall proceed safely from chaos to order in order to accomplish a great and noble work for God and man. With this confidence—a sacred trust born of his friendship with the Lord of Life, and with faith in the nobility God has placed within his soul—he is able to fabricate according to the divine design.

The *Religio* Art Experience

The works that I accomplished during my embodiment as Paolo Veronese were the manifestation of my absolute faith in God's ability to perform through me whatsoever he desired. It is this essential faith that each man or woman who espouses the noble cause of enrichening the quality of life upon the planetary body must have in order to sustain the necessary matrix for the completion of his work.

It has been my experience that to be successful as an artist in the service of the Christ, one must imbue the figures and forms that he portrays on canvas with the qualities of faith, hope, and charity, which quicken in all who see these works of art the response that lifts the heart and propels it into spiritual dimensions. I would say that one must also endow his creation with his own momentum of creativity and that unless he espouse the cause of ennobling the souls of others as a part of his creative endeavor, he is not fulfilling his raison d'être.

Whatever the artist desires to communicate must be infused within his work at the time of its creation, for it is not possible to do so at a later date. If at that moment his thoughts and feelings are chaotic, his work will also be chaotic. If they are harmonious, his work will also be harmonious.

Likewise, he who would perfect the technique of recording in Matter form the ideas of God and man—of "making art," as we might say—should realize that he can never communicate to form and substance that which he has not first experienced within himself.

Only by reaching up into a realm higher than himself, into the dwelling place of the angelic hosts, into the habitation of the Most High God, only by penetrating cosmos and gaining proximity to those who have approximated the consciousness of God, can the artist convey to others through his work the divine experience. This is what I would term the *religio* art experience, whereby all who look upon his work, no matter what their conviction, have a religious experience, a communion with an aspect of being that is beyond themselves, an aspect that they would not contact under ordinary circumstances.

Life Is an Outpicturing of the Divine Art

Thus the true work of art can be nothing more or less than a catalyst whereby the human transcends itself and becomes one with the Divine. The true work of art must convey a universal principle through the presentation of a personal and particular aspect of life. It must take the individual from the specific to the general, from the personal to the impersonal, without binding his consciousness to doctrine or dogma, without confining his soul to planes of consciousness not native to its own.

The true work of art has many meanings for people of diverse backgrounds. Allowing for the confluence of multifaceted ideas through the one Mind, it serves to integrate humanity into the body of God, captivating souls at various points of the upward-moving spiral, the great Godward cycle of individual initiation and fulfillment.

Each individual aspect of the grand mural of life can also be tested according to these criteria so that every man and woman might know if his life is an outpicturing of the divine art. For although all men and women are not artists in the usual sense of the word, they are apprentices of the Master Artist, commissioned by the LORD God himself to practice the divine art of refining their nature, their thoughts, their feelings, and their entire being, that they might make a unique contribution to the mural of life.

One might say that mankind become less and less of their former selves and more and more of the Greater Self that they seek to be as they accept the role of being a contributing artist of the divine panorama and as they recognize that it is the acts of God through man, the works of art wrought by His hand through the hands of man, that communicate the higher life to all.

The Divine Art Is Waiting to Be Born in Every Man

To follow the Christ in the regeneration,[6] to follow his star to the throne of God, to be raised from the dead—these goals, set before man as hurdles of the Great Law, are the divine stimulus of excellence. In striving to attain them we are reminded of the strivings of others on the Path, such as the Apostle Paul, who said, "I count not myself to have apprehended: but this one thing I do, forgetting those things which are behind, and reaching forth unto those things which are before, I press toward the mark for the prize of the high calling of God in Christ Jesus."[7]

Thus man must think and feel, know and be, and see and manifest that aspect of God's consciousness that desires to communicate unto them newness of life. For the divine art is waiting to be born in every man. The spirals of regeneration press upon his mind and heart, exacting the excellent manifestation of God in man.

Man seeks to be a chalice. He already has a chalice—the chalice of his consciousness. True it is that the consciousness is in the formative state, and this is precisely the challenge of life, the challenge of being an artist of the Spirit—the perfecting of the chalice through the mastering of the divine art.

There is an ongoingness about the divine art. There is a sense of progressive fulfillment that seizes the consciousness of the one who seizes it. Those who fail to apprehend the purpose of life as an opportunity to engage their total being in the flow of the divine art soon lose that sense, and their creative faculties become stultified. Thus man himself, by his failure to enter into the cosmic flow, stalls his own progress and stills the natural and progressive movement of the soul.

The Transition of Man from the Spiritually Inactive to the Spiritually Active State

There are times when, by reason of an inner prompting, man engages in the necessary act of retrospection and introspection, when he ponders that which has transpired in his life—his losses and his gains, his forward and backward movements, his past and present levels of attainment—and just what he is and where he is as opposed to what and where he would like to be.

By so doing, man can assess his rate of progress and take steps to counteract all that detracts from his pursuit of primary goals. Not as a continuing process but as a periodic self-evaluation, this examining of one's motives and acts, past and present, can be extremely useful as the disciple prepares himself for the progressive cycles of initiation, which sooner or later come to everyone on the Path.

The transition of man from the spiritually inactive to the spiritually active state should be automated under the guidance of the Holy Spirit. When a pillar of fire or a pillar of cloud[8] begins its forward movement before his consciousness by night or by day, man must be ready to follow. It does not matter what the world thinks. To the soul in pursuit of spiritual Reality, human opinion is of no consequence. His constant prayer is "Lead me from the unreal to the Real! Lead me from Darkness to Light! Lead me from death to immortality!"[9] And always it is God who leads and man who follows.

Art Is Eternally Progressive

It is the education of the young that I would speak of, not of the young in body but of the young in heart and of the young in spirit. For they recognize that the Lord of Creation has appointed elder bards of cosmic art to preside over the universal order and that as master artists they are eager and willing, under divine direction, to teach mankind how to realize their cosmic potential and to bequeath to them their own momentums of cosmic achievement.

Neither I nor any other ascended master has ever found fault with man's adoration of the Christ, whether this be of the universal Christ or of Christ Jesus born in Bethlehem long ago. In his own expression of the depth, the height, and the riches of God, Jesus has said again and again, both to us and to his embodied disciples, "It behooves every man who would pursue the divine art to summon the original creative power, which 'before Abraham was, I AM,'[10] the creative wisdom, and the creative love that were inherent within the mind of the Creator before form was."

Just as the universal Christ is in us all, in every master, in every angel and the blessed elementals who sustain the petals of a rose and the boughs of the pines in the forest, so light and life and intelligence pervade all substance. Man should seek to communicate with these aspects of God's consciousness with which He has endowed both the spiritual and the material creation, for even that which appears to be inert matter is imbued with the universal Christ consciousness.

In accepting the form consciousness of the master of love who walked the shores of Galilee two thousand years ago, man often neglects to realize the imbuement of the entire creation with light and its manifold reflections by the Lord of heaven and earth.[11] But through the initiations leading to God-mastery, man discovers the penetrability of all substance and being by the universal God, by the universal Christ, by the person of the Christ in Jesus or in any man. For to be a joint heir with him means to be one with him in thought, in word, and in deed.

The divine art is dynamic beyond the ken of mortal thought. Through the outreach of his consciousness, man comes to definite conclusions regarding his place in the great cosmic flow. Thus he achieves an ongoing expression of the divine symmetry. For art, both material and spiritual, is eternally progressive.

February 20, 1972

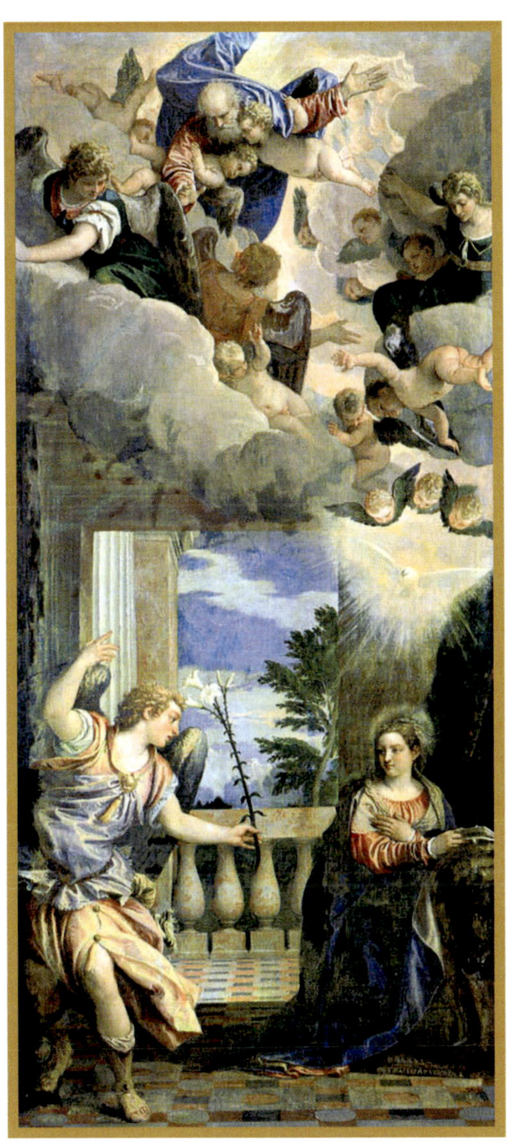

The Annunciation, 1583

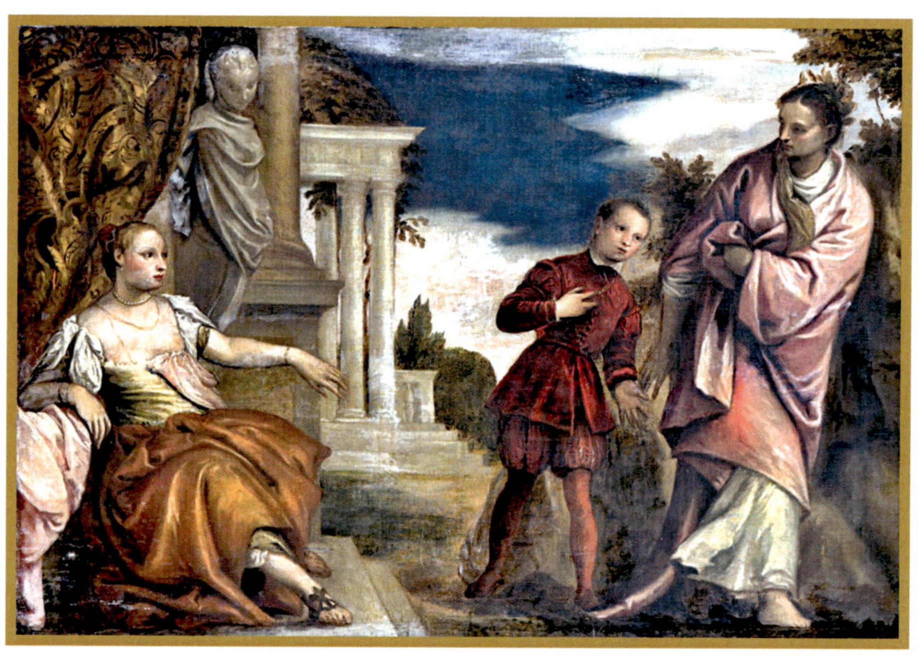

Young Man from the Sanuto Family Chooses Virtue over Vice, c. 1565–70

Jewels of the sacred fire, crystallized teardrops of the love of heaven descending to the planet, to the heart of the Mother of the World, are a consummate realization... of the care of God, not only for the lilies and the sparrows but for men made in the divine image.

CHAPTER 6

The Mighty Magnet of Universal Love

O infinite hope, how beautiful are thy strands of descending love! How beautiful is the ladder of light, adorned with the flowers of striving and becoming! How beautiful is the flow of angelic grace unto the heart of the world!

And I speak now of the love of the heart of God for humanity and their present state or dilemma. I speak as though it were a matter of the tears of God falling for the errors of man. And as they descend—beautiful, radiant, fiery drops of light and life—they are seen as crystallized jewels of the rarest beauty, descending with the dawn of new hope unto all. I pause, then, this moment to pay homage to them. [6-second pause]

Jewels of the sacred fire, crystallized teardrops of the love of heaven descending to the planet, to the heart of the Mother of the World, are a consummate realization (for those who will permit their consciousness to accept it) of the care of God, not only for the lilies and the sparrows but for men made in the divine image. A more beautiful image is not possible to conceive of.

A noble exposé of the fragrance of the Holy Spirit as the principle of cosmic adornment, consideration, and care of God for his creation is perceived. And it must be perceived through a mirage and barrage of human concepts even involving the Godhead or the principle of evolution without God.

It is unthinkable that men and women, possessed with a true sense of the greatness of even the physical manifestation, let alone the spiritual, should conceive of the universe as having created itself. And yet, as God has ordained it, as Spirit has directed it, each man *will* become a joint heir with him, hence the creator of all things that were, of all things that are, and of all things that shall be.

The Spirit Most Holy, Most Loving and Kind

And it is to the beautiful sense that we dedicate ourselves this day, to the sense of the consummate ability of the Holy Spirit to release its radiation and fragrance into the heart of man—the gold and the frankincense and the myrrh—which (in adorning the heart, covering it also with the aloes of the oil of peace) may bring to that heart a realization of the cosmic fortress in which there is the ivy of perennial green, the strength of the fruitfulness of God in his abundant release of life, drops of life unto men and women, so that they may perceive these and go and do likewise with the fruit of their life and of their identity.

For love is needed in the world as never before. It is a love that will comfort the lonely yet not involve itself in their acts of mistaken identity. For humanity today is experiencing a case of mistaken identity in the nature of God and in their own nature. They do not understand who they are or who God is, nor do they understand en masse the power of the I AM Presence.

Yet many are emerging, as though it were from a chrysalis, out of the generation of man into the universal regeneration of the Christ consciousness. It is as though the Holy Grail were enhanced and were aglow once again in the world order, the perception of universal love pouring forth and streaming forth, creating a mystical search for the love that is identifiable with each man.

I am Paul, and my love is also consecrated to the identification of God, the Spirit with each of you—the Spirit Most Holy, most fragrant, most loving and kind. And when I speak of the loving-kindness of God, I think also of the words "His mercy endureth forever."[1] The mercies of God have made it possible for a host of inequities and little slings of outrageous fortune[2] and darkness to also carry many of you, from time to time, far afield of the goal intended for each of you. But I speak of the magnet, the mighty magnet of universal love, that by its radiance has drawn you still, like the Magi to the star, and has also magnetized your hearts with the power of right direction.

The Triad of Light, Life, and Love

When you were momentarily in darkness, the greatest hope of your life was the glimmer that flashed forth of the light. And it is ever so. For light is identifiable with life and simultaneously with love. The triad of these three brings to man the power of the consuming fire of his nature that will remove the dross and leave the pure, refined gold to act as an ornament unto the beauties of the Spirit descending from above.

Light, when it descends in vision or in sleep, may bring to each individual a greater release of God-strength. For when the waking consciousness is momentarily set aside (either in sleep or in vision by distraction and its principle), man is able to perceive the lodestone of the greater light and the effulgent roses of the light that descend from on high from the heart of God.

Angelic cherub faces peeping through the streaming light speak also of another evolution—one spiritual, not one carnal. And there is hope in man that he may not only preserve his present life unto that point where he can transmute it into everlasting life, but he will also enjoy the precepts and principles of everlasting life in the here and now, where the fruit of the divine art may become manifest in the radiated release of his God Presence, invoked by him at his moment of need.

The Release of the Outpicturing of Your Divine Identity

We think not only of each of you but also of those whom you can influence, those whom you can influence for the beauty of the eternal Presence. We think of the great release that comes about as a result of the union of heaven and earth, and we see that release as streaming forth not only over the margent of the world but in the hearts of all mankind embodied thereon.

For the world is a terrestrial globe of hope whose symmetry may be questioned by some. For there are banal influences in nature that manifest as a result of gross distortions in the God-concepts vouchsafed to every man originally but so traduced because mankind has accepted the ill-born fruits of the mass consciousness. We urge upon all, then, the acceptance of that lofty flow of cosmic thinking that will regenerate the individual world of self, hence the whole world also.

As there is a tie between the self and the universal Divine Presence, so God himself, through the electrode of your own being, will flash forth into the world the renewed lightning of cosmic intensity, the universal resurrection of God upon the planetary body, delivering man from all evil desires and creating in him a new realm of spiritual desires—the desire for the perfectionment of reality in his being and his soul.

The *power of love* suddenly is captured by the mind! And the chalice thereof, the fiery chalice, raises its heart in cosmic laughter: "I AM *free,* by divine desire, from all that binds! My heart, my mind, my soul are one with universal purpose! No more blinded by the miasma of the world, I stand awaiting thy release!"

O cosmic wind of Holy Spirit most brilliant, thy glow—like eastern sun, like lightning, like swift wind—comes out of the east into the being of man. And this I cherish. For in this I stand, not as a will-o'-the-wisp to be commanded by banal influences, by darkness and by the curse of darkness, but by the fruit of the light—fruit and flower and movement—garnering in man those precious gifts which God has given so wonderfully to all. Yet men have not received them, for they have seen naught behind the pall but darkness and confusion, chaos and stubbornness.

Now all will be released, as man will God and Christ confess and see at last that light will live to bring forth its bower of gifts, its power and shower of holiness, of wholeness. And man at last will stand in the place where the Lord lay to consecrate, this blessed day, the new experience of each who comes as the prodigal son[3] returning to oneness.

And aloft, alight and bright with new hope, the star is lit. The taper in the heavens that stands as a candle to the universe is lit by the hand of God. Its light shall beam afar and *all* shall live beneath its rod. For its rod is the rod of comfort, of divinity, of the beautiful sense of consecration of worlds without end.

As we begin now the process of release of the outpicturing of your divine identity through your mighty I AM Presence, we urge upon you all the acceptance of those things that count and the forgetting of those things that hinder, that you may come always to that realization of your universal bliss, which is the comfort of divine love to all, the expansion of the fragrance that existed before the fall of man into dark densities and the abuse of heaven's purposes. We urge upon you all the acceptance of this gift, so tender yet so fragile.

Be imbued with the Holy Spirit. Be consecrated. Be whitened. Be one with. Be divine. And be not the victim of the shafts of darkness in the world that seek to turn you aside from the divine tide, the flow of beauty and might and wisdom.

God is beauty. God is might. God is wisdom. All these three are to be found in this unity amidst diversity. Perceive it as the subtle shade of cosmic iridescence that illumines all, that is the vital wings' glowing purpose, fires majestic, strength untold.

I thank you.

February 27, 1972

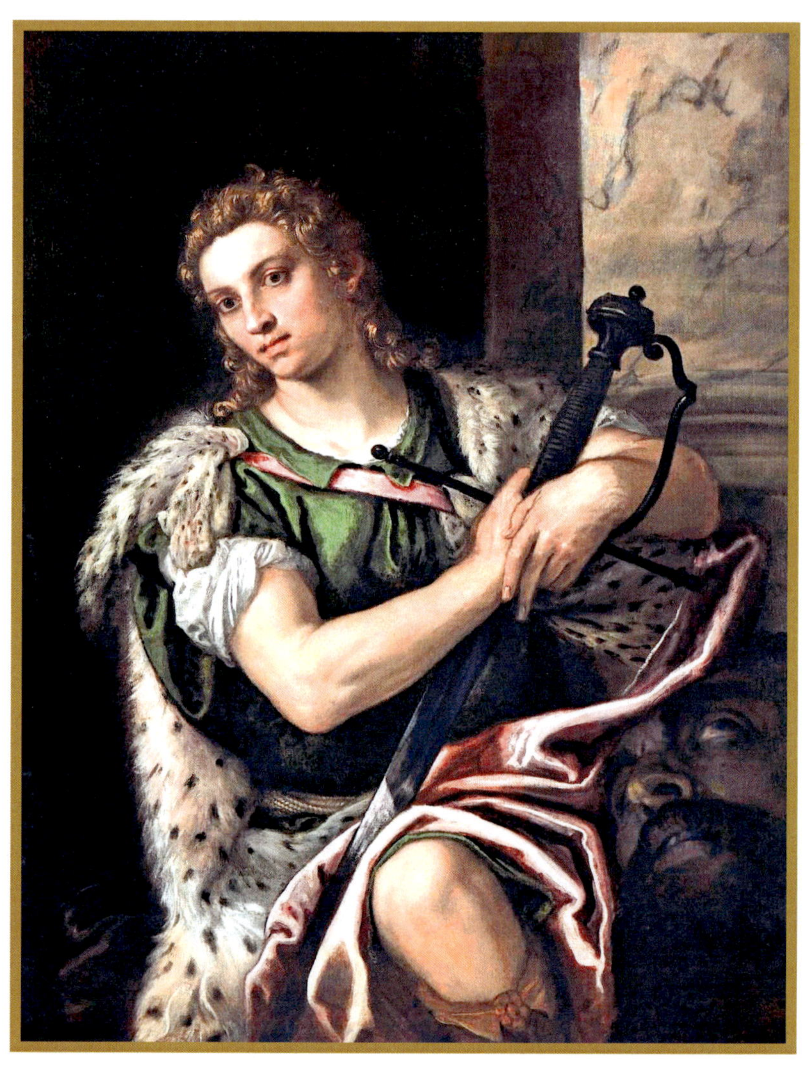

David with the Head of Goliath, c. 1557

You are all painters, after a fashion.
You are all possessed with many of the selfsame qualities of the Godhead in lesser measure, but you are also endowed by God with all the qualities of the Godhead.

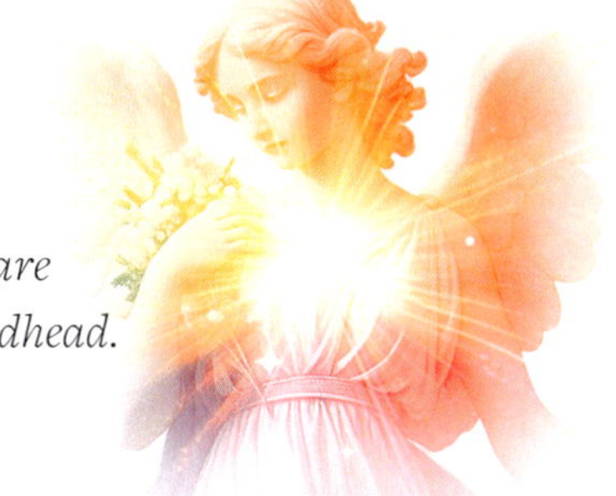

CHAPTER 7

The Divine Artist Within

Gracious, divine ladies and gentlemen, I come to you today to speak of the framework, the historical framework of the present hour and the magnificent pigmentations that can appear upon the canvas of your present life because you believe that the colorations that presently exist are the same beautiful texture and consistency as in days of old or in the days of the beginning of life.

One of the great problems of humanity is that they seem to regard past ages as possessed with a special quality of calmness or of violence that exists as a challenge to the present moment, causing them to feel that this present moment is different from the past.

We want all to understand, and understand clearly, that each moment is endowed by God with the same abilities—the same abilities to transcend tragedy, the same abilities to rise above circumstance, the same abilities to expand the domain of consciousness into the heart of divine thought and to bring that thought down as an endowment of this precious jewel, the jewel of the present.

Mankind should understand that the reservoir of the past holds a certain charm and allure, for it represents an era of completion, whereas that which has not yet become reality represents the opportunities of the exercise of the imaginative faculties, the endowments of God resident within the soul.

You are all painters, after a fashion. You are all possessed with many of the selfsame qualities of the Godhead in lesser measure, but you are also endowed by God with *all* the qualities of the Godhead. You simply have not yet learned to express them and to release the thoughts that are Godlike into the atmosphere, because quite frequently you regard yourselves as such a lesser figure than God.

Remember the parable of the talents[1] and try to understand that the endowments that God gave to you were intended by him to represent that final achievement, which is the reunion of the prodigal son with the Father.[2]

The Endowment of a True, Creative Artist

Mankind have asked for and have received certain experiences in the world of form that are intended to challenge the very life within them, to exercise its higher ranges rather than remain fixed in its consciousness and immovable.

The ability to be mobile, the ability to expand the consciousness is the endowment of a true, creative artist, one who can understand that that which has never been within the range of that consciousness *can be,* which will endow man with the ability to draw forth from the Universal the elements of life that he requires at a given moment and to show them forth upon the screen of his life.

It is not enough to simply aspire. Mankind must understand that in addition to aspiring, they must be able to act. And that action must be the action of God, as though the "tracements"* of life were by his hands, the tracements of thought by his mind, the tracements of identity by his identity, without for one moment allowing oneself to fall in consciousness into the pitfall of the human domain, the carnal mind, the strange experiences that never teach but always maim.

Rather, let mankind understand how quickly, if they will, the mind can be endowed with those delicate and fragile qualities of cosmic upreach that enable man to become creators of their own destiny.

*"tracements": a coined word that could mean traceable elements; the fundamental cause of one's actions, characteristics, patterns, qualities

The Cosmic Energies of Inspiration

As we pause now to summon the cosmic energies of inspiration and pray to the angelic hosts to increase the tempo of your own realization of the actuality of God, we ask you to put aside those temporary chastisements (even those you deserve), and reckon at last with that magnificent event when you have laid aside all weights. And as was long ago said, "The weight of sin which so easily besets you,"[3] you will find at last that you are a God-free being, and out of that domain of eternality, focalized into the area of the present, you will successfully demonstrate that mastery and God-control that as a divine matrix will assist the forward evolution of the soul.

You will have those magnificent passions of cosmic gratitude soaring within the domain of memory and consciousness that will elevate you, ennoble you, and endow you with a greater ability to use those talents that you have been given and to realize that the expansion of those talents into the domain of the world is a part of the drama of this age.

As was said long ago in Shakespeare, "Each one has his exits and his entrances,"[4] so let me remind you that whether those exits appear to loom before you as a fearsome manifestation or whether the domain of those entrances can be kept before you as an entrance into newness of life, you will be able to exercise the same God-control of your emotions, of your feelings, and say:

> *O Holy Spirit, endow me with the ability to work the works of God before my fellowmen, not as though it were mine in the outer physical sense, connected with cause, effect, record, and memory of my personal person, but only because it is the will of God working through me to endow the whole of life with that "encanvassment"* of Reality that is the transcendence of God made manifest in the face of life, with all of its temporal viciousness.*

Often I was challenged with the opportunity to portray human viciousness and violence in my paintings. That which I so frequently

*"encanvassment": a coined word likely meaning the expression or capturing of a quality or attribute as on canvas, whether on the physical or etheric plane

portrayed of constructivism in the world was the reality of God that is the reality of past, present, and future. For all divine Reality has forever existed. It is simply that mankind have failed to outpicture it upon the screen of their own life.

The Structure of Man's Identity Is One of Universal Grandeur

We come not to chastise but to teach. For when the healing arts are practiced upon the soul and the unguents of the Spirit are released by mind and heart—accepted and made a part of the contract of universal peace with the universe from the heart of God—each individual will understand that all that has been is a part of the range of his experience, one day to be a transmutative catalyst that will release only the goodness of perfection, the perfection of God into the manifestation of his consciousness as drops of peace and life.

When mankind understand these conveyances that are ever the activity of the higher powers of the universe, they will see that all lesser things—which they have clung to as though it were a temporary sustainment—ought to be abandoned in the face of the ocean of universal manifestation, that the soul of God ought to be the pond in which the soul should swim, that the consciousness of God ought to be that in which the soul is bathed, that the mind of God ought to become the sustainment and strength, yea, even the happiness of the very bones of man's existence. For the structure of his identity is one of universal grandeur.

The Strength and the Courage of God Is the Fabric of the Soul of the Divine Artist

Spanning the pages of history and all events, man is able to transcend the fashion of his immediate life and raise himself in consciousness into that splendor of the divine domain in which immortals dwell. So long as he dwells in the veils of mortality, so long as he holds a consciousness of death and the cessation of his life, he will not be able to summon those pages of reality that see his life as coming in intervals both of day and night, with a certain promise of the eternal dayspring from on high that shall visit him in his weakness and raise him into his strength.

For the strength and the courage of God is the fabric of the soul of the Divine Artist, and the Divine Artist does execute upon the individual screen of man's life the manifestations of His perfection, yea, of His perfection forever. There is never a moment when the soul in reality is separated from God, for with the separation thereof, even the soul would cease to be. God sustains and God radiates.

Does man, then, learn to possess the capacity to receive, to still the voices of the outer mind? The voices of darkness that are heard in so many lands and in so many minds are stilled now, for the permanent day of God burns as a taper of Reality in the sanctuary of his Being.

Then the healing arts and unguents of the Spirit will be accomplished and the veil between the Holy of Holies will be rent in twain[5] for each individual as it already manifests in the universal Christ pool of Reality, troubled by the vibrations of those angels of record who see clearly the activities of man that have been and those that should be. And in this area of contrast, the angels of record draw forth from the heart of the living God the projection of those actions that now shall accomplish in the domain of individual life and in the domain of universal life that which is the holy will of God, that which is to be found within the pigments of life, within the stroke of the master's brush in the master's hand.

For as all things manifest in their full, intended perfection, man will see at last that God intended from the Beginning the domain of perfection for all and that that outworking in experience, which takes place now, is the result of the failure of mankind to comprehend the immensity of the divine power that heaven has placed within their reach—yea, within their grasp.

I have said, then, that this is so because I have learned through divine experience that it is. I trust, through the power of faith and your belief, that you shall cancel out and nullify the power of your unbelief. For man possesseth both, yet at given moments amplifies first the one and then the other, rising and falling in consciousness. Man is intended to be as stable as he possibly can be, for "a double-minded man is unstable in all his ways."[6]

Hold Full Faith in the Immensity of the Divine Plan

Will you, then, forsaking the outer conceptions that have held you trapped in the mires of life, hold full faith in the immensity of the divine plan for yourself, for the universe? And because you make peace between your heart and the heart of God, will you allow the flow of those increments of immortality to seize you utterly and to lift you up and shake you as a fleece until at last you see the Son of Righteousness shining in his strength?

You see the beauty of life spread before you upon the grass and in the heavens and in the domain of your hope for the future. And in your determination, without wane, you shall find that which you seek and you shall manifest that which God seeks for all—which he has ever sought, which he has ever hoped for, which he always remains in consciousness.

O beloved hearts, I make this plea for the grand activity of the artistry of the universe created by the Divine Artist within.

Thank you. *Dieu vous garde.*

October 29, 1972

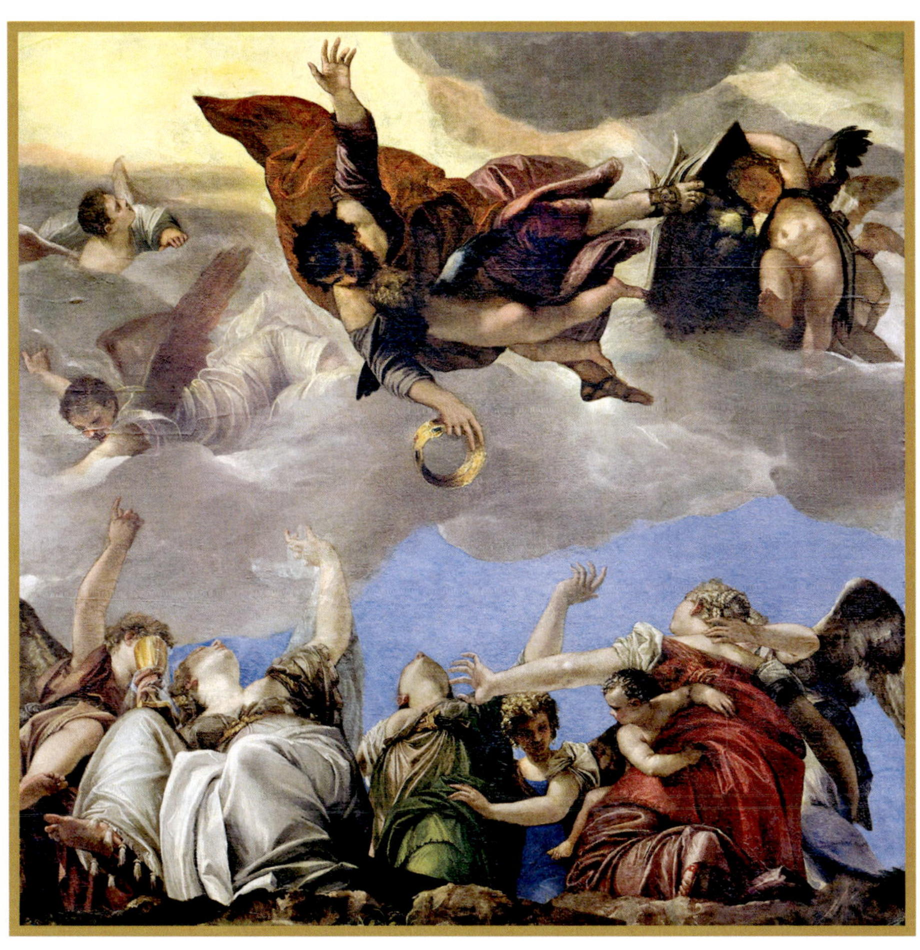

Saint Mark Crowning the Virtues, 1556

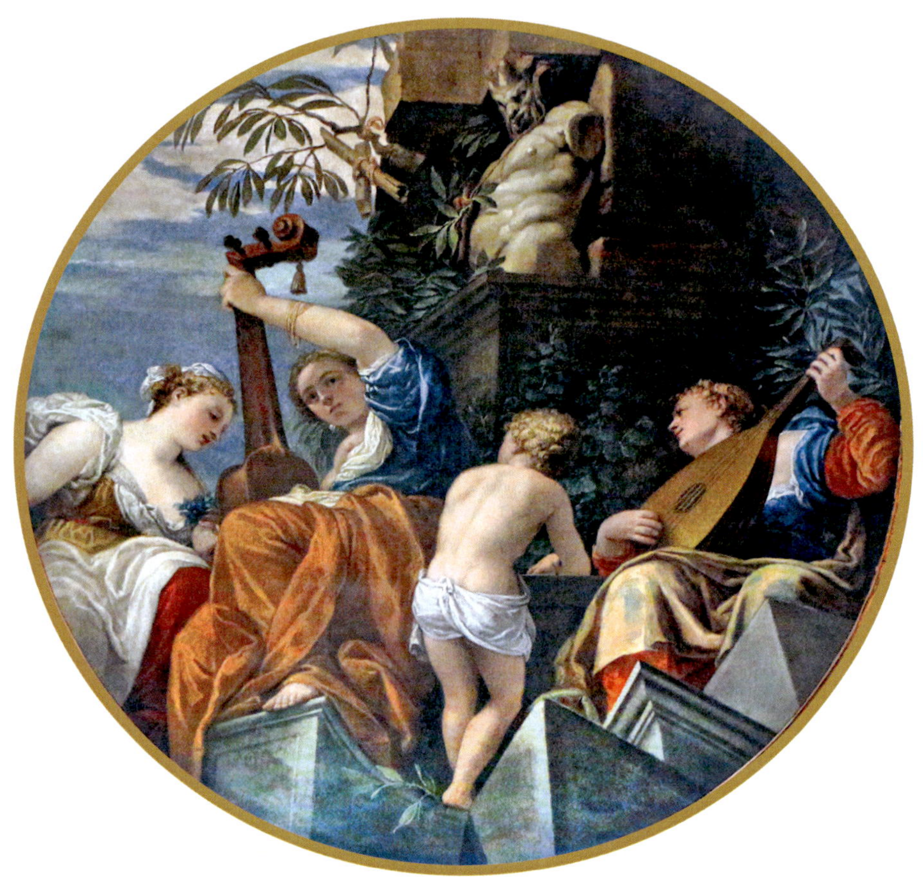

Music, 1557

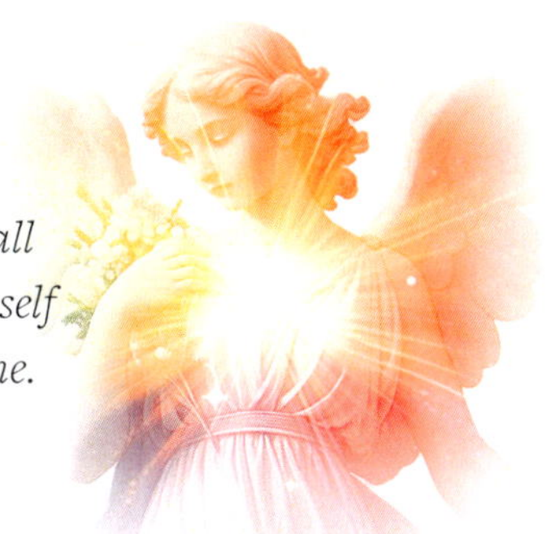

God in the perfect balance of universal love, wisdom, and power has already given the greatest valentine of all to mankind when he conveyed the very thought of himself and his potential to the blessed individuality of each one.

CHAPTER 8

The Greatest Valentine of All

To All Who Love,

The bounty of life is found in love. If a panacea exists, it is love and the feeling thereof. Such delight is in love that it floods the mind and heart with expanding vistas of new hope, even when hope seems far away. There is a joy that kaleidoscopes memory, past and present, into the glass of the future as pink mayflowers falling like snow in an azure blue sky bringing intimations of a golden age to come.

Love is the sun of that perfect day when civilization will have passed through its long night of degradation into a perennial sense of spring and of eternal summers that makes eternal life worth living. The segments of men's lives that are their yesterdays, their todays, and their tomorrows are time-spatial sequences that should mark a passing from glory unto glory,[1] making every intimation of heaven believable to the outer consciousness.

The wonderful world of childhood is great because of the mystical sense of being and of believing in the permanence of life at the same time that its ongoingness is assessed by the soul as joyous expectancy and spiritual advancement. Such ideas permeating the body and the mind of man produce, even within his physical form, the fragrant hope that, in rivulets of joy, surges with the currents of a mighty river through the whole being. Washing away troubles and cares, hope creates a vanishing point for darkness and a search of far horizons for the faintest star of joy and light.

A Portrait of Divine Love

So wonderful is the concept of a true spiritual valentine winging messages of love from heart to heart that it is my desire to portray for you a portrait of divine love. One day, regardless of outer circumstances or who is to blame for them, mankind will clearly see that the omnipresent, omniscient, omnipotent God, in the perfect balance of universal love, wisdom, and power, has already given the greatest valentine of all to mankind when he conveyed the very thought of himself and his potential to the blessed individuality of each one.

The heavy clouds of worldly condemnation, jealousy, and egotistic judgments are seldom seen or felt by the insensate ones who create them. These are quick to rationalize all they do as being within the province of their rights, but they seldom understand that what they give to others is what they themselves shall ultimately receive.

The law of currents indicates clearly that the course of all energy, whether it be qualified with shadow or with light, flows back to its source. Inasmuch as God is the author of only loveliness and perfection, only loveliness and perfection can be known by him, expanded by him, and returned to him. As Above, so below, all virtues and vices return to their authors. Thus mankind's heavens as well as their hades are either of their own creating or of those dark spirits that in past ages rejected God and survive to the present day through their vampirism of the energies of embodied mankind.

When the day dawns that mankind learn to repudiate darkness and not to personalize it, they will no longer feel the need to express condemnation; hence they will no longer receive it on the returning current. All may then perceive, if they will, the loveliness and perfection of the law of love. Nature will produce abundantly for man, and the joy of the Lord will fill the heart of every tiny babe at birth unto the fulfillment of his cycle.

The advent of the infinite flow into the finite consciousness will surely erase all the works of darkness that now loom so large in the world, replacing them all by the miracle sense of the divine potential. The nearness of the angels and mankind's invisible teachers will enable humanity to at last become the recipients of the boundless energies of the universe, restoring their soul faculties and returning to them the magical age of innocence. But their energies will not be engaged in the protecting of a sand fort from an ocean that will ultimately wash it away, but instead their energies will be engaged in the building of foundations of freedom upon the bedrock of truth, not merely as man sees it but as God sees it for every one of his children.

To Each Individual There Is Given the Opportunity of Embellishing the Universe

As your beloved friend El Morya saith, a thrust for a purpose will establish in you that inward sense that, in its plasticity of direct apprehension and divine knowing, can find acceptance for ideas that are not earthy, but heavenly. The refinement of the senses of man is a magnificent gift of great import in precipitating the divine art or the art of being divine.

Men need never fear the heavenly consciousness, for all that is of God is worthy of being cherished, and to each individual there is given the opportunity of embellishing the universe. Men furnish houses, array themselves in fine linen, and deck their halls with festoons of gaiety. Let them understand the art of becoming a decorator of the universe and of becoming an interior decorator of their consciousness. Not only will the self benefit but also the universe, which has need of those who value supremely creative innocence and the will to become the handiworkers of heaven.

For this cause were all born. For this cause did man come into the world, that he, identifying with the Christ consciousness, with the most tangible reality of the living Christ, might be engaged in his Father's business, the business of permanently creating in the world beauty and the divine sense of beauty as a memorial to the correct use of the many gifts of life. Of these many gifts, love is the greatest[2]—and all may receive it, and all may give it.

Devoted to the Christ cause of all, I remain

Paul the Venetian

February 11, 1973

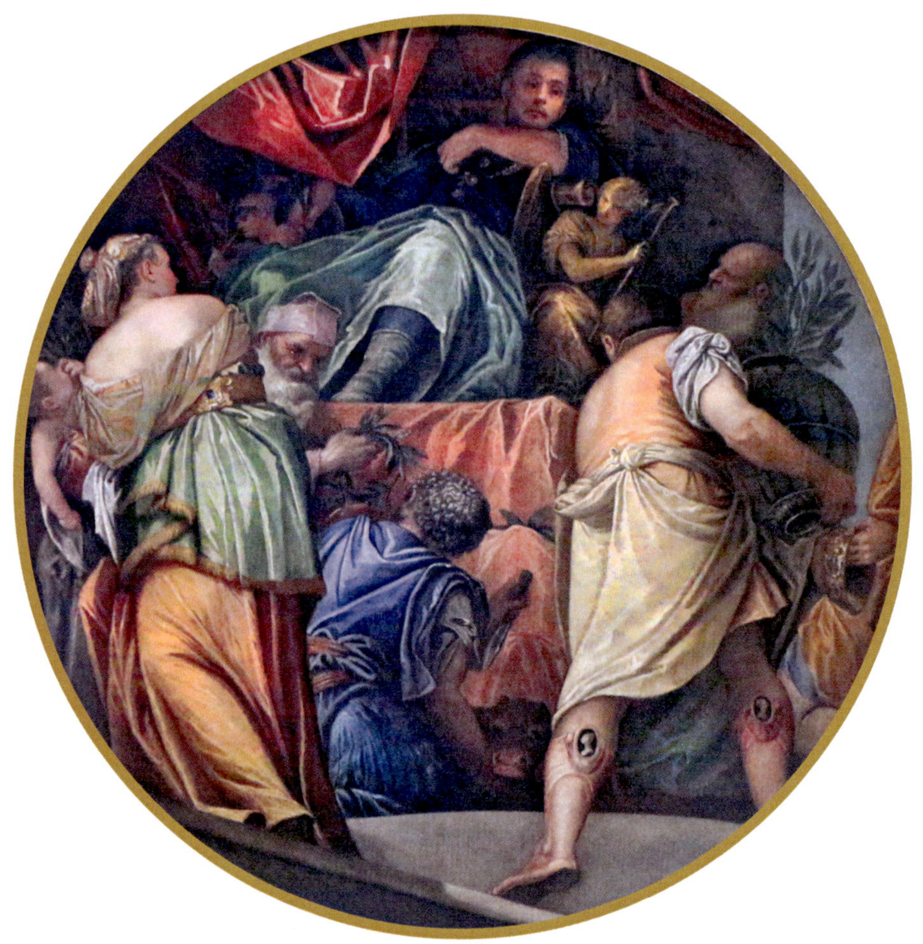

Honor, c. 1556–57

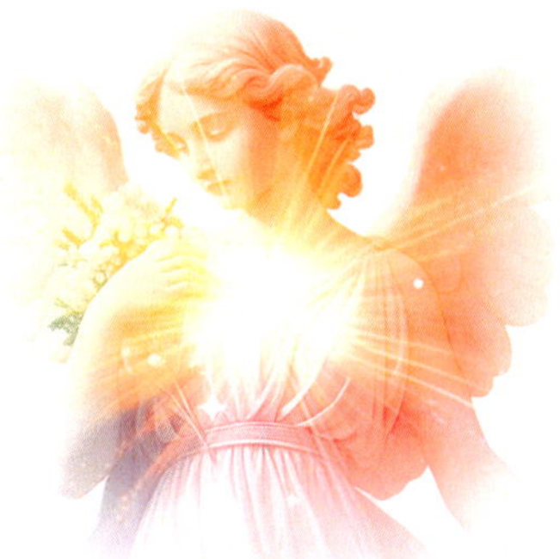

To acclaim the universe within and without as God's and then to use it to implement his glory—this is the great satisfaction of the devotees of beauty.

CHAPTER 9

A Dispensation from the Lords of Karma: To Call the Children of God to the Heart of the Mother

To Those Who Would Be Strengthened in Love,

As the Word of the LORD came unto Daniel saying, "O man greatly beloved, fear not: peace be unto thee, be strong, yea, be strong,"[1] so I come as the Lord of the third ray of God's divine love to strengthen the children of God by the power of the LORD's strength wherewith he strengthened his prophet of old.

Children of the light, attention! In this hour of world travail when there is taking place in the hearts of men and in the heart of a planet the chemicalization necessary to the transfiguration of all, I would impress upon you the very patterns that issue from the heart of God—patterns that, as floral cups, are made up of the exact geometry that is required to sustain a momentum of love upon the planet in the last days.

Precious hearts, it is one thing to have in the mind an idea of love, to think of love, to accept love when all is going well. But I would train you to magnetize love as a vortex of pulsating light essence that is not moved—that cannot be moved—come what may. To sustain a focus of love when all the world is confounded by the volleying of their hatreds is the calling of the avatars and of their chelas, who count not the cost as they give their all for the salvation of a planet and its people.

Patterns of Loveliness

Now then, I would take you into my drill sessions. Yes indeed, we do drill in my retreat. Those of you who think that we spend all our days and nights in painting and sculpture and the divine arts must realize that each of the seven rays issues forth from the white-fire core of God's being, and in that white-fire core is the full complement of his consciousness. And so I have an army of beauty-bearers, those who bear the consciousness of beauty to mankind, and they do march in formation and most lovingly come under the disciplines of Serapis Bey.[2] For they see that out from the flaming center of ordered purity comes forth the pattern whereby they can not only precipitate beauty but they can also release it to mankind and impress it upon the consciousness of the race.

Patterns of loveliness are the salvation of mankind, for each perfect design that originates as divine blueprint within the fiery center of life and is then embellished by the adoration of the cherubim and the flaming pink angels presents to the consciousness of mankind a passion for living, for striving, and for reaching the ultimate goal of reunion with the God Self.

To some, these patterns come and are perceived by the outer consciousness. For others not yet quickened by the immortal rays of beauty, these patterns enter the subconscious as cosmic rays do penetrate the earth and are absorbed by all the inhabitants thereof. But one day the force of these impressions must cycle to the outer consciousness, there to impel the mind and heart to be all that God designed for that lifestream.

The Necessity of Disciplines in Outpicturing Beauty

In our drill exercises we impress upon the neophytes as well as the advanced disciples in our retreat the necessity of disciplines in outpicturing beauty. We drill the mind through meditation upon perfect forms. We drill the emotions in God-control, and we show how each one may command the perfect feelings of God to be the receptacles of God's light within his consciousness and how he can, in the name of the risen Christ, refuse to admit aught else, especially the teeming emotions of the mass mind.

This can be done, precious hearts. Do not doubt that you, even in your present state, can rise quickly—no matter what your level of attainment—to greater self-mastery and greater control of the fires of creation. For when you come right down to it, the fires of creativity held within the forcefield of a man determine what he can accomplish in his earthly span.

Some dissipate their creativity in lust and worldly desire and worldly pursuit, in greed and selfishness and in acquisitiveness, which is the disease of the human race. We then must exercise the mind in nonattachment, and our devotees give mantras to affirm that "the earth is the Lord's, and the fulness thereof; the world, and they that dwell therein."[3] They must come to understand not merely intellectually but also in their feelings that because all things are God's, all things are theirs to command and to use to amplify his will and his wisdom. To acclaim the universe within and without as God's and then to use it to implement his glory—this is the great satisfaction of the devotees of beauty.

All then is seen as flow, and the exercise for the etheric body is to plot the flow of God's energy as it comes forth from the divine memory bank, as the electrons flow—mighty electrons as cosmic beings, cosmic masters, tiny electrons as sparks of love descending and ascending on the ladder of hierarchy—from the Great Central Sun all the way to the very fiery core of the planet Earth or a million other planets scattered throughout the galaxies. Thus the fourfold consciousness of man is expanded through discipline. And as it expands, God's beauty is heard resounding down the universal highway of the advancing mind of God.

Our Call Goes Forth to the Children of God

The fresh glory and triumph of our messenger[4] has prompted the seven chohans, the Maha Chohan, and the World Teachers to pay tribute to the victory of the God flame within him in this current series of *Pearls of Wisdom* begun by beloved El Morya two weeks ago. By the pressure of the love of the messenger ascended and the messenger unascended, the chohans and their Lord, working together with Jesus and Kuthumi, have received from the Lords of Karma a dispensation to go out into the highways and byways to call the children of God to the flame and the heart of the Mother.

As the Master Jesus commanded his disciples to "cast the net on the right side of the ship,"[5] so the Cosmic Christ, Lord Maitreya,[6] has commanded us in the name of the ascended Lanello to cast the net of our consciousness into the right side of humanity's being, there to produce the tenfold opportunity for mankind, through intensive study in our retreats, to balance their karma in these latter days when the judgment of souls draws nigh and all are required to be ready to meet the Son of God in the air[7]—that is, in the purified mind of Christ that they have acclaimed and must claim as their own.

By the power of the seven rays from the heart of the Maha Chohan, by the illumination of the Buddha through the World Teachers, we stand in life this hour to anoint each child of God to receive the tabernacle of the two witnesses[8] within his being. Our call goes forth to the children of God across the margent of the world and to all those who will hear and respond to the calls of the students of light to come Home. And all who answer the call shall receive the blessing of the seven chohans and the opportunity to attend classes in our retreats.

If you are ready for the disciplines of love, then I invite you to come to France, to the Château de Liberté. Come on wings of song and wings of glory. Come on the coattails, if you will, of the newly ascended master Lanello, who in other days of nobility and grandeur brought the culture of the Mother to France and the love of the Cosmic Virgin to her altars. He who so recently walked in your midst as a beautiful example of the eternal triumph of truth over error, of eternity over time, of life over death, will also welcome you here and address you on the beauty of the abundant life.

I AM and I remain the advocate of the strengthening power of love before the God of your universe,

Paul the Venetian

March 25, 1973

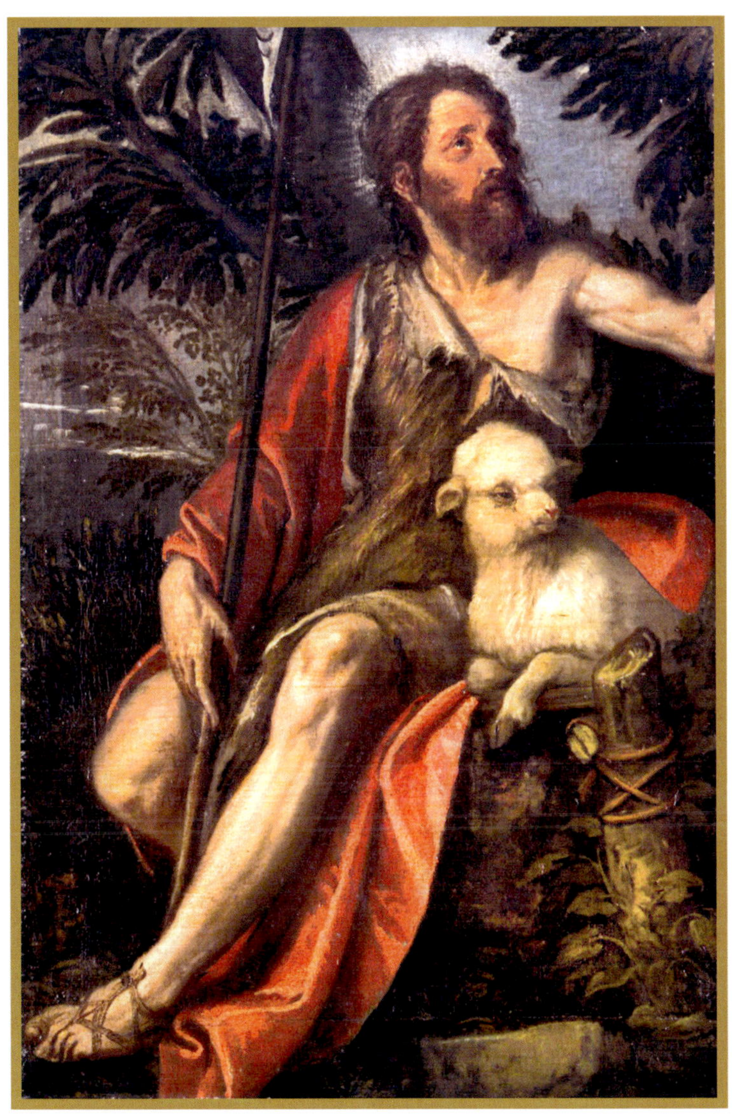

Saint John the Baptist, 1545

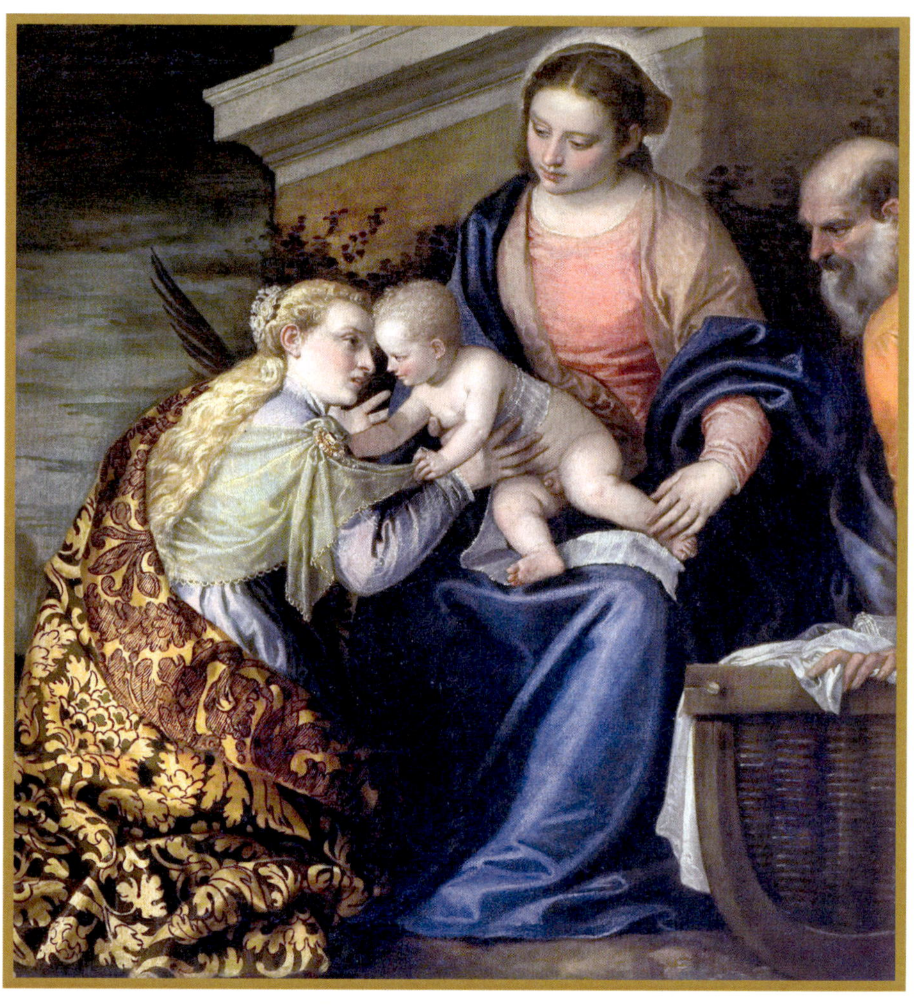

The Mystical Marriage of Saint Catherine, c. 1560–65

To enshrine beauty... call to Sanat Kumara and Lady Master Venus for the enfoldment of the Christed ones so that beauty might be preserved as the matrix of the soul, the cell, and the atom, and as the particle of identity of each evolving one.

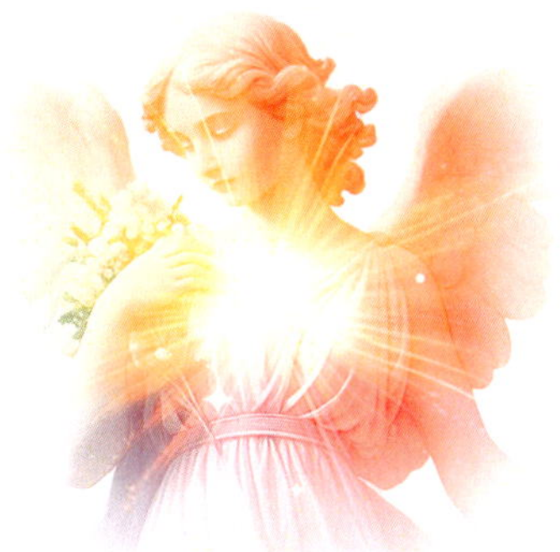

CHAPTER 10

The Beauty of the Cosmic Christ

By the power of beauty, the worlds were framed and creation was formed, individed into the four planes of Mater, each plane reflecting the divine effulgence, the beatification* of the face, the very living Presence of the Father-Mother God.

By the power of beauty, worlds are perpetuated. For by the true image of the Christ, which beauty is, man is able to hold the immaculate concept of perfection, and it is that concept held within the All-Seeing Eye of God by which the fire of the atom retains the destiny of its immortal birthright, the Image Most Holy.

Therefore when the forces of darkness desire to destroy all that God hath wrought and all that man has wrought, the first procedure that they take is to destroy beauty—beauty in the mind, beauty in the heart, beauty in the consciousness, beauty in the hands. For without the image of beauty, man cannot sustain civilization, man cannot sustain himself or his creation or his world.

Therefore I urge all students of the light, during these hours and days of transition,[1] to forsake not beauty, to enshrine beauty within the soul and heart, to display objects of beauty—images of the Christ, the masters, and the saints—in order that the refinements of the soul, which are the building blocks of reality, might continue to take place even while the outer consciousness is involved in adjustment, in change,

*having attained the blessedness of heaven

and in transmutation for the sake of greater beauty in the future, for the sake of future glory and a future heaven won by working the works of God's hands upon earth as the hands of man, by working the works of God's heart upon earth as the heart of man, by working the works of God's mind upon earth through the mind of Christ made tangible and real in the mind of man and in the mind of woman.

I AM the beauty of the cosmos unfurled before you as the mighty wind that rushes across the margent of the world, bringing good tidings of the Holy Spirit to some, and to others bringing the foreboding of their own returning karma. Thus beauty is as beauty does. And the peace—the silence in the eye of the atom, in the eye of the Presence, and in the eye of the wind—is the silence of the Godhead that declares I AM WHO I AM. I AM WHAT I AM.

Preserving the Christic Pattern of Each Root Race

Thus the immaculate image of perfection is brought forth in the undulations of the mind of God as these are released by the seven archangels, the seven beloved chohans, and the seven mighty Elohim.

The four hierarchs of the root races are gathered in cosmic consultation this day to determine what the greatest outpicturing of the destiny of the fourth, fifth, sixth, and seventh root races shall be and how it shall manifest and how the Christic pattern of each race shall be preserved through transition and through all forces of darkness.

On the agenda of their meeting is the consciousness of beauty and how it is to be preserved and ensouled, how the culture of the Divine Mother is to be pursued under Lord Himalaya,[2] Vaivasvata Manu,[3] the God and Goddess Meru, and the Great Divine Director.

There is some sense of urgency among hierarchy this day as Helios and Vesta have released the mighty currents for the New Age.[4] So there are some destined to reveal the plan majestic who are caught up in the whirlwind of human travail, human consciousness, mortality, death, and decay. Young and old alike, these need your prayers and our intercession, which is awarded by the action of your prayers, your decrees, and your invocations.

Thus, hearts of light, never was the need greater. Never was the hour more urgent. For those who have plotted against the Woman and her seed have determined to destroy the opportunity of the root races to embody and to perfect the noble plan released from the heart of Helios and Vesta to each lifewave, that the current cycle might be fulfilled.

Discover Natural Beauty Once Again

Thus I have come this day pleading before mankind—those who are gathered here and those who shall hear this dictation—to enshrine beauty, to call to Sanat Kumara and Lady Master Venus[5] for the enfoldment of the Christed ones so that beauty might be preserved as the matrix of the soul, the cell, and the atom, and as the particle of identity of each evolving one.

Beauty must be invoked as the bulwark of life as it is known on Terra. For if beauty be shattered and be no more, then what can be left? What can continue? What can be preserved for the next two-thousand-year period?

I say that so much of modern art and modern music will fall and be consumed by the weight of its own discord. Truly there is very little of worth except that which came through the artists of the Renaissance and the Baroque periods, for these preserved the geometry of the divine science of the Divine Mother.

Therefore return to nature, to the forces of nature, to the God of nature to discover natural beauty once again as conceived by God and executed by the salamanders, the sylphs, the undines, and the gnomes.

But look not upon the creations that they have brought forth under misdirection from mankind through mankind's misuse of energy. Look beyond the gnarled oak, the poisonous plants, the ferocious beasts. Look to the very core of nature and find there the heartbeat of God that establishes the rhythm of true art and the archetypal patterns of the Holy Spirit that are released from the very center of the earth.

Do you desire to journey to the center of the earth? Then I say, you must first retire to the center of the heart, to the white-fire core of all true being. And there, secure in the secret rays, in the white-fire core, you shall discover the center of all worlds and you shall perceive how you can traverse matter and enter the very heart of all life everywhere, anywhere.

Thus the center of being in the earth is just God's heartbeat away. And if you will make your heart beat in consonance with God's heartbeat—through *love, love, love* for one another, *love* for all life—then when the need arises you will find the little elementals only too willing and ready to guide you to the haven of safety in the center of worlds within worlds, through beauty and art, through the love of cosmos.

Make friends with these gentle souls. Work and play with them. For one day you will find that they will prove to be your guardians, your guides, your friends along the pathway Home. Invoke their presence, then joyfully seal them in the violet flame* and watch how your tasks grow lighter, your creations more beautiful, and how nature and the cycles of sun and rain, of harvest and grain and precipitation will all follow the great heartbeat of God and the rhythm of cycles.

To Love Is to Be Truth in Action

I come to you to acquaint you with the love of God, to bestow upon you my momentum of love, my mantle of emerald hue, which brings the power of precipitation, of love from the very heart of cosmos to you.

For to love is to be truth in action. And thus the great emerald ray and the emerald stone is worn by devotees of love, devotees of beauty, for they understand that love is nothing unless it can be brought into manifestation as a mark of truth, a mark of beauty written upon the air, written with great care, written from the mind of Christ, written from within each heart. For beauty is written in the earth, written as the stone of great worth.

Beauty is written in the water as the mark of heaven's rejoicing. Beauty is written in the fire as the smile of elementals and fiery salamanders dancing. Beauty is written everywhere—everywhere that God does write and man does write. Beauty is made manifest as the power of the Holy Grail, the cup of Christ that you all shall share, drinking, each one, partaking, each one, of the elixir of the Body and Blood of Christ that is the beatification by the power of alchemy, the transubstantiation whereby the body becomes the manifestation of

*For a decree to the elementals, see p. 244.

the soul, obedient thereto; whereby the emotions, the mind, and the etheric feelings, the etheric records do become one with the light-pattern of the soul.

Awaken to the Beauty and the Glory of the New Day

Thus in Holy Communion with the Holy Spirit you are transformed as in the twinkling of an eye, when the last trump shall sound.[6] So you are transformed from glory to glory each time you partake of the Lord's cup and then awaken to the beauty and the glory of the New Day, born again! And in that rebirth you shall behold your own Christ Self face-to-face and there see the Image Most Holy that is then transferred upon your own body and you become one with the immortals, walking the earth as masters of time and space. Honoring the cosmic clock,* so you become, in the place of dominion, masters of that clock.

I say to you, each one, come to the heart of beauty. Come to my retreat. Come to the Château de Liberté and there receive the lessons in the divine art for which your souls long and for which your hearts and minds yearn to express in form.

So be the living example of the Mother, of true beauty to all, and crest the tide to the golden age by the victory of the fohatic light of the design that is the inner key of light's release into your world, into your consciousness, into your planetary body, into the solar system, into the galaxy, into all of cosmos.

So beauty is the great mesh through which God releases his light, his wisdom, and his power. Thus does all energy precipitate and coalesce as the beauty of the Cosmic Christ.

I AM your servant of the third ray of God's love and I remain your brother on the Path, beckoning you Home to the arms of Liberty, where you will stay, nevermore to roam.

July 15, 1973

*For more information on the cosmic clock, see p. 283.

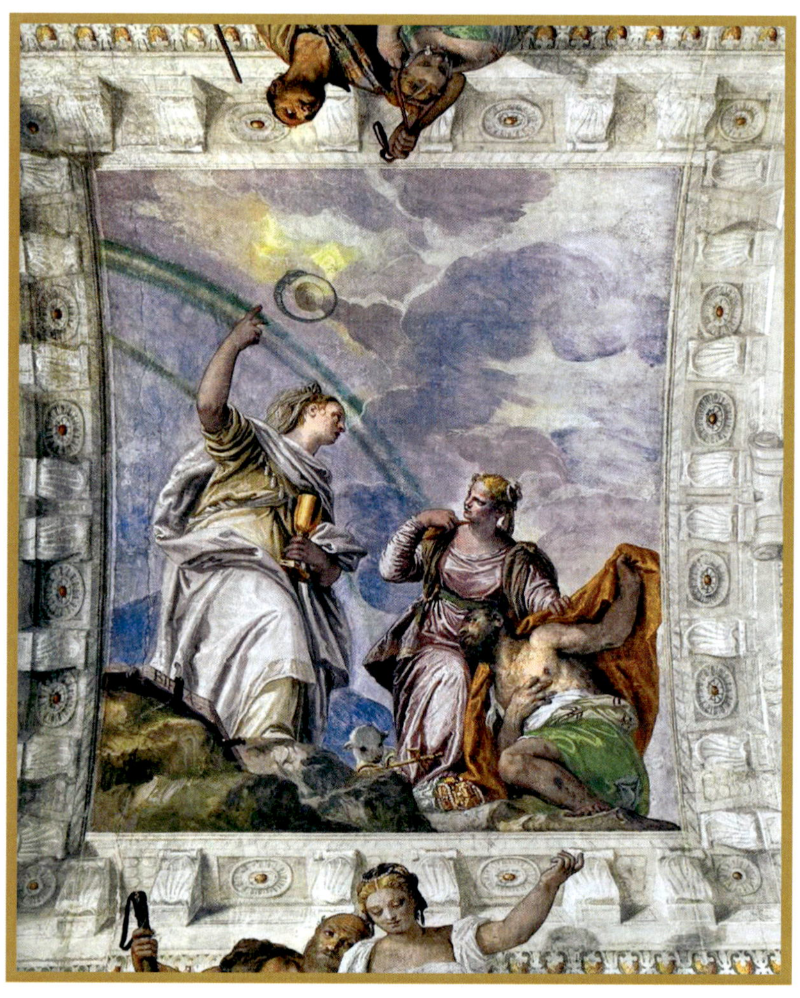

Mortal Man Guided to Divine Eternity, c. 1560–61

I am here to tell you that locked in the heart of every one of you is a unique idea of love that you can bring forth for the benefit of your fellowman and the progress of the culture of the Divine Mother.

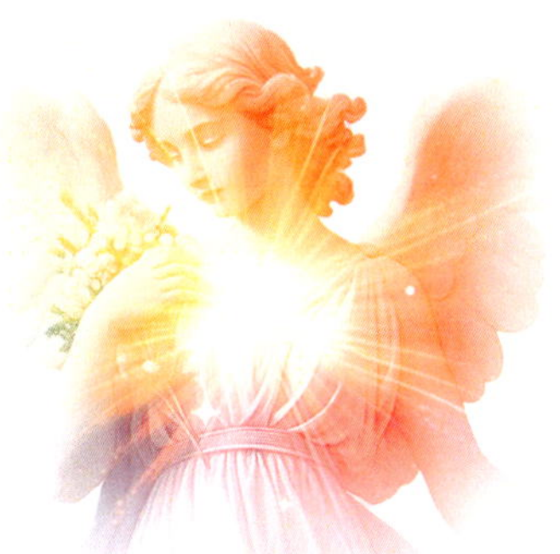

CHAPTER 11

The Art of Living Love

Good evening, ladies and gentlemen. I come in the flame of love to adorn you with the sacred adornments of the God of love.

> As fires of creativity flow
> From this sacred God I know,
> I bring to you an impartation of the soul—
> 'Tis the fragrance of Alpha and Omega
> That will make you whole.

As love is the flowing essence, the ephemeral quality of God, as it is the movement of the wind and the flowing of water, it requires the greatest of discipline to be able to retain—to have and to hold that love that is so tender, so gentle, and yet the ultimate expression of creative fires. Those who are the greatest artists, poets, and musicians who use the flame of love to implement an idea of God are those who have the greatest discipline—discipline of self, energies of self, of life, even of time and space.

I come, then, to bring to you an understanding of this discipline so that you will understand that discipline is not something to be feared, but discipline is the Law, the fulfillment of love. Discipline is a grid, a forcefield that is necessary in order to have the flow of love and to retain the flow of love.

You notice all around you where there are undisciplined lives how love flies out the window, how love is compromised and perverted and then lost. Where energies in motion are undisciplined, where there is not a chalice that can contain the liquid fire of love, mankind lose that love.

And so they are happy for a day or for a week or for a year, but to be happy for eternity means that love must be ensconced in a discipline that requires self-sacrifice. To continue to receive love, you must give love. But love is given in rhythm, in measured harmony, in increments of gratitude and a bursting forth of joy—a bursting forth that seems uncontrolled yet that proceeds from the bubbling fountain of the heart, the heart that knows that it is in that God-control of energy flow.

Understand, then, that when you discipline your energy, your supply, your expression, the hours of your day, your service to life, you are increasing your capacity to release love. The more you are disciplined, the stronger are the grids of consciousness. And to have a strong consciousness, as strong sinews, enables you to balance megatons of the light-force that you call love.

Alas, so many are destined to carry the pink flame. So many have incarnated on the third ray who are my chelas although they know it not. And they are in walks of life where they are expressing that creativity of love in various ways.

But because on Terra there is such difficulty on the part of lifestreams in their handling of the currents of love, many who should be masters of the flame are now in states of degradation, having perverted that flame. Thus their bodies are in states of disintegration and their minds are filled with foul spirits and the mutterings of those spirits.

All of the Science of the Aquarian Age Is Channeled to Mankind as the Flame of God-Love

Because love is such a powerful force, precious ones, its abuse results in a very severe karma and a deprivation of life and the life force. Therefore, you see, all of the science of the Aquarian age, given at the hand of the alchemist Saint Germain, is channeled to mankind as the flame of God-love. For out of love is the fulfillment of the Mother flame of every invention, every aspect of divine Reality that is waiting to be lowered into manifestation through the creative genius of many among you and many among mankind.

Unfortunately, due to the educational systems of the world and the equation of certain mass concepts and certain omissions of concepts that ought to be taught from childhood, mankind have a misunderstanding of native genius and they are not taught of the talents of the Lord given to each one, nor are they taught how to release those talents and those flames of their innate God-reality.

People feel a sense of worthlessness and that only the few have the ability to invent and to create. But I am here to tell you that locked in the heart of every one of you is a unique idea of love that you can bring forth for the benefit of your fellowman and the progress of the culture of the Divine Mother. It may be an invention, it may be a poem, it may be a geometric design, but it is a gift that only you can bring forth. Unfortunately, many of you have held that gift in your heart for a succession of embodiments simply because no one has told you that you could release it, that you could bring it forth, that you are beings of ultimate creativity.

The Art of Living Love Is to Be Creative

Why, creativity is the nature of God—your Father, your Mother. If God be creative, then you are creative. In your hands, in your eyes, in the movement of energies through you there is creative flow. And if you have the discipline here below, you can realize beautiful thoughtforms in Mater [Matter]. You can release those things that are not for profit nor for the trade and merchandising in the world that are here today and gone tomorrow. But you can release something of enduring worth, a pearl of great price, something that will transcend the fads of the times and move across the centuries as a permanent contribution to the race of mankind.

And so, as I looked upon you in analyzing what my message

should be, it was first of all to tell you that the art of living love is to be creative. And the art of being creative is to be self-disciplined. And so now I have given you an entirely new reason to be self-disciplined—not because if you sin you will die, not if you sin you will be punished, but simply because if you are disorganized (and this is a sin against the order of the cosmos), if you are slovenly in your personal habits, if you allow yourself to be moved by every little current and every little sway, you will lose the fires of love that will give you the greatest enjoyment of your life—the fulfillment of your creative destiny.

Now self-discipline becomes a point of enlightened self-interest. To move toward the fulfillment of your divine blueprint and your divine plan can be accomplished in the greatest beauty and joy of the fire of love if you will only take me into your daily invocations and give generously of the "Introit to the Holy Christ Self"* so that you can receive directly from your Christ Self the impartations of genius that are native to the "droplet of identity"—and this is what you are in this vast ocean of God's being.

To come into union with the Christ flame is to move with love.

Why cannot you walk the earth as Christed ones? What is hindering your manifestation of the Christ? Only the ignorance, the banality, and the sleep of the ages; only because your billboards and your media are not constantly telling you that you can become the Christ. They tell you other things and you fulfill them out of the hypnotism of the mass consciousness.

Well, I tell you, the media were given to mankind as a means of disciplining self, selfhood, and of releasing to mankind the messages of the ascended masters, the Elohim, and the angelic hosts.

Can you imagine if every time you turned on the television set the announcer said, "You can become the Christ," you would begin to believe it! It would become a common fact—no longer startling or astounding. Well, turn on the television set of your inner being, of your etheric body. Tune in to the teachers in the retreats of the ascended masters and hear these teachers as they teach classes in ascended master law.

---

*The decree "Introit to the Holy Christ Self" can be found on p. 245.

You Have a Body That Is Functioning at the Frequency of the Ascended Masters and Their Retreats

Here I am releasing an opportunity for you to realize that there is an invention right within you already functioning, a means of contacting through the etheric body—by a mechanism and an electronic frequency far above the physical plane—the octaves of the ascended masters.

The ascended masters have retreats on the etheric plane, do they not? This you know. You also know that you have an etheric body. You also know that things equal to the same thing are equal to each other. If you have an etheric body, you have a body that is functioning at the frequency of the ascended masters and their retreats. You have been told that your soul, using the vehicle of the etheric body, can journey to those retreats while your physical temple is at rest.

Well, then, since there is in reality no time and space, realize that at any moment of the hour or day you can be in the presence of your teacher. You can be in that retreat through your etheric body because there is no time or space at that plane. And you are where you will to be, where you think you are, where you feel you are.

It simply takes the practice of projecting the mind's eye to that physical point, that geographical location in time and space that is the coordinate of the retreat that is on the etheric plane. And then by an inner key that I will allow you to receive from your own Christ Self, you can be transported in frequency, in consciousness, through the ear and the eye and a congruency of your chakras with the ascended masters to their inner retreats. And so, you see, creativity can flow, flow, and flow through you.

The Elementals Are Tuning In Their "Radio Sets" to Play the Hail Mary

There are so many simple truths that ought to be broadcast across the radio waves. I am delighted to hear the Hail Mary coming forth, entering the atmosphere. And do you know that the elementals (nature spirits, beings of fire, air, water, and earth) are tuning in their "radio sets" to play that Hail Mary and to give it with the Mother of the Flame[1] and the sons and daughters of the flame as that recording is played each morning?

Do you know, then, that the elementals rejoice to see the media, the airwaves, used by the frequencies of the ascended masters? For they know that this will lead to their freedom, to the resurrection and the life within them whereby one day there will be imparted to them that threefold flame that will be the gift of immortal life.

And so, let the waves of the air, let the plane of the mind conduct now that which is in the mind of God that is transferred to and through your mind.

A Transfer of Energy of God's Mind to All Minds on the Planet

So let us have an experiment, for do you know that my pink cape is lined in green? And I am a scientist of the first order, and you need not relegate me to the exclusive corner of being an artist. For I am a scientist as well as an artist, and I rejoice that both faculties have been given into my hand by the Great Logos.

Let our experiment be the transfer of frequencies through the lobes of the brain and through the mental body. Let there be a transfer through your minds by the momentum of my love that is God's love, by the momentum of the emerald ray of precipitation. Yes, let there be a transfer of energy of God's mind to all minds on the planet and to the mental belt. And let there be a permanent recording in that belt this hour of the geometry of love.

The geometry of love is the art of living love according to the sacred science, the science that was taught by Melchizedek, king of Salem and priest of the Most High God[2]—the science that is practiced by artists and artisans of the Spirit.

So let the chalice that was released many years ago as a thoughtform now be given here below as a chalice for the mental body, as a chalice for the mental belt. And let that chalice be for the elixir of love. Let the chalice be a disciplined forcefield given to you at my hand and yet that you yourself must fashion. For this chalice will not remain with you unless you reinforce it by daily application to the discipline of the flame, specifically with calls to the white-fire core made with Serapis Bey and the ascension flame. For this chalice is composed of ascension fire.

As water seeks its own level, so the flame of perfection seeks its own level. And since the level of mankind's consciousness is at the level of imperfection, all that is perfect that is lowered into form must either be reinforced each twenty-four hours by those in embodiment or, if it is not, it will return to the higher octaves.

You might say, then, that this is a decay rate in reverse, for of course perfection does not decay; it simply withdraws. Particle by particle, then, the chalice will return to the level of your Christ flame unless by invocations to that Christ flame you continually reinforce in the physical octave the atoms and molecules of fiery light that compose the chalice.

Now, isn't this an interesting experiment? It's almost like going the opposite way on a moving conveyer belt. If you don't keep moving and keep decreeing, you will lose the ground that you have gained. And that is almost how it is prior to your ascension. It is as though you were on an uphill climb and as though that belt were continually moving, so that once you get on the belt you can never stop. For to stop is to move backwards with the automatic reverse trends of civilization that move down, down, down the mount of attainment.

And that is why progress is the law of being in infinity. Unless you are forever transcending yourself, you are not coming into the perfection of the Christ flame that is continually gathering more of itself, more of God's Self-awareness, continually becoming more and more of God until God in you is the All-in-all.

So I come to release creative fires. I could release much more. But I am limited, not by the laws of cosmos but by karmic law—the law of your own being. For your own being has a law of its own, and each individual has made that law of himself according to himself and his own self-discipline.

Therefore, where there is the presence of sin, impurity, human consciousness, past records of karma that remain untransmuted, the law of your being is written that the ascended hosts cannot pour an increase of love into your forcefield until you show that the love that you have already received—albeit it is now misqualified energy—is or shall be in short order returned to the flame, purified, multiplied as an offering on the altar of the LORD.

In reality you are chalices filled with love. But you have inverted those chalices and made of them the entire complement of the electronic belt—the record, the memory of all past misdoings contained in the subconscious at the level of the astral plane.

Now, then, if you think about it, all you have to do is turn that chalice that is upside down right side up. Let the sacred fire pour in, let the misuses be consumed, and you will have megatons of cosmic love at your disposal and a new law of your being—the law of infinity won here below as you become the electrode for the sendings not only of angels and elementals but of mighty cosmic beings, Elohim, Mighty Victory,[3] and the very God of very gods himself.

Accept the Challenge of Life to Liberate God's Energy

See, then, karma as the opportunity of God's own love to fulfill his science and to learn the art of living love.

Will you not think of me as you come across those jagged patterns and emotions in your world? Think of the rose of my heart and the delicate petals. Think, then, of taking that energy and fashioning the beautiful rose, even as the lotus grows in the swampland and out of the mud comes forth the beauty of the light of living fire.

So, you see, you can plant a garden that grows from the energies of the electronic belt. You can sow love continuously. You have a reservoir of light on high in your causal body. It has been told to you. But I would remind you that every erg of energy that is transmuted in answer to your call is money in your cosmic bank account. It is money that can be drawn forth and multiplied for the bringing in of the kingdom of God.

Therefore, accept the challenge of the hour to go back and undo those misqualified energies that you left behind on the trail of life.

Where you have walked away from karma, go back and fulfill that karma. Be the one who has dominion. Accept the challenge of life to liberate God's energy, to use that supply for the bringing into manifestation of the City Foursquare.

If you have walked away from a situation, a karma, a marriage, a family, a job, a business where you should have fulfilled the transmutation of love, you still have time in this life to go back and be the living presence of the Christ. And then you will see that to go back does not mean to compromise, but to go back means to take your stand with the sacred fire, to compel all human creation to move into that flame. And let the flame take that energy and place it upon the altar of the LORD. This is the cosmic honor flame as it is outlived in love.

The Staying Power of Love

As I have watched and seen among mankind how there are some of such endurance and such long-suffering who take upon themselves perhaps the brutality, perhaps the insanity of another part of life, uttering not a word of complaint nor having a feeling of self-pity, I have said these are they among mankind who are counted among the saints. For their way is the way of transmutation by love, and they almost allow themselves, as it were, to be flagellated for the Lord. And this is not a disturbance of the psyche nor anything to do with masochism. It is in many cases a legitimate expression of selflessness.

And often in the outer consciousness these souls have not the least understanding except an inner conviction to remain. They have the staying power of love. And by allowing themselves to be the forcefield on which there is outworked certain energies of the mass consciousness, they win their immortal freedom by the flame of love. And so, then, I would give you this understanding of a path—a path that is won through sacrifice, through selflessness.

There is also the path of God-justice and the flame that refuses to allow itself to be trampled upon by the human consciousness. This, too, is the legitimate stand. You see, when you are a pillar of fire and it appears to the world that injustice is being practiced against you, it is not always injustice from the level of the eye of God in the inner flame.

For mankind do not see the action of transmutation whereby the flame infolding itself, involuting within, is drawing into itself that substance, even as your body is the buffer for that energy as it returns to God for its freedom in love.

And therefore, you must weigh in the balance of the scales of Libra each decision of your life and you must come to know that the flame of God-justice is the flame of God-mastery that is a gift to you because you have conquered in love and in the art of living love.

Let the pyramid of life now be upon you. And let the flame in the heart of the pyramid as the resurrection fire resurrect within you the full complement of divine love.

I Want You to Be, Through and Through, the Frequency of the Christ

So I am your chohan of the heart. And as the pink flame of the heart is the frequency of love to the world, may I come into your heart at least on Monday* to be received there in the chamber of the heart so that I might release to you at the hand of your Christ Self the energies of love so necessary to reverse the course of the cancer that is eating away at the body of the world?

Do you not understand that all of the problems of the planet on a planetary scale can be transmuted in the flame of love? This will take place more and more as you bring your consciousness into congruity with your Christ Self. In some of you that Christ Self is hovering perhaps an eighth of an inch or a hundredth of an inch from full congruency with all of your chakras and your mind and heart.

Call, then, for the transmutation of the blockages to the meshing of your consciousness with the consciousness of the Christ. Call for that Christ flame to press in and through you. Call for that Christ consciousness to take over your life, to purge you of all darkness.

I want your hands to be the hands of your Christ Self. I want your very skin to pulsate with the frequencies of the fire of that transparent one, that image of life. I want you to be, through and through,

*The seven rays are released on the seven days of the week. Monday is the release of the third ray.

the frequency of the Christ. For by that love, the planet will be transformed and mankind will know that love has returned. For your own Logos, your own self-awareness in the Christ consciousness, is the fulfilling of the Law as Above, so below. It is healing. It is science. It is victory. Love is the All-in-all.

As we have communed in love, as we are one in love, we cannot be separated. And therefore, consider your life a continuation of the flame that we have shared this day and know that I am aware of you, each one, intimately—of your problems, of your past, and of the potential of your future. No matter what you have been, you can be better and life can be better and fuller from this moment on because you have accepted my love.

Do not, then, be ashamed, for in actuality sin is not real. It is a forcefield of energy that must be consumed. But you have the flame of the sacred fire that is real, that is all of your reality. You have but to consign the past to that flame, your will to that flame, and let that flame reveal the firing of God's will within you.

So I am your chohan of love. Remember, I live in love and I have, by the grace of God, at my command the energies of love from the Great Central Sun for the healing of your heart, for the healing of your soul and your mind.

Won't you prepare yourself to receive more love? Won't you invoke the fires of transmutation and come to my retreat and knock on the door and say, "O beloved Paul, here—I have transmuted another sphere of energy. I give it to you that I might receive God's love"?

And I will take you by the hand and show you my castle. I will show you the works of art that have been brought forth by chelas unascended and ascended. And we will go through many rooms, and lastly I will take you to the room where there is that frame that hangs. In some cases it will be an empty frame. In some cases it will have a canvas in it. It will be your frame, the frame of your identity waiting for you to bring forth the genius of your soul. And when you see that frame, if it is empty, you will want to fill it.

You Can Draw the Image of Your Own Christ-Perfection

And so I will take you to that place, "The Atelier," where you can work with other artisans who are learning the art of living love by the discipline of the hand and the discipline of expression so that you can draw the image of your own Christ-perfection. And when it is the best that you have to offer, it will be placed in your frame.

And when you come again before that frame after many months of purging and self-purification, you will say undoubtedly, "Beloved Paul, may I have another opportunity to express my Christhood, to draw the image of myself? For I have perceived a new aspect of that image and I would like to have this, my best offering, now placed in my frame." And of course you will have the opportunity.

Of course, those who come for the first time and find the canvas in the frame are those who have come before in other lifetimes or perhaps in this one. And you do have a record of your self-awareness there, and you may or may not be pleased with that record.

A certain few among you have been artists in other civilizations on Atlantis and in South America, and you do have in your frame an expression truly worthy of the Christ. In some cases, you have lost that memory. In other cases, you have retained it. And so you will rejoice to see the continuity of your soul's expression and how you have been fulfilling a path of destiny for so, so many incarnations. And you will say, "I am grateful for these many opportunities to perceive the Christ, but now I would enter the wholeness of immortal spheres."

And so your time is coming to an end when time and space will be no more of your experience but only infinity here and now, eternally the expression of your soul's creativity.

I am, then, the discipline of the white fire. I am the science of the emerald ray, and I am the filling of the cup of consciousness with love's creative fires. I am the fulfillment of the law of your divine being.

I am Paul, a teacher of love.

October 14, 1974

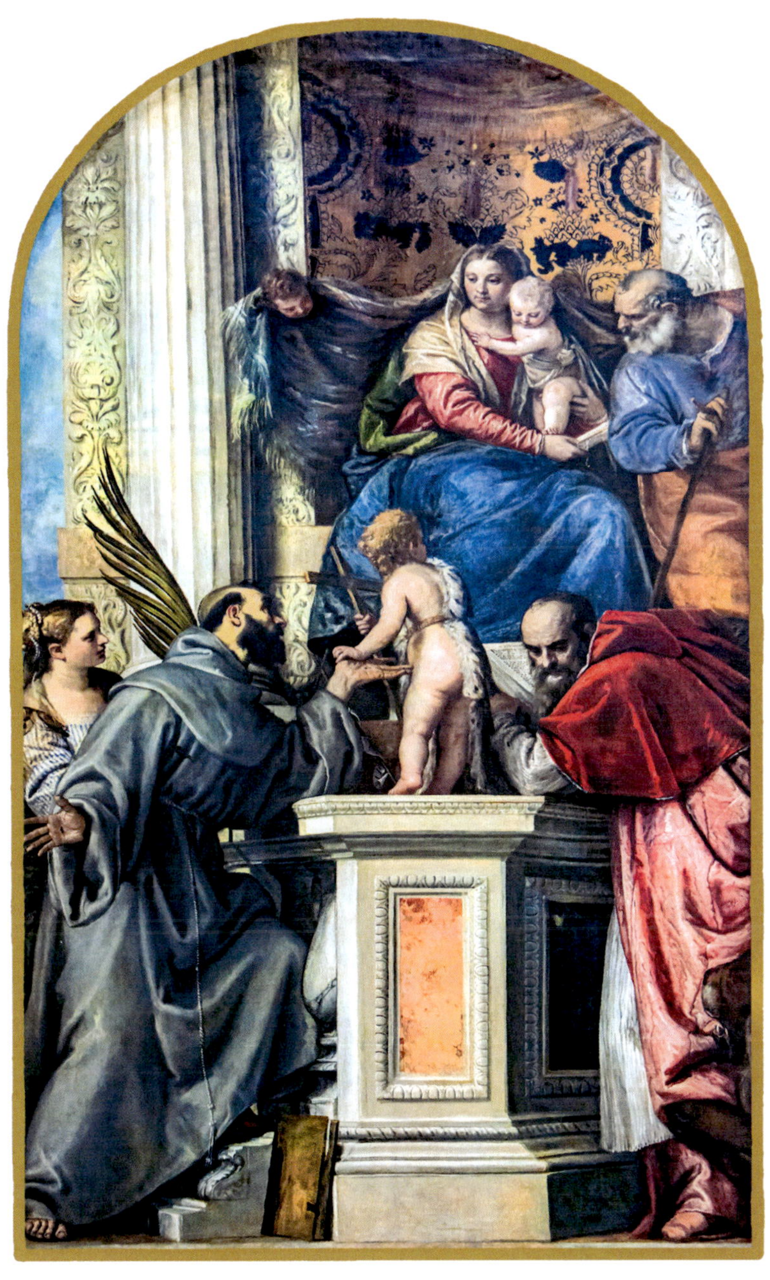

Madonna and Child with Saints Joseph, Justine, Francis of Assisi, John the Baptist Child and Jerome, c. 1562–64

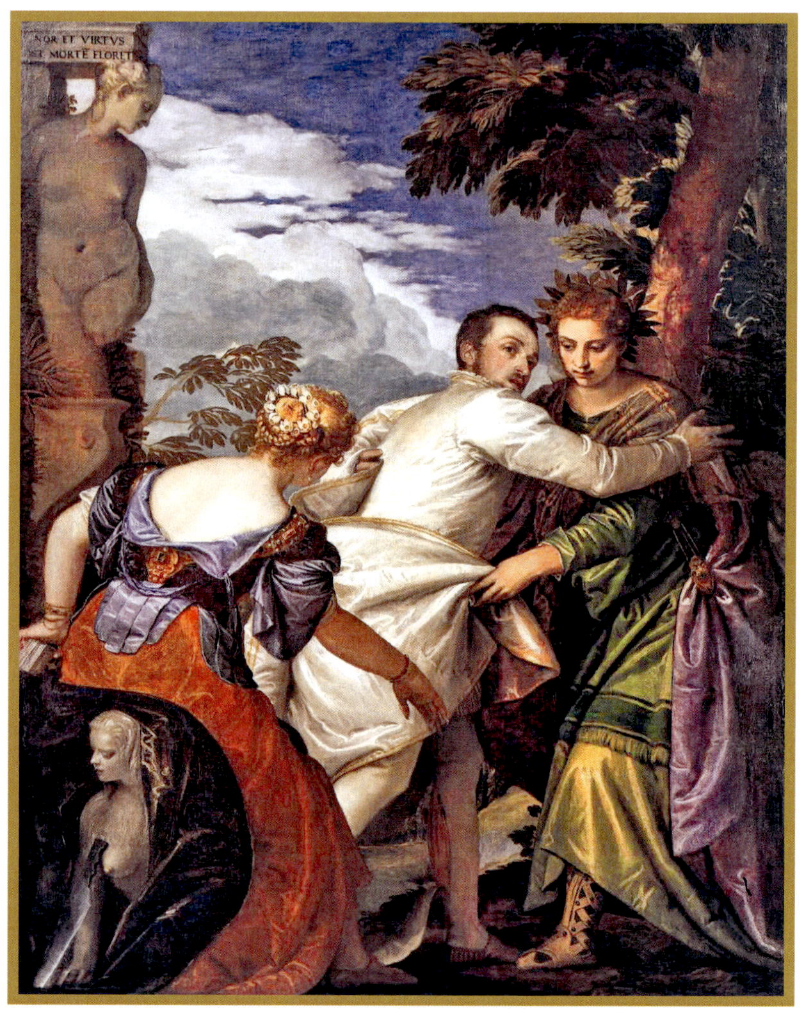

Honor and Power after the Death of Flourishes, 1567

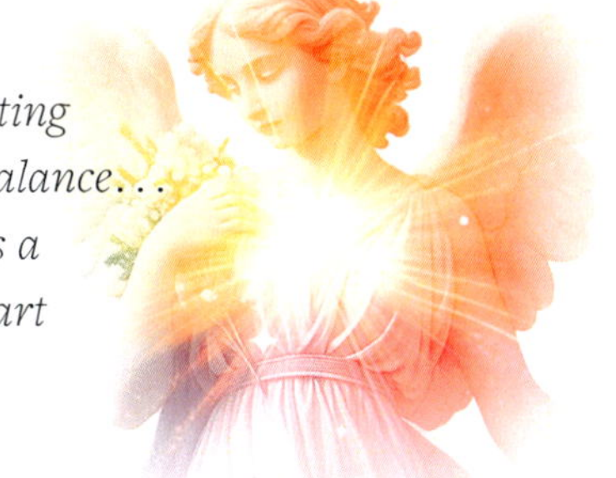

I come in the flame of art—art as more than a painting or a sculpture but art as a way of life, as a way of balance... and as a way of setting before the eyes of many souls a glimpse of infinity, a point of contact with a higher art that they cannot yet perceive.

CHAPTER 12

The Revolution of Love

Art Is the Precipitation of Love in Form

Let love burn on within the heart, and give fuel to the fire of love.

Never stop loving. For if you ever stop loving, you will stop living. Love is your very life and the energy flow of your consciousness. Love gives birth to selflessness, to that surrender that your soul craves, to every sacrifice that the Path requires.

If you stop loving, some souls will be lost. For there are souls in this world who depend upon you for the release of God's love. They depend upon the smile, the comfort, the helping hand, the concern, the care.

It is true that God is everywhere. But then electricity is also everywhere, and how long was it before one man decided to unlock the energy potential?

And so, you see, there are those who really do not know how to tap the source of love, and therefore you are that source. Even though you know you are but the vessel and the pathway for the flow, souls will see you as the source. For from their vantage point they cannot see beyond your position in hierarchy.

And so you have recognized the source of your love as the masters and cosmic beings beyond the masters, as the Solar Logoi beyond the cosmic beings, and as the Elohim that surround them. And one day you will see that they too are the instruments of a greater love, and you will see them as a greater and greater source.

Art Is the Precipitation of Love

Beloved ones, your love is the hope of hierarchy. And this is hierarchy—that we can come to you to release our love and to thereby find an opening in consciousness through which we may nourish mankind.

I come in the flame of art—art as more than a painting or a sculpture but art as a way of life, as a way of balance, as a way of movement within balance, as a way of portraying energy fields, and as a way of setting before the eyes of many souls a glimpse of infinity, a point of contact with a higher art that they cannot yet perceive.

Art is the precipitation of love in a form that communicates in the silence, in the knowing, and also in the thunder and in nature and in starlight glowing.

Art is a vehicle that God uses to convey himself to you, to convey *yourself* to you. Art as music and as dance and as drama—art as the portrayal of life—is the pink-flame way of instructing mankind in the discipline of the Law that is necessary for the bringing forth of the highest creativity in the individual.

There are art forms, and forms of art. To find these essential forms we look to nature, to the patterns of the Holy Spirit. We look to subatomic particles. We look to the basic geometric forms, to the golden ratio of the release of energy. We look at pure forms in nature. And we, as the artist who is the instrument of the Greater Artist, portray a fusion of these forms from out of the formlessness—a symmetry of manifestation through which a special dispensation can flow—a special release of light, a special release of victory.

This, then, is the light of manifestation. This, then, is the light of action—that you would come into the third ray and that you would portray in that ray a portion of the Infinite that otherwise would remain unexpressed and unrecognized, like the light that shone in the darkness, but the darkness comprehended it not.[1]

The Light Is Flowing and Yet It Is Confined to Imperfect Matrices

And so the light of the pure art of the Creator is shining upon this world, and yet that light is a banner that is not unfurled. It has not been seen, for those who have the ability to portray the light are not portraying the forms. The light is flowing and yet it is confined to imperfect matrices, imperfect patterns. And the artists of this decade, the artists of the Spirit intended to incarnate, they have come. And yet they have taken on the ways of the world.

And so, you see, the young who have the sense of art have been trained in forms that are patterned after the disintegration spirals. They have identified with discord, even with the patterns of the microbes of disease. They have tied into the manifestations of the misuse of the sacred fire. They have tied into the downward spirals of civilization, and sometimes, very oftentimes, their art is an expression of the human effluvia that hangs in the astral plane. And because their soul sensitivities have not been developed, have not been sensitized, they have psychic senses that tune into the astral plane, and thus there before you is the chaos and the confusion that is the misuse of the Mother flame.

When souls gaze upon these forms of art and take them into their subconscious, they outpicture in their auras—in their creative flow, in their energy flow—this effluvia, this misqualified substance, and the substance of the pattern behind that manifestation. And so there is a programming of the mass consciousness through imperfect forms in art, of patterns of the astral plane in music, in dance, on stage, in sculpture, in still life.

Therefore mankind are outpicturing those patterns at an alarming rate. There is the schism of consciousness. There is disease. There is the breaking down of the four lower bodies. These art forms are conveyed in advertising and they are conveyed in the voodoo cults, in satanic cults as perverted rhythms.

Everywhere in the world there is seen the desecration of the Mother flame through imperfect art forms, simply because of what has been called "the great divorce"[2]—the divorce of the soul from the Holy Spirit, from its patterns and from the patterns of nature.

Children Must Take In the Patterns of Nature

Therefore understand that for the true art of the golden-age culture to come forth, mankind must make contact with the Holy Spirit and return to the assimilation of God as Father and as Mother, as Christ flame, and as the fusion of that flame in the cloven tongues of fire.

Children must take in the patterns of nature, of the flowers and of the trees, of the skies and of the stars, and even the patterns and the formations of the stars in the heavens. Let them gaze upon a blade of grass rather than upon that discordant art form or that discordant music, so-called. Let them learn to listen in the within to the music of the spheres. Let them learn to hear the sound of the electrons whirling in their orbits.

Let the children meditate in silence, for they have come forth from the retreats of the Great White Brotherhood, and there they have been taught the art of meditation. There they have been taught to go into the silence of the chakras, of the Sun behind the sun, and of the secret chamber of the heart.

Do not burden their souls by leaving the radio or the television on or the tape recorder or the record player running in the house day and night. Let them have surcease from all sound so that they may hear the sound of the voice of God.

Children need to be free from the bombardment of their consciousness with all sorts of harmful images, those that are at the level of awareness and those beneath that level, at subliminal levels that come through the television. Even frequencies that are harmful to the consciousness passing through the television register in the subconscious.

You must understand that these children, who are being born and who have been coming forth for the last decade, are highly sensitized to cosmic frequencies. When they are subjected to imperfect art forms and sounds and images, there is a dulling of their inner senses, a pressing down into the within of those abilities of the soul to contact cosmic levels of awareness. And do you know, it has already happened that many of these souls of light have had their sensitivities destroyed for this incarnation because of unwise parents failing to respect their child's silence, failing to respect the time and the space, the cyclings of the consciousness of these souls.

Understand, then, that a child of God coming into incarnation to fulfill the flame of genius in the arts, as a means of communication to mankind, must be carefully sealed in the immaculate conception of mother and father.

Let the soul live in the veils of innocence. The veils of innocence are layers of consciousness from the etheric plane that seal the soul in the swaddling garment, like the placenta, which is like unto the Central Sun. These veils of innocence will seal the soul in its internal destiny and will allow the soul, at the point of maturation, to contact threads, to draw upon these threads, and to weave into Matter a solar awareness that will be to the benefit of all mankind.

It is music and art and forms that govern the flow of mankind's energy, especially their feelings. The angels, such as the great artist Michelangelo, an angel, took incarnation to show mankind the perfect forms of God and man that are in the temples of light, where mothers and fathers are taken to contemplate the divinity of the soul aborning.

You see, the feeling body of mankind is a giant sea of energy, a tremendous power in the desire body. And this power must be channeled, and it is always channeled through feeling. Whatever can arouse the feelings of mankind and cause these feelings to be free-flowing into patterns, this will control the destiny of the individual soul.

You Must Keep On Loving

When we see masses of young people gathered at festivals where discordant rhythms and sounds are put together as music, when we see thousands allowing the entire contents of the emotional body to flow into these patterns—and then we see how these patterns containing this energy are released into the astral plane, becoming a floating grid and forcefield that endangers the very equilibrium of nature—we wonder, "How can we bring in a golden age?" For golden ages are always noted for the flowering of creativity in the soul, for the release of creativity. This is that love burning within your heart, that love that must burn on.

This is why you must keep on loving. It is because the release of love to mankind will evoke a response in the desire body, and hopefully that response will be a return, in kind, of love. And when that love is flowing and you extend the form—the cup of your consciousness as a chalice—then the love of mankind that pours into that chalice of your being can be raised on high to God as an offering, as an energy that is surrendered, so that God himself may then pour this offering into the perfect art forms of the Christ consciousness of mankind.

We who serve on the third ray look for the revolution of love. We look for love as art and as the discipline of art to take command of civilization, to draw mankind away from their anxieties and their tensions, to heal the hearts that beat out of rhythm with the cosmic heart, to heal the bodies where cells are in rebellion to the divine blueprint.

We look to art and music coming forth out of the genius of souls now in incarnation and coming. We look to this to restore a planetary momentum of movement toward the Source, of creativity and all that leads mankind unto that Source—the noble, the true, and the virtuous. This is that which will usher in the golden age.

Art must be a form, whatever its expression, whereby the soul can get onto the spiral that is cycling toward the center. And the perfect art is the art that keeps the attention from point to point, making that triangle of manifestation in the painting or in the sculpture—the trinity of the threefold flame of life. Art is a point of meditation upon the life within.

Why is it that the students are not able to visualize the internal realities of being or to meditate upon the symbols of nature, the geometric forms of the flowers? Why must they always have an image physically before them?

Fohatic Keys Locked in the Soul

Sadly, I will tell you. It is because there has not been stored within their subconscious the perfect forms from childhood on, which would relate them to the fohatic keys that are locked in the soul.

A fohatic key is an energy pattern more complex than even the formula or the program of a computer. A fohatic key is a series of frequencies, of energy cycles, and these keys are in the I AM Presence and in the Christ Self.

Souls who have attainment on the Path have these keys locked in their chakras and in their auras. And when they do, they are able to release enormous quantities of energy to mankind. These are the ones who rise as the teachers, the avatars of the ages, the prophets, the Christic ones, and the messengers. They have an extraordinary focalization within their auras of energy fields, which cosmic beings use to release the light of the Great Causal Body.

Now, the incoming souls have these talents and fohatic keys locked in their causal bodies. By meditation on the Word and the Logos, on geometric symbols, on life itself as God, you can draw forth from out of the very own causal bodies of these incoming children the forcefields that will enable them to use their auras as the aura of God, to use these coordinates as the coordinates of cosmic consciousness in order to release to Terra the necessary energies for a transition into the golden age.

The classical forms of art, the great works portraying the Madonna that were released in the Renaissance—art forms that portray the family and happiness and joy, light colors and nature, the birds of the air and the beautiful cloud formations, beautiful children and beautiful faces—these should be in the nursery, in the playroom, in the recreation rooms. These should be in the classrooms, where the children can tie into that art and remember those periods in the etheric plane when they lived in the etheric cities and also journeyed to the etheric temples, where they have seen the world's greatest artists and their paintings.

Call to Me to Paint the Portrait of the Christ Self

These children also spend a season in my retreat, where they have the opportunity to paint the image of their own Christ Self, their own Real Self. And there is that image and that painting, as you have been told,[3] for each chela of the masters. And every chela is invited to return now and then, as cycles of progress are traversed, to repaint that painting when an increased awareness of the Christ Self enables the vision of the inner life to take form and to be drawn forth through the etheric body.

I have contemplated releasing, through an artist of the world, the image of the Christ Self, and I have thought of sending forth a call to chelas on the Path, who are the artists, to call to me to paint the portrait of the Christ Self—an image that every soul will identify as his own Christ Self.

This painting would also be a mirror. It would have locked within it some of the secrets that the artists in my retreat have—the ability to allow the beholder of the work of art to find himself, to see himself, to extract from the painting a portion of his own causal body so that each individual who gazes upon the same painting will see a different image according to his own inner attunement with the Christ flame.

I have thought, then, to sponsor an opportunity for Keepers of the Flame and devotees of light to make their renditions of the Christ Self and to send them to the Mother, at Colorado Springs,[4] so that the concept of the Christ Self might become nearer and dearer to the hearts of children.

If you would like to do this, please do. For I will be with you to instruct you, to inspire you, to release to you the image of your own Christ Self. And that image will be an archetype of the Christ consciousness in all mankind.

Now as I am before you, having been given the opportunity to convey the emerald fires of precipitation for the precipitation of the divine art, I choose to release to you, through my chakras, a key—a fohatic key of light. It is for the release of the divine art in your four lower bodies. It is for the alignment of those bodies according to the symmetry of the soul and the blueprint of the soul. It is a key to cherish and to love. It is a key that, when used, will restore your energies that have flowed in patterns of discord at every level, will restore your outer senses in order to key into your soul senses so that your soul can perceive beyond the veils of nature to the patterns behind the forms.

This will restore in you the sensitivity to love, to *real* love, and it will enable you to let that flame burn on. It will make of you, each one, an electrode for the golden-age art, and it will reverse the spirals of the degradation of that divine art coming forth from the purity of the Mother flame within you.

It Is the Hour of the Breaking of the Spirals That Do Not Fulfill the Law of Life

I ask that you make fervent calls to the Brotherhood, to the entire hierarchy, to release the violet flame in order to transmute all discord that would be transferred to the eye or to the ear or to the soul senses of the little ones and of the sons and daughters of God. For the bombardment of consciousness is great. And so I am a part of the rescue mission to rescue souls from this confinement of their energy flow to imperfection.

As you look about you in the cities, on the billboards, in the windows of the shops, you can scarcely find a pure form of art. You can scarcely find a trace of the ascended masters' consciousness in that which has come forth from the pen or the mind of those who are in advertising art, in sales, in public relations, those who control the images in the media.

Let this spiral be broken. It is the will of God. It is the hour of the judgment and of the breaking of the spirals that do not fulfill the law of life.

I ask you, then, to be instruments for the judgment, which is the flow of love for the restoration of Terra to the divine art.

I thank you, and I bid you good evening.

October 11, 1975

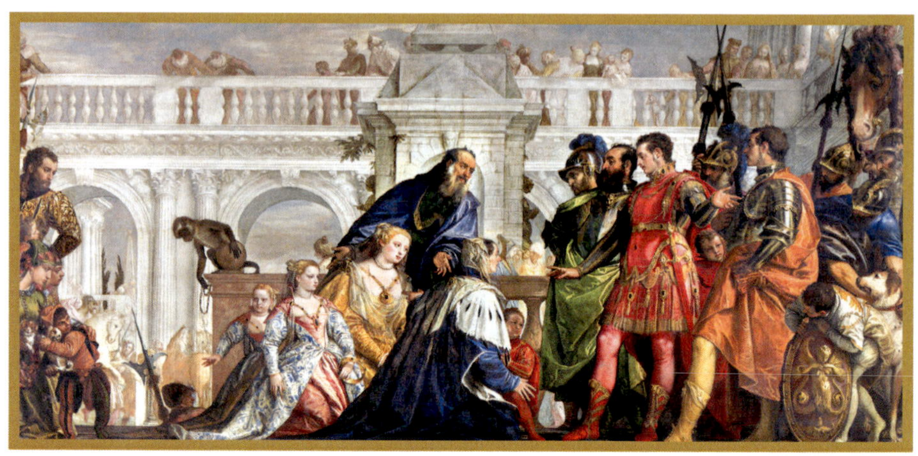

The Family of Darius before Alexander, c. 1565–67

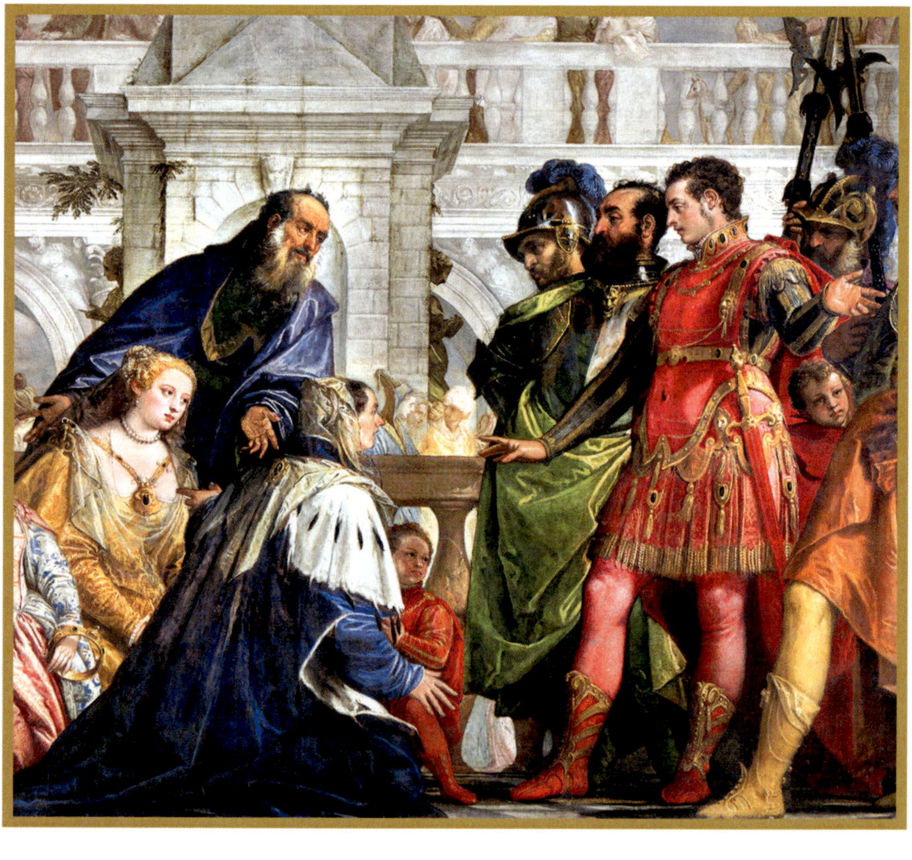

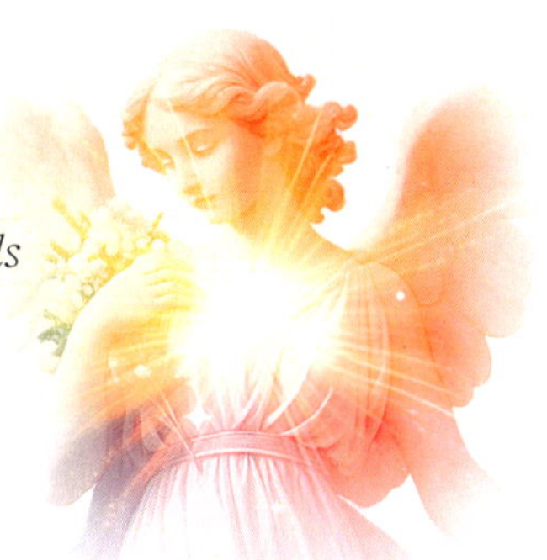

Do you know that when little children gaze upon the paintings of the saints, of Jesus and his lambs, their souls see beyond the painting into the inner octaves of light?

CHAPTER 13

The Beauty and Truth of Love

O Lord, thou who art the author and the finisher of our faith, I am come in the flame of love to address thy sons and daughters. I am come to infuse them with the love of my heart that is the foundation and the culmination of the beauty of life.

O Lord, I pray to thee that thou wilt place within this message thy message of the beauty of love. I place upon the altar the beauty of my heart, the beauty of my soul and of my ascension and of all that I AM. Almighty One, let it be transferred by thy love to these chelas of love this night.

Most gracious ladies and gentlemen, I greet you in my love for your life and for the evolution of your soul on the path of love. The initiations of love and all that it entails are taught at my retreat, the Château de Liberté. And I call you to my retreat to be representatives of love to earth. I call the students of Summit University, all Keepers of the Flame, and all who love love just for the sake of loving love.

I call you because of my concern for the little children and the distortions of love that are being placed upon them even from the moment of conception and certainly from the hour of birth. I am concerned for the disregard of the science of love, which God himself has formulated in the vast panorama of nature and in all with which he has surrounded man and woman for the fulfillment of their love.

I am concerned with the distortion of both form and formlessness. For instance, the work of many modern artists is an attempt to portray on canvas formlessness. Indeed, God embodies the quality of formlessness, and it is true that a transfer of the flame of formlessness can be made to the canvas.

But, precious ones, the lowering into manifestation of this dispensation of art, which ought to be the art of the New Age, has been set aside by the coming into manifestation of the false hierarchs of the third ray. These false prophets of love have infused the consciousness of today's artists, for the most part, with an awareness of the astral plane and the endless miasma of portrayal of the imitation of formlessness, which is not an imitation at all but a counterfeit of that creation out of the mind of God.

The fascination with horror and with the ugly is a symptom of the psychology of the age and of the devastation of the soul that lives in separation from the Mother and in rebellion against the Mother.

With the forcing of the chakras by the taking of violent drugs, the Holy Spirit energies of love have been taken by force, and the forcefield of the Holy Spirit—as Alpha and Omega (the plus, the minus polarity of the sacred fire) within the chakras—has in many cases been torn or shattered.

The Absolute Distortion of the Flame of Living Love

And thus Pandora's box has been opened, and the open door is through the chakras of those whose consciousness is half within the physical plane and half within the astral. And the juxtaposition of these planes at obtuse angles has created a warping of life that is not the warp and woof of creation but the absolute distortion of the flame of living love.

I trust that you well realize that I know that I am risking my popularity in being truthful this night. But did you know that the brothers of our retreat wear the emerald band and that our understanding of truth is that it is the other side of beauty? For to us, art must convey the truth of God and the truth of life, and this is true realism. For realism is the reality of God and not the unreality that is continually changing and that passes away as transient.

That which is portrayed on canvas today is in many instances no better than the sewer itself. The sewers of life and of the astral plane are being poured out from the palette to the canvas and from the canvas to homes of all classes. Hanging on the walls of the American home, such paintings are the foundation for the perversion of the consciousness of the Christ and the Buddha within the Holy Child.

As you well know, the fallen ones who perverted the great civilizations that once existed on the continent of Africa did so through the perversion of the art form, through the perversion of the love ray.

It seems that the children of light and even the sons and daughters of God have neglected this one great truth—that beauty is in the eye of the beholder and that *as a man thinketh, so is he.* And as a man thinketh *in his heart,* so is the transfer of that thought to the canvas of life through the vision of the All-Seeing Eye of God focused through the third-eye chakra at the brow.

We Must Clear the Vision

In order to portray beauty, one must have a vision of beauty. And so, you see, we use the emerald ray—first the vision, then the transfer of the vision to the canvas by the technique of the Master Artist himself.

I am a chela of Almighty God. And Almighty God has tutored me, heart and head and hand, in the way of transferring to the canvas, even in the ascended octaves, the most magnificent manifestations of himself.

Therefore, for the clearing of the stream of the flame of love within the heart, we must work backwards *and* forwards. We must clear the vision, for the vision is polluted. And the polluted stream comes from impure motive and the perversion of love. And so we work from the without to the within and from the within to the without.

We must mop up the mud of mankind's misqualified substance in all of the chakras. And I tell you, precious ones, you can get along fairly well without the functioning of a number of your chakras, for instance, when you perform tasks such as driving your car. But if your windshield is covered with mud or ice or snow, you can go nowhere before clearing your windshield. And so you carry implements with you and you use your windshield wipers.

But I tell you that the sons and daughters of God are not using their windshield wipers for the clearing of the third eye and the seat-of-the-soul chakra for the penetration of that which is real. And if they did, they would be here by the tens of thousands, for they would see clearly the great work of light and the release of light of the Great White Brotherhood.

But the false prophets of love have seen to it that the windshields of the children of the light have remained muddied. And therefore the vision of their souls is retained inside of a very narrow room and a narrow space, and they cannot see beyond that narrow space or beyond the immediate presence of the false prophet of the arts of love.

It is important, then, that you become the ones who clean the windshields for mankind in order that this magnificent focus of the All-Seeing Eye of God,* which I myself have guarded for you and for the Mother and her children, shall now become the focal point for the most glorious equalization and manifestation in form of that God-vision, which is the foundation of victory. For right within the very eye of God is the vision of the fullness of his manifestation within the City Foursquare.

Therefore, intensify the calls to Cyclopea,[1] and include in your calls to Cyclopea a call to me that with that vision will come the joy of beholding the beauty of God.

How sordid life is when mankind prefer the ugly to the beautiful. It is because they are uncomfortable in the presence of true divine beauty—because their very auras are the ugly manifestation of ugly thoughts and feelings, and the heavenly patterns and the divine image are an offense to their lesser sense of selfhood.

Let Us Pray for the Little Children

Let us educate mankind and elevate them to the inner standard of the universal Christ. And let us pray, then, for the little children. For the fallen ones know that these little children will grow up and come into their own to take their place, where they will be called of

*A large portrait of the All-Seeing Eye of God by Charles Sindelar is a most beautiful and powerful focus of God's abiding vision.

God to carry the torch of freedom that you now carry. And if their perception of the love flame within them is warped by all of these distortions of truth and beauty, then I tell you, they will not have in mind and heart the necessary chalice or grid or forcefield to be the instrument of the arts of love in the day at hand, expressing truth and the inner symmetry of beauty in design, architecture, fashion, and in that symbolism that is embedded in advertising and the communications media.

The children of earth are being mercilessly subjected to a completely thought-out plot of the fallen angels in their midst to hypnotize their minds, to hypnotize the subconscious. And these fallen angels combine the distortion of art with the distortion of music—music, the God-intended manifestation of the All-Seeing Eye and that which carries the flame of beauty in formulas of sound and rhythm or mantras of the soul—yantras of the Spirit.

Combining music, then, with true art as formulas of the Word, there is the double stimulus to the soul to go back to the white-fire core of the Central Sun and to contact the very heart of beauty itself. And so, you see, as you combine music and art in your own meditations, you find the inspiration of worlds within worlds, which you once knew but which have been cut off from you by the outer appearance world and senses dulled thereby—undiscriminating, untutored.

Let us proclaim, then, once and for all, that for the purpose of the geometry and the mathematics of building the intricate patterns of the soul and the consciousness, there is nothing that can replace classical art and classical music of the highest order.

The days are long gone when the chelas of the ascended masters were concerned with popularity. Let your homes be filled, then, with the music that has been brought forth by the chelas of the ascended masters in all past ages. And let your children be filled with the sound of this music, which transfers to them in the Matter flame inner keys of their own causal bodies—fohatic keys that release the sacred fire to heart and cell and chakra and every brain molecule by sound and imagery.

This Beauty and This Truth of the Higher Octaves Must Be before the Children from Infancy

Do you know, precious ones, that the great musicians have actually tapped the causal bodies of the saints and the lightbearers to bring forth that "music of the spheres"? And the spheres of which they are speaking are the spheres of the causal bodies of ascended beings and of unascended souls of light. And so, in the great symphonies and piano concertos, the little children often hear music that they heard when their souls were cradled in their causal bodies of light. Now, it is this beauty and this truth of the higher octaves that must be before the children from infancy so that they will know the voice of inner conscience and of the Almighty and of their mentors, the ascended masters, when they come of age.

As there is a dearth in the land of souls who will give their life for beauty and truth, for love itself that is unselfed, I ask you to come into the awareness of the living flame of love as it was set forth in poetry and in prose by Saint John of the Cross.[2]

Learn what it means to pursue the beloved—the Holy Christ Self who is the "hidden man of the heart." Learn what it means to be impassioned with the freedom of the soul to love God and to love him in every part of life. Let the Holy Spirit that comes to your heart through the third ray be for the refinement of your appreciation of the deeper mysteries, sealed—until you love enough—in the secret chamber of the heart. As you learn to appreciate beauty, precious ones, you become sensitive to fine detail, to workmanship, to the crafts, and to the culture of the Mother.

Life is not intended to be gross or crude or dull or dense. But it is intended to be in power, in wisdom, and in love—and in the delicate flame of the zephyrs and the strong winds of winter—the most magnificent release of light whereby the thousand strings of the harp of your soul might be played in order that your inner ear might appreciate a thousand chords of God's cosmic consciousness.

When children have placed before them from birth the images of lesser or incomplete forms, such as animals having human traits and sympathies, or gross features, comic strips, cartoons, and films that are made in a distorted (sometimes hideous) portrayal of life that is unreal, they do not develop an appreciation for the qualities of the saints—qualities that build character and self-esteem, opening channels for independent, creative thought stimulating new solutions to old problems.

Do you know that when little children gaze upon the paintings of the saints, of Jesus and his lambs, their souls see beyond the painting into the inner octaves of light? For the little ones do retain that connection with the inner spheres whence they descended into form, and the inner world is so real to them that they do not often speak of it because they think, in their innocence, that everyone around them has the same perception. And it is only after three or four years of incarnation that they begin to lose that ability to see through the eyes of the soul beyond the veil.

But alas, in this hour we are finding that that soul faculty of perception and penetration beyond the veil is being destroyed from the earliest months of life and the physical senses are not being developed in conjunction with the development of the inner senses of the soul. When the physical senses are not developed and the spiritual sensitivities are not stimulated, then the relationship between the inner and the outer development is practically nil.

The inner development of the soul must parallel the outer, and vice versa. And therefore if there are not manifestations surrounding the child that key the inner development of the spiritual centers called chakras, then that development will be bypassed and it may not take place in that given lifetime. The cycles missed may be beyond recall.

And so, you see, the keys to cosmic consciousness must surround the child in the earliest years. The period of gestation through the age of seven affords the most creative hours of the child's entire incarnation. It is during this period that the life patterns are set.

The Misuse of the Fundamental Principles of the Law of Precipitation

And so, beloved ones, although you know this law, I repeat it tonight because I desire to bring to the very fore of your attention the fact that civilization in America and in every nation on earth is being destroyed in this day and age by the fallen ones' manipulation of art forms from their positions of power both in and out of embodiment. *I say it is being destroyed, and I mean every word of it!*

The downward spirals of darkness come from that which contacts the eye of every single individual in embodiment. Look at the billboards. Look at the newspapers. Look at the magazines. Look at the use of motion pictures and tell me how often you see a pure, undiluted, unperverted thoughtform of the ascended masters' octave. So often there is beauty portrayed, but that beauty in nature or in man and woman is perverted because it is used to sell sex and death and cigarettes and liquor and every form of violation of the chakras.

And therefore as the souls of individuals cry out to drink in beauty and the only beauty they see is in association with perversion, they therefore take in both. And thus there is the magnetism of beauty to which the soul is receptive, and upon the tail of it comes the trigger of the thoughtform of black magic, which, as you know, is the misuse of the science of imaging or projecting upon the screen of life through visualization a desired manifestation. People do this all the time. They simply see themselves accomplishing their goals and then they set about realizing them in a practical manner. This is "eye-magic" as the "I" images the will or intent of the soul.

The misuse of this science for factors of control and the manipulation of people's tastes, preferences, and decision-making through advertising or any means becomes, as you can see, a violation of the All-Seeing Eye of God, who holds the immaculate concept for the whole of creation. This violation affects everyone at the level of the third eye and seat-of-the-soul chakra—even as the malpractice of this science of imaging involves the misuse of these chakras by its practitioners.

This misuse of the fundamental principles of the law of precipitation, or alchemy, is indeed a form of black magic, which individuals unwittingly practice upon themselves even as they are the hapless, unsuspecting victims of such abuses through the media.

How long can this continue? It is gaining momentum. It is a downward-moving spiral. And today the art culture that was born out of the drug culture has become a style and a way of life that has left its mark on everything, even to the clothes and accessories you wear.

And that which was once shocking is no longer shocking because the senses are dulled, the ears are dulled. Even the physical ears are no longer as perceptive of sound as they were a decade ago. And thus, the inner ear listening to the inner voice is also burdened, even as it is stunted, by the absence of proper stimuli in early development.

Precious ones, I could go on and on. But I come upon the sweep of love of Lady Venus, of Chamuel and Charity, and the great love that you have brought to this conference.

As Lord of the Third Ray, I desire to make practical to you the science of love, which is connected with the science of vision, in order to make you understand that living the way of love is going out and taking the action of the Holy Spirit and moving into society and challenging those conditions that are the very destruction of souls and that are making inroads into a way of life that even in this hour of the Dark Cycle (noted for the accelerated return of personal and planetary karma) could be a way of light and beauty.

Make the Fiats of Love with Me That There Be the Shattering of the Forcefields of Darkness

I appeal to you, then, on behalf of the children of earth and on behalf of souls of light whose vision is being tampered with in this very hour. Will you not, then, make the fiats of love with me that there be the shattering of the forcefields of darkness and of the veils of illusion and of the membrane of density's distortions that cover the all-seeing eye, the third eye, of the beloved souls of light on earth?

> *I call, then, in the name of Almighty God, to the entire Spirit of the Great White Brotherhood. I call to Saint Germain for assistance.*
>
> *I call to Freedom for assistance. And I, Paul, stand before the Lords of Karma this day and I make my plea for freedom—freedom for the souls of lightbearers from the perversions of vision, of beauty and of truth, freedom from the perversions of the beauty of the chakras of God in their body temples.*

In the name of the Mother, I send forth the lightning of the mind of God to shatter the forcefield of human bondage! And in the name Jesus Christ I say: Shatter the forcefield! Shatter the forcefield of human bondage!

In the name of the Christ, I, Paul, demand the binding of the false hierarchs of love by the archangels of love, Chamuel and Charity! Let them be bound this hour. Let blue lightning from the Great Central Sun explode as the fireworks of the Fourth of July. And let the exploding and the imploding of light be for the shattering of forcefields out of the depths of death and hell that are spawned by sinister forces of anti-beauty, anti-love, and anti-truth.

Blaze forth the light! [repeated 20 times]

Beloved ones, I would explain to you this element of the science of the spoken Word. When you give a series of decrees or fiats for a specific purpose and you are tackling the entrenched forcefields of darkness that have existed for thousands of years as an astral belt of effluvia surrounding planet Earth created by the mass consciousness of human hate and hate miscreations, you need a more than ordinary science and expression of that Word of the LORD for the protection of your soul as you ascend Bethany's hill with Jesus.

When you give a concentrated series of fiats such as this action of "Blaze forth the light!" or any short decree for a specific action, if you will give it in rhythm and continue to give it and visualize the Holy Spirit moving against the entrenched darkness of the earth in all areas where love is perverted, even in the areas of pornography, prostitution, gambling, organized crime, drug trafficking, child molestation and child abuse, you will do much to assist the hosts of light to alleviate the suffering and burdens of the planet and the children of light.

All of these areas, through the perversion of vision, are become the perversion of the culture of the Mother, the body of the Mother, the innocence of the Mother and the child. To tackle them you must be prepared to grapple with the most vicious forces of the astral plane.

I tell you, precious ones, that to defend love is to take on the sinister force itself. Do not marvel, then, when you are met with opposition. For the greatest of saints have described that opposition to love and the coming of demons and discarnates moving against this mighty work of the ages—the restoration of divine love to a planet and her people.

It is time, then, for those who have learned of the armour of Archangel Michael and the use of his flaming blue sword and of the action of the Great Blue Causal Body to stand forth in the flame of wisdom and wise dominion and call upon the Trinity to tackle now all that is pitted by death and hell against the pure love of Father-Mother God, of twin flames, of Mother and child, of Guru and chela and the youth of the world.

So, before you begin, give this call to the Captain of the Lord's Hosts at home or in your car:

Lord Michael before, Lord Michael behind,
Lord Michael to the right, Lord Michael to the left,
Lord Michael above, Lord Michael below,
Lord Michael, Lord Michael wherever I go!

I AM his Love protecting here!
I AM his Love protecting here!
I AM his Love protecting here! (3x)

Precious hearts, the attack is on love—divine love blazing from the hearts of God's people as the nucleus of the New Age. Therefore, say with me, in the name of Almighty God, and visualize the great blue sphere from Alpha and Omega—

Blaze forth the love! [repeated 22 times]

Use this technique, precious ones. It is for the transmutation of energy fields of darkness. By the rhythm of the sphere of love from your causal body, you will invoke an action of the blue-lightning angels of the first ray serving under Archangel Michael who, by the power of the will of God, will break down forcefields of misqualified substance so that the violet-flame angels and the legions of Astrea[3] can come back again and again for a whirling action of the sacred fire as they hold the balance for your soul's liberation from all evil on the first and the seventh rays.

You have been told of the blue lightning wielded by the LORD's hosts and its shattering effect upon negative forcefields most dangerous to society—even toxic waste and radioactive fallout. And indeed, the cosmic blue lightning of purity is an action of sacred fire incomparable. Now, coupled with the sphere of love and the relentless love of the decreers of the Word, you will see a magnificence of love never known before and a breaking down of all of those vortices of darkness spawned by the fallen angels that are pitted against the souls who are making their way to the light of their mighty I AM Presence.

I am Paul. I seal you now in the third eye. It is a seal of beauty, a kiss of love. And it is my hand cleaning the windshield of your consciousness.

AUM . . . Ma-ray.

July 3, 1977

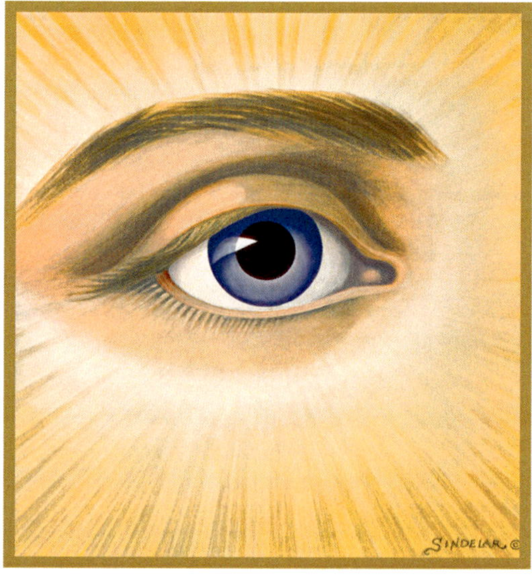

The All-Seeing Eye of God, by Charles Sindelar

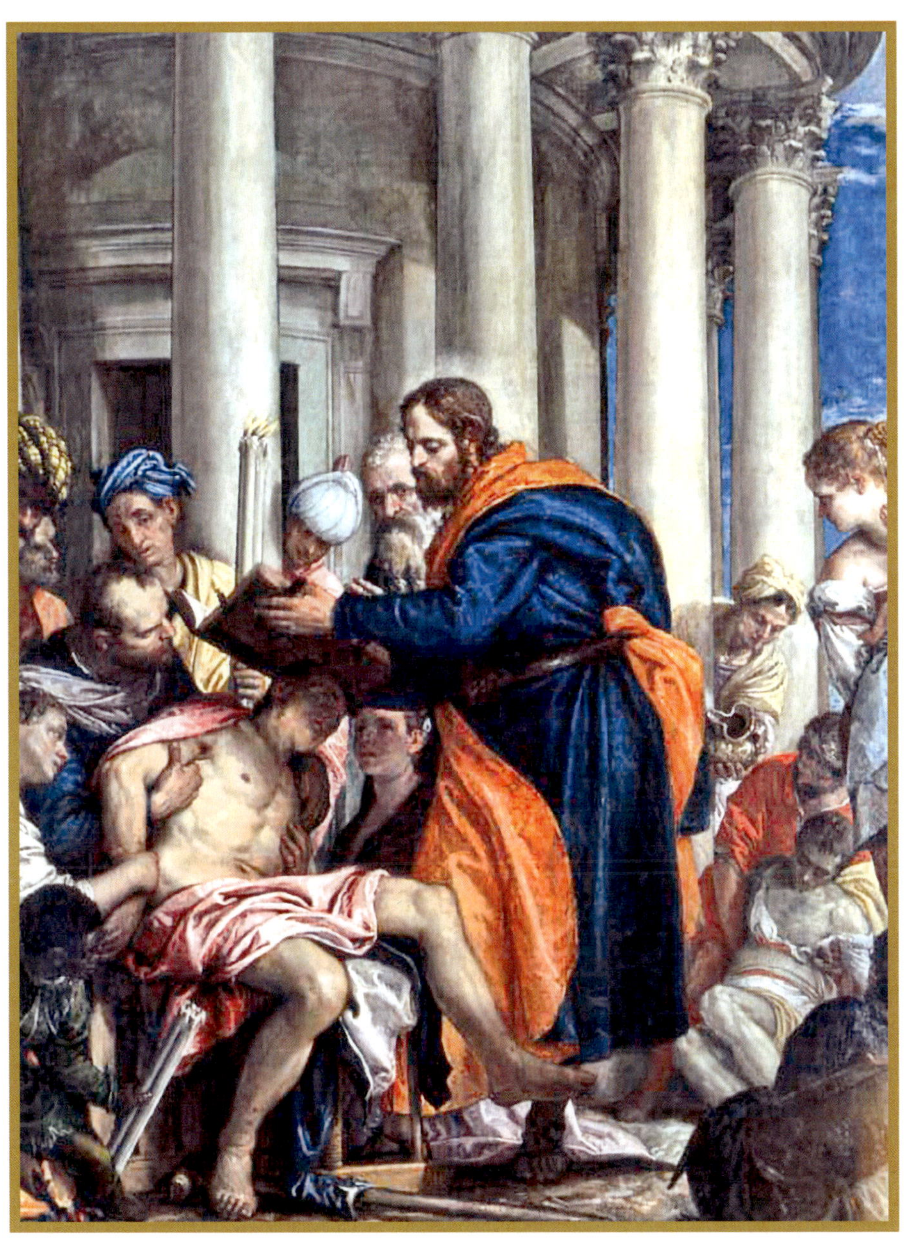

Saint Barnabas Healing the Sick, 1566

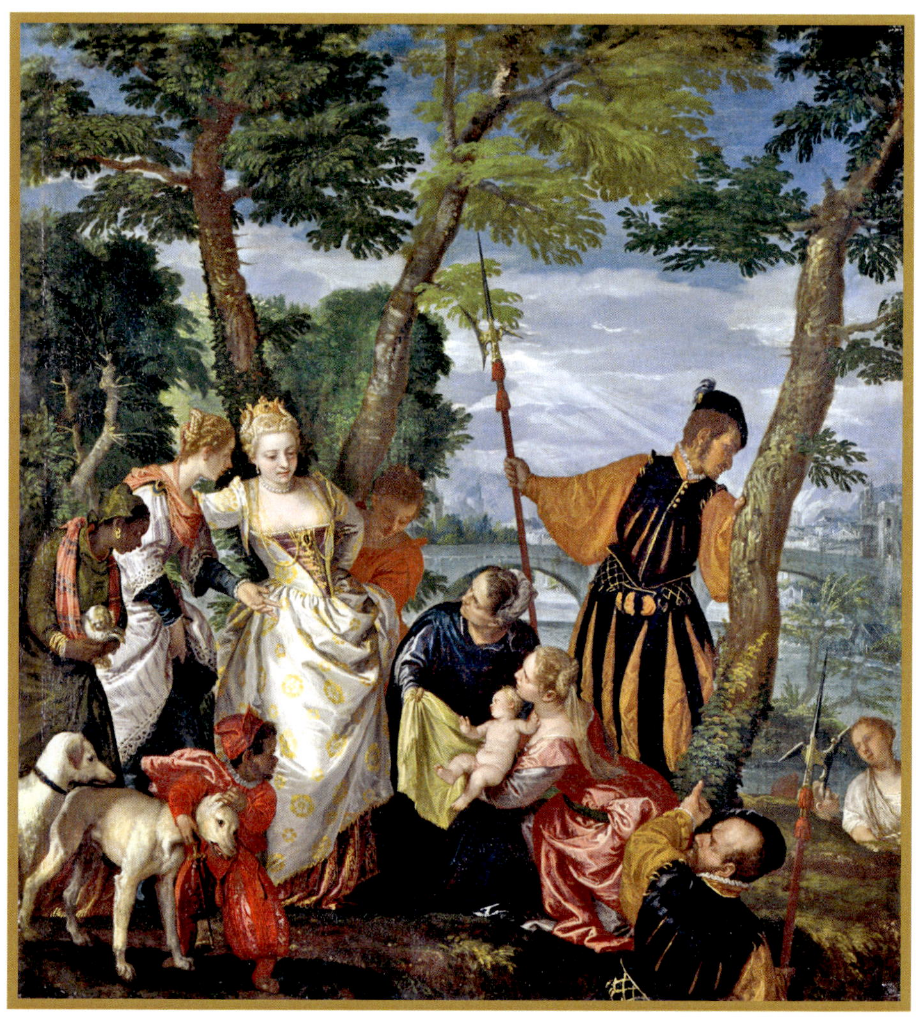

Moses Saved from the Waters, c. 1570–80

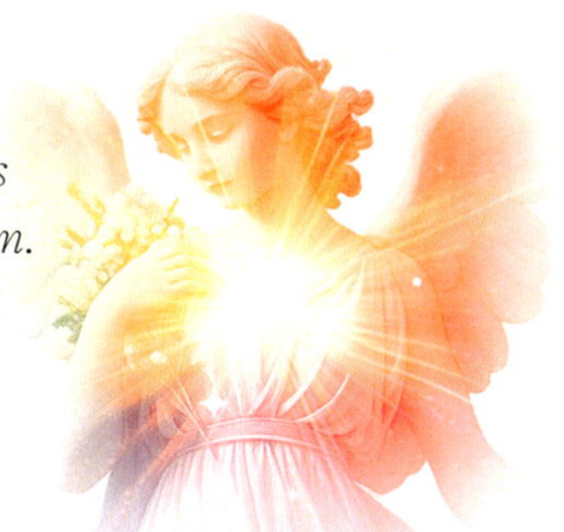

Let those who would enter the circle of love be the lovers of God—in love with him, longing for him, desiring him. Let them become the lovers of his Mother, the universal Mother of worlds, whose radiant face emits the light of his Son, her Son.

CHAPTER 14

The Face of the Son of Man

Beloved of My Heart,

I am the lover of your souls, though you know it not. For I am one of the ruby ray—a son of the Holy Spirit. And on the third ray, love is the fulfilling of the Law.[1]

Some have said, "We have a right to a relationship with the Great White Brotherhood." As those who sense themselves losing their hold on life cry out the more loudly for human rights, we are reminded of a king whose motto was *Dieu et mon droit.*[2] Thus he acknowledged two sources of power: God the Almighty and "my right."

The right of the individual to be king derives from the anointing of the Lord and from the freewill initiative of the soul to exercise "my right" to rule in the footstool kingdom[3] because he in Christ has assumed responsibility for others as for himself. The king in the service of the Lord Above and below is exercising his right to be his brother's keeper. Thus have we called you, under the office of the Lord Maha Chohan, to be Keepers of the Flame of Life on behalf of every part of life, as he who would be chief disciple among you must be the servant of all.[4]

This is the calling of love unto the children of God who would enter the path of discipleship on the ruby ray and thereby accelerate unto that sonship conferred by the face of a Man, whose face is the image of the Lord Christ. But who has the right to be servant? Only he who serves because he loves.

Superficial Love

My beloved, even in the ranks of chelaship there are those who serve but love not. Thereby they lose the right to serve within the hallowed circle of our love. Oh yes, there are those who would and should "do good," human for human, in the outer courts of life. Outside of Eden it is better to do good than to do evil, and there are avenues of service that in themselves become the world guru unto those who are yet learning to love.

Even as I say the words, the saying is strange to me: "Learn to love." Must the creation of love learn to love? Even the angels of the third ray must pause in their ministrations to earth, so startled are they by the absence of love because men and women have forgotten to love. And in their forgetting to be kind and gentle and sweet, they have actually forgotten how to be tender and compassionate to the aching hearts who are so alone.

As love begets love, so the children and the children's children [of these men and women who have forgotten to love] lose the habit of the rituals of love, and the caring expressions of life that convey the cups of love and the love-light of angels are fewer and farther between. These are replaced by the mechanized love of the television and motion-picture screen or a mechanized performance of niceties exchanged in surface relationships, where the inner cords of love that bind souls together in His all-consuming Presence are simply absent.

The superficial love given even to the Christ Child is so apparent in the distortions of life on earth. While he is adored as the God of very gods in all the pageants and pleasures of the season, the face of that Son of man appearing over and over again in the little child is desecrated and his presence denied by the Josephs and the Marys who are culpable because they have conspired with modern Herods to take the life of the little child as soon as it is born.[5] Such is the consciousness of idolatry that can never enter into the portals of perfect love, where the Guru of love awaits the coming of his true chelas.

Reverence for Life

There is a town called Litchfield in the United States, whose custom it is to award to the firstborn child of the year with gifts and good cheer. But what do you think, to the dismay of the angels of love who make their rounds? The town fathers considered it inappropriate that the first child of the year to come to Litchfield should receive that prize. And why? Because that child was born out of wedlock.

Scarcely the days have passed since the celebration of the Christ Mass, when the maiden, the blessed Mary, had the courage to bring forth her firstborn son under circumstances not entirely in keeping with the accepted norms of the day.[6] The Wise Men honored him with gifts. Where are the wise men of Litchfield who will not honor the spark of life and the holy breath of God that breathes within the little child, whose Father and Mother are God?

Reverence for life accords the right to be revered. Those who have no self-respect—because they have believed the lie that God does not live in them—will not respect another part of life in whom the living Spirit dwells. And who can say how long ago the living Spirit vacated the temples of the town fathers of Litchfield? Every child of light becomes the judgment of this world through him who is Christ the Lord of each little one.

Angels of the love ray are bearing gifts to the little child denied by callous men. Would that the Christ in him should speak and write, with handwriting in the sand, of their own misdeeds and misdemeanors of this and previous lives, then they too would shrink into the night of their own creating before the light of the eternal Virgin's oneness with the Holy Spirit. Then they too might hear the words of Christ unto the beloved Magdalene, "Where are those thine accusers? Hath no man condemned thee? . . . Neither do I condemn thee: go, and sin no more."[7]

If Jesus came into the world not to condemn the world, but that the world through the incarnate Christ might have eternal life,[8] then why, oh why do those who cry out the loudest for human rights deny the divine right of being unto one another?

The Sphere of the Cosmic Virgin and the Manchild

We celebrate the glorious thoughtform of the year 1980 that has descended by the hand of the Solar Logoi unto our Lord Sanat Kumara and was unveiled by the Lord of the World, Gautama Buddha.[9] Indeed the figure eight is become the object of our adoring—the sphere of the Cosmic Virgin and the sphere of the cosmic Manchild. This royal reintegration of Life with Life excludes no one but includes all—all, that is, who have not forgotten the flame of love.

The Manchild in the lower sphere is the symbol of the God-identity of every man, woman, and child, worlds without end. Those who love not the Mother cannot enter into the womb of her cosmos. They cannot be received of her to receive the initiation of the Manchild, nor can they interact with her in the glorious ritual of the resurrection, which our Lord Sanat Kumara has delivered to you in his magnificent message, "Drink Me While I AM Drinking Thee."[10]

Do you know why, my beloved, the subject of the Virgin and Child has enamored artists for thousands of years in every culture, even before the birth of Jesus Christ?

It is because the oneness of mother and child best illustrates the most fundamental desire of the soul for that sublime union with God, and on earth there is no other relationship that so fulfills the need to reenact the figure-eight flow, which is the foundation of every particle of the Matter and Spirit creations. *Drink me while I AM drinking thee.*

As the blessed child drinks in the nourishment of life from the body of the Mother, so the Mother drinks in the light of the Manchild, who nourishes her soul with the light of the heavenly Father incarnate in the blessed Son. The Mother is the eternal servant of the Father. She is the life-giver unto the whole of creation and every creature. Therefore she is the most beloved, the archetype of the original chela.

The Mother, who is the all-love of the cosmos, excelling and excelling in all life as her heartbeat becomes the heartbeat of her offspring, is the dearly beloved of the Father. As Christ is the head of the Church and the Saviour of the body of baptized believers,* even so the husband, endued with the Lord's Spirit, is unto the wife the ordained representative of the Father.[11]

*Christ is the light of the soul individually and collectively in the community of the Holy Spirit.

Twin Flames Bear the Relationships of Alpha and Omega One to the Other

Now Adam (archetype of Father whose Selfhood includes that of Mother) became the first chela of Maitreya, and as such he was the Lord's representative unto Eve. She then became the second chela in the order of the Edenic hierarchy and was subject unto him—and should have remained so—as unto the Guru. So it is the divine plan for twin flames, who bear the relationship of Alpha and Omega one to the other.

By and by in the cosmic evolution of twin flames, the Lord of the household transfers to the beloved wife the full mantle of the Guru. And lo, in the Matter spheres it is Mother and the Mother flame who becomes the Guru unto all of their children. And she, the servant of her Maker who is her husband,[12] now becomes the lord of his vineyard.[13]

So it is with the ascended master Ramakrishna,[14] whose spouse and beloved twin flame, Sarada Devi, remains unascended in the community of lightbearers, wearing his mantle—she the anchor of his love; he the lifeline of her anchor.

Thus the Maha Kali of the East,[15] the great brooding Mother of all worlds, becomes the highest object of the devotion of gurus and chelas alike. For she and she alone holds in her heart a crystal point of light that is the image of Ishwara—Ishwara, the Lord of all worlds Above and below.[16] He, whose image is the face of the Son of man, takes up his abode in the heart of Mother. By this, by this, she alone is Guru.

I speak to you of love—love that is the foundation of the Guru-chela relationship. I speak to you of the love of the Father for the Mother and of the Mother for the Father, each one the servant of the other, each one the Lord of his domain. As the Father reigns in Spirit and the Mother reigns in Matter, so in the divine embrace both are the center and the circumference of worlds aborning and worlds dying.

To Enter the Circle of Love

Now, my beloved, who do you suppose has the right to enter into the divine embrace with Father and Mother? Is it not the little child who has entered into the fiery ovoid of the Manchild?

The little child who follows after the Mother in imitation of her service and her love, holding her garments, going wherever she goes—this is the little child who is caught up into the arms of the Father and to his throne.[17] This little child may claim his inheritance, for he has lawfully walked the path of service in the footsteps of his Father and his Mother and their mutual adoring in the service of one another.

This little child is in love with his Father and his Mother. This adoring one is become the chela of the divine lovers. In him, therefore, reside the cloven tongues of fire.[18] And when the Father and the Mother withdraw to other octaves of the Spirit-Matter universes in their ongoing service to life, it is the little child, the chief disciple, who now wears the mantle of the Guru in the earth. And the face of this Son of their *man*ifestation reflects the Father-Mother and their individed Holy Spirit.

There are some who have related themselves to the ascended masters of the Great White Brotherhood by outer signs and symbols. They have not been called, but they have chosen to enter in. They say, "My right is to choose to be or not to be in the service of the light." But the light responds, "You have not chosen me, but I have chosen you."[19]

The creation, after all, does not sit in the judgment seat that is reserved for the God of all. These who have not been called say, "We will come and see whether or not the Lord's Spirit is truly present midst this people and this messenger." But they themselves have never witnessed to that Spirit, which comes only to those who have the love tie to the Father-Mother Person. After all, would you go to the wilds of Kenya to hunt an animal you had never seen? Undoubtedly, you would return with the official report, "No such animal exists," though you had been surrounded by a herd of them.

Why do I speak to you of love, my beloved? It is because so many have been toiling to enter in. They come. They go. They bask in the light. They store the light. They go out on the high seas of life, the proud captains of their ships. But when their batteries run low and they are high and dry on some desert isle of their fantasy, they suddenly return.

They knock upon the door, expecting to be received as before, expecting to have access to all the light and love of Father and Mother. But they have loved neither light nor love nor Person of the Great Guru in his first and foremost chela, the beloved bride who wears the mantle of her Bridegroom.

And all at once they cry out, "My right, my right!" And in the night their voice is heard receding with the receding wave, while vestal virgins keep the flame of the Maha Chohan with the perpetual word, "My God, my God!"

Let those who would enter the circle of love be the lovers of God—in love with him, longing for him, desiring him. Let them become the lovers of his Mother, the universal Mother of worlds, whose radiant face emits the light of his Son, her Son.

Let the lovers of the Mother care for her children—feed them and clothe them, tend them when they are sick, bring them gifts, and honor their presence in life. Let the lovers of the Mother go to the many crosses upon the hill and receive her sons and daughters into their arms as they take them down from the very nexus where they have left them long ago. So let them bear their burden in the hour of their crucifixion and they will bear the burden of their light in the hour of their resurrection.

Such is the ministration of the servants of love. Such is the wisdom of the wise virgins,[20] the souls of men and women who are the real and living chelas of the Guru Ma.

I AM

Paul the Venetian

I am choosing my chelas of the third ray to enter in with me into the bridal chamber—my retreat, the Château de Liberté. Here by the disciplines of love we will study the art of freedom and once again present the image of Mother Liberty to a world who must come to know her sons and daughters in the face of the Son of man.

January 20, 1980

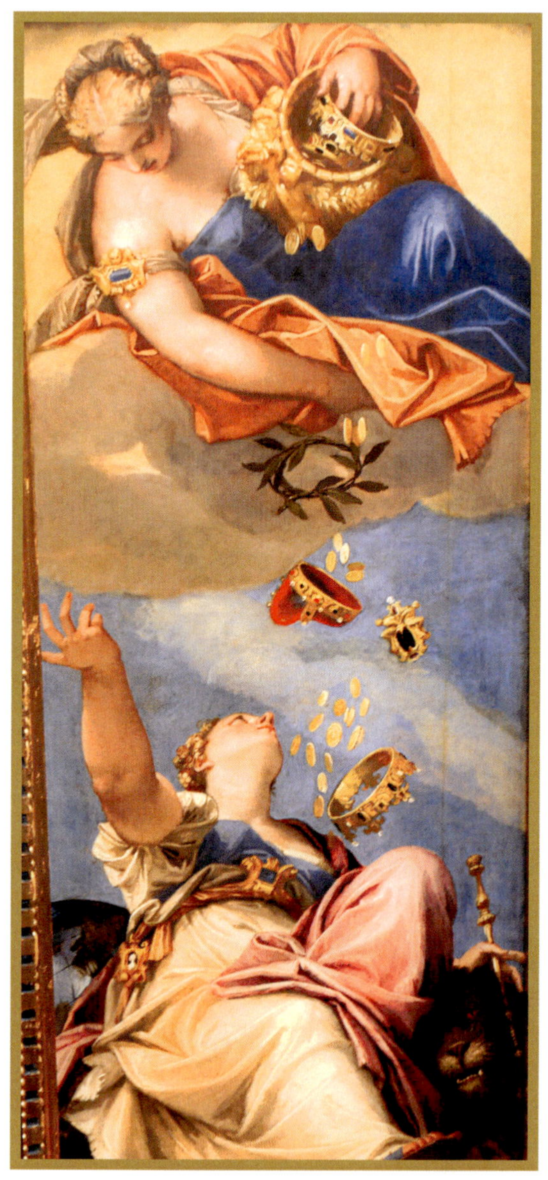

Juno Showering Gifts on Venice, 1553

See how the mountain calls! And the call of love is to those who respond to a vibration that is compelling, and contained within itself is the ray of love that shows each one the blessed teaching.

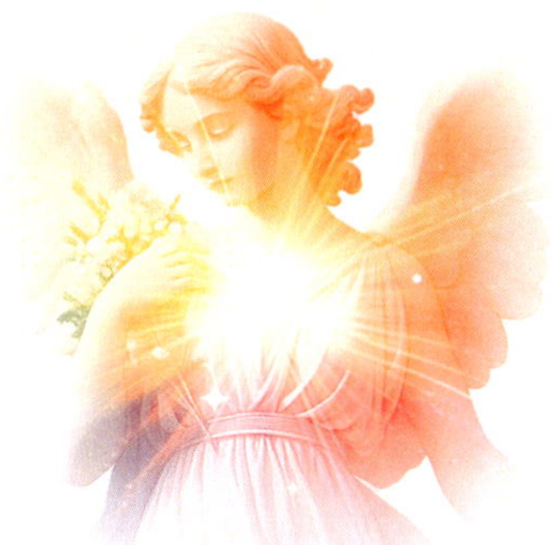

CHAPTER 15

Message of the Chohan of the Third Ray

The Next Step

As you listen, my beloved, to the cadences of the music, you hear another anthem of the free.[1] The repetition of the theme in joy and in acceleration is understood by the free to be the repetition of the mantra whereby the beats of the hours and the days and the years must reconfirm in this Matter vessel the true freedom of the soul:

I AM the power of light that makes you right.
I AM the power of light that makes you right.
I AM the power of light that makes you right.

The fiat of the I AM is a descent, a continuous stream of spheres of light, each one itself a world of love, each one containing the very necessary I AM affirmation for the confirmation of your liberty in this hour.

This I would teach you—that as you are one with the inner Guru, the Christ Self, and communing under your own vine and fig tree, you must begin to generate the mantra of the word of love—the mantra that affirms the very next point of attainment, the very next step until you come to the place where you no longer think and exercise deliberation in taking that step, any more than you would in merely walking down the street. It becomes the response. The thought before the act is already contained in the act in the state of descending—right, left, right, left.

And thus, you see, there is an I AM affirmation for the next step that you see on your path—a door that must be opened by your hand, a step that must be taken.

Therefore, in the motion of the descent of the spheres of light there is also the mantra, the I AM affirmation that affirms that right step just before the moment that the step is taken, and also congruent with that step. Therefore when you listen to the music of Beethoven, you hear a thousand million cadences of the rhythm of your heart pronouncing the I AM Be-ness, the I AM affirmation that "I AM the fullness of perfect love in this act, in this. To the right, to the left—I go, I move, forward marching!"

And thus, you see, when you are not in form and not fit, physically or otherwise, sometimes you tend to contemplate the next step from the armchair of life, and it is a bit too much of an exertion to get up and begin those exercises and begin the movement of the heart. Therefore sometimes acts are performed mentally or in the future and they die, never coming to full physical manifestation because there is a confusion concerning action and thought.

Thought is action in the process of formation, but it is not action and therefore cannot yet be counted for good karma until the act truly is the fullness of a deed—heartfelt, contemplated, affirmed, and thrust forward.

Love in Action

Thus, I come as the chohan of the third ray. Some of you know me very little and some not at all. Some of you know me only in your own exercise of the prerogative to manifest the action of love.

Now, the fullness of love cannot be love unless it is action. Contemplated love or the mere repetition of words may occupy one's fancy, but love in action is the measure of a heart united with mind and soul.

Therefore as I come, I bring to you perhaps an understanding of your own soul's psychology in relationship to El Morya and beloved

Lord Lanto.[2] For you see, your hearts wax fervent in love for the will of God, in joy in the presence of El Morya, and in the study of the wisdom teachings. But there is a general confusion, if I might say, among the students (which is akin to the confusion on this planetary home) that the contemplated action, the happiness, the enjoyment of another's attainment is the equivalent of the attainment of the third ray—love itself.

Some actually suppose that the words "I love you" carry the full force of its commitment and fulfillment. Not so. It is a mantra that must be fulfilled by a keen perception of the needs and demands of every part of life and what ought to be the next givingness of self. Therefore, you see, it is easy to mistake one's contemplated love of the masters, the activity, the messenger, and so forth, with an inaction that does not complete the cycle.

Here, then, we roll up our sleeves and realize that the love of the third ray and its chohan, its disciplines, its chelas, must now carry forward those plans, those teachings, those advices given, already recorded, that now deserve to be made physical. And the measure of everyone's cup of love must be that which is brought forth and brought to the full flowering and the fruit of the Tree of Life.

Let us, then, carefully define what are those spirals yet to be completed—the contemplated life's journey. Each one has a sense of self-knowledge of that which is to be accomplished. Do not think that thinking about it will make it so! Thinking about it and yet not achieving it will result, in the hour of transition, in the necessity of going back to begin again, to start again, and once again to understand that the mighty work of the ages must be here on earth a shrine to the living, to the free, to the little ones, and to the LORD himself, who dwells with his people.

The Step Not Taken

Now, therefore, I would converse with you concerning the *step not taken*—the step contemplated and often resisted until resistance itself becomes habit and a momentum and a coil wound tightly around the spine of being. And this pole of being, then, once set with that habit, becomes an act no longer reviewed or questioned. It simply becomes a self-acceptance: "Well, this is the way I am. People will have to accept me the way I am. This is my level of service. This is all I intend to give. Others will have to do the rest."

Well, the fallacy in this is not self-knowledge and defining one's potential, for it is good to understand one's capacity and not to commit to more than one can. But the fallacy is, beloved hearts, the sense that one can rest on any plateau or arrive at a set of definitions for one's life or personality, seal them with a sealing wax, make the imprint of the seal of oneself and say, "As it is, so it is. So be it. I have spoken."

Now, this is the human ego that would hold captive and prisoner the soul to a certain level of the knowns, a certain level of stability. But unknowingly it would keep the soul there and it would convince the soul that no other progress can or should be made and that its current level of attainment is sufficient unto all things.

How can this state of mind, I ask you, be reconciled with the upward-spiraling, self-transcending movement of the galaxies, of God himself, of the ascended masters and their circles of chelas—all of whom and all of which are moving through cosmos at colossal speeds toward the Central Sun?

Let us take care, then, that self-assessment does not result in the inertia of rest and that such inertia is not confused with the lawful state of samadhi or of nirvana. Contrary to any human opinion whatsoever, these higher states of consciousness are those of movement even within the point and the heart of rest.

The Inner Vow to Become All That You Are

I trust, then, that you will understand when I say that I have come to spin your tops! I have come to increase the movement and to give you the inner sense of timing, a timing that reflects now your I AM Presence and the inner vow to become all that you are. Why, becoming all that you are—this is what you sing and dance and pray and live and work for! But this becoming is a movement requiring diligence and an intimate knowledge of the ruby ray, which is always self-sacrificing.

Each day when you come before the altar of your I AM Presence, remember: It is the hour of sacrifice. It would be well to consider, "What shall I sacrifice upon the altar this day?"

Perhaps I needn't tell you, but I shall. In order to set now a new forcefield and point of the eye of this mystical body of God moving together, we must first, of course, have had to accelerate and adjust the alignment of our own messenger. And therefore it does become apparent in her heart that many who come here come desiring to bring bag and baggage of a former life, considering that the former attainment is also acceptable for the new matrix.

It is as simple as this: You cannot pour the old wine into the new bottle.[3] You cannot say, "Montana, here I come, just as I am. Take me or leave me, but here I am!"[4] You must also realize that there are certain ways of consciousness, certain devious ways of avoiding the encounter with your own Christ Self that simply must go. They must go into the flame if you would truly find a new place in the Sun.

If you would truly rise in chelaship and follow the seven chohans to the heart of the Maha Chohan, you must come up higher. In fact, this higher ground is a compelling of the Lord that will also keep away those who have thought to indulge the outer senses in the presence of our angels.

Therefore, see how the mountain calls! And the call of love is to those who respond to a vibration that is compelling, and contained within itself is the ray of love that shows each one the blessed teaching, that shows each one how to do better and more and therefore to unfold that golden light that Helios and Vesta hold in store for each and every one.

The Way of Love

My service to life and to you, then, is to show you the way of love, especially to coalesce the teachings of the Lords of the first and second rays. For here at the point of love is the leap, then, into the fiery core of Serapis Bey, and then the going forth therefrom to bring into precipitation, by the light of the fifth, the sixth, and the seventh rays all that has been builded from within.

Why, this is the moment to step forth and to realize that no longer are thoughts or dreams or wishes to be left in jars upon a shelf and admired as a collection of some long-lost culture of ancient Egypt or Greece or China. Now these vessels come alive! They are dancing vessels! They are the singing hearts of chelas! And the mystery of the within, the message of good fortune, the mantra that is stolen away, hid there by Buddhists who also pray, may now become a daily experience. And this, ah this—this, my beloved, becomes the magnet to draw here, then, other souls and magnets who are of those who espouse the sacred labor and, not in words but in the labor of the soul and the heart, do teach what is the component of being and of life.

Let us begin, then, at the beginning. For the Lord of the first ray does teach students to refrain from all criticism, condemnation, and judgment. Yet when individuals choose, they will criticize the director of their study group or their teaching center[5] or someone put in charge of a committee.

They do not consider it criticism but only "constructive suggestion," while the one criticized is bowed down with that condemnation and therefore not able to perform his or her best. His or her performance may indeed become worse and worse, while others—their voices becoming shrill and dissonant—will continue to cry out in condemnation. This often occurs where the best servants do their best and can do no more, for life or breath is not available to them, as they have already given their all.

In some areas these servants might well be God-tutored and shown a better way by those who think they know better, and sometimes they do. But they have not drawn that full measure of devotion from the very fountain of the heart in order to fill their own cup and then to give of that drink to the brother who is servant in our retreat.

I would say this, then: It is high time that those who think they know better come and join and give their service willingly and realize that whatever the office that you aspire toward—whether teacher or minister or any other level of professional esteem within this activity—you must come and begin at the beginning and become the servant of all. And resist not, then, that service, nor expect others to do for you what only you may do for yourselves.

The Calling Must Be from the Heart

Now, there is from time to time created, by the absence of love or a true acceleration on the Path, a schism between those serving on our staff and those serving in the field. This, however, is not created by the devotees themselves, who are the tireless ones, but often by those who are offended in themselves when they see such servants and cannot bring themselves to give that measure of service! Therefore they must find fault with our staff, concluding that they are fanatical or impersonal or too solemn or too busy to give them the time of conversation.

Well, perhaps their busyness is a path of initiation that ought to be tried out! And perhaps their labor is long and hard spent because they also need reinforcements, but they would never ask for help in that task. They themselves understand that the calling must be from the heart and there must be the response of the heart.

Therefore, let not those who have chosen a way of living, a living therefore that is lawful in the keeping of their own households and families, disparage a service and a countenance of those who are facing other situations and other tests.

These two paths are lawful in their own right. And, as a matter of fact, the keeping of the flame of family requires a great deal more than many have put to it who have chosen it as their way. And if they were to do so, they would find themselves also far more busy and in need of greater devotion to truly bring forth the fruits that they ought to bring forth in the exemplary way of the following of, in imitation of, the divine family.

The Seven Rays

Let us realize, then, that when we are on different rays, each one of the seven rays themselves requires its own discipline and its own several initiations. Let us be their understanding. Let us therefore have an understanding, one with the other, that some of you must accelerate with individual chohans in order to expiate past karma and gain a mastery you do not have. This calling ought to be respected, whether you are on the staff or not on the staff or in any form of membership in this community.

The messenger and the ascended masters give to all the freedom to establish themselves at any ring of fire in proximity or distance from the sun. As you can see, the planets are also so arranged. You are free to be on any one of the seven rays, and the chohans and the messenger will receive you and attempt to give you that for which your soul is asking and that which you may need, though you know it not.

I am certain that you can all remember the wonder and the awe of entering the first grade, graduating from kindergarten and coming into that first grade in the first day of primary school, your eyes full of wonder, not knowing or even being able to imagine what could be coming in this schoolroom or what you might be learning or what would qualify you for the second grade. This is something that each must also understand in the path of chelaship.

When you lovingly take a hand of one of the chohans and you also understand the messenger as your guide, do not be surprised that the tasks and the exercises and the ABC's of that classroom might be thoroughly unknown to you, unexpected, perhaps distasteful. You may remember being set in the corner or being put out of the classroom because you refused to do your mathematics or your sums of addition or to do your penmanship properly.

Thus, we find that the little child is ever-present in the soul, no matter how old the adult, and sometimes resists the first steps of the lessons that must be taken and taken again until they are perfected. And therefore adults who have become sophisticated in other areas are sometimes more difficult to train and discipline, especially in our retreat of the third ray, because they cannot believe that they do not have the attainment that they think they have.

They cannot believe that they do not have the ability to assess their own position on the Path or their own vibration, that they do not know the difference between a criticism that is utterly destructive and the careful analysis and constructive contribution that ought to be given from the wisdom and compassion of the heart. Therefore, you see, we have those even with professional standards who expect to be received on the basis of the training of the outer mind, when in fact they must begin with Jesus, before the hierophant of Luxor, at the very first steps of application.[6]

The Stairway of Love

I go over these as the first notes of the piano, the scale of C major, so that you may realize that there is a time to begin again and to review the very first lessons of life—to realize that when you come complaining and "throw energy" because things are not as you expect them and you heap upon our staff that criticism, it does not go unnoticed. And you place yourself on record with the recording angels that you have not understood what is energy, what is discord, what is the release of a little bit of tantrum, a little bit of an emotional thrust from the belly to intimidate and to demand that others should march and dance to your tune immediately.

If this is to be a community of love and a community of our co-workers that can carry the day and deal with the planetary counter-forces moving against the Christ, then each one must come to grips with the third ray of God's love, with me as its anointed chohan, with the Maha Chohan, and with the love attainment of all other ascended masters. For I assure you that none enter heaven without passing through the most arduous disciplines, ranging from the petal pink of the love ray to the intensity that reaches finally the piercing, almost sharpness, of the ruby ray, which when the sacrifice is not forthcoming we must enter in and strip from the disciple (who calls himself disciple) those things that, my beloved, ought not to be.

Let charity and givingness be without dissimulation. And let us realize that pride itself, pride in one's own ability to direct and correct others, is the first condition that must go before the ascended masters and before their chelas.

Let each one then consider starting at the bottom of the stairway of love and enjoying each upward step. Let there be a savoring and a resting at each step, as with each Montessori exercise so joyfully entered into. Let us not skip the steps and leap and bound with pride that we may move as a mountain goat or a she-lion. But let us know that every step contains the lawful angles and the mathematics of life, and fifty steps higher one will need the fortitude gained on the second step of life. Therefore, let us not overlook these lessons.

Alas, beloved ones, it is almost without exception that here and there in past embodiments you have skipped a step or two, and this is why you find yourself sometimes doing something for which you have such a stinging remorse within your heart, as the hot tears run down your cheeks and you realize the word that has escaped your mouth or the sharp feeling that has crushed another. You long to draw it back and you say to yourself, "How could I have let go of something that so easily has hurt another?"

A Rolling Stone Gathers No Moss

Well, my beloved, have compassion for your own soul, and self-correct. It is because of a lost step. Go back, then, and learn the art of patience and of the lever of control of the movement of forces in your being. Do not allow yourself to be triggered by sudden information that someone brings to you about another, which may or may not be correct, exaggerated, distorted. But rather, hold the reins of an emotional fury. Hold back, then, and in wisdom consider all things. And let only the word of the innermost presence of love be the healing in every situation.

This, then, this great determination of my heart to make you one and to bring you into a closer bond, is truly what I long to do and what I must do. But as I said in the *Pearl of Wisdom* that the messenger read to you, which some of you heard and some of you did not (for you do not have all the control of your thoughts that you ought to have and therefore the mind wanders and you do not hear each cadence).

Thus, I reiterate that we cannot teach those who are not willing to be taught, who do not acknowledge the need to be taught, who do not incline themselves, and who do not reach forth, then, and understand that the step must first be taken, as the boot must be tried on for the boot to fit, and the step taken is to become the realization of self-mastery.

No one ever learned to ride a bicycle without getting on and beginning to pedal down the street. So it is with the next step in life. We are here to teach, but if you are confirmed upon your level of the rock and say, "I will build my fortress here so that none may enter and move me where I would not go," I assure you that the masters do withdraw and you are left in your fortress on the rock for a thousand years or more, as long as your soul desires not to move on.

This, then, breeds attachment to the rock and to the house and to the castle and to all the pets inside. Somehow the longer you stay, the more opportunity there is for the moss to grow. And so we say, "A rolling stone gathers no moss." Perhaps it is good for those who contemplate the larger initiations of the third ray to remember so simple a statement so common in your land.

Light the Candle of Love

I AM Paul the Venetian. I have waited to take your hand for many a year. In the name of the chohans, in the name of the Path, you have rejected my hand and said, "Aha, I have free will, beloved Paul, and I will do my thing now for this year and the next. And when it suits my purposes, I will come and I will lay my thing upon the altar of God."

Well, blessed hearts, the proving and the refining of all things must be ongoing, and therefore indeed by free will you may be preparing a precious gift for God. But sometimes the giver of the gift does not assess the need of the one to whom the gift is to be given, and often we are given gifts that we do not need at all, while our children on earth suffer and have great need and are hungry and crying in the streets. And somehow there is not sensed in that seemingly mundane or menial task that herein lies the greatest glory of all—to be the servant of the orphan, the widow, the needy, and the humble of heart.

As Confucius said, let us start. Let us begin at the beginning,[7] where the need is greatest. Let us come to understand the need of the Lord of Life, who dwells in the heart of the little child, of one's companion, of the friend, the stranger—and last but not least, the need of the heart of the messenger and of the masters. For all have needs, and in filling these the entire body of God moves forward.

You see, when the needs are not met, as you know in your own soul—if you are hungry, you cannot work; if you are tired, you must first rest; if you are cold, you must warm yourself before you have anything to give. Therefore, if the needs of the total community and the organization are not met, you cannot crack the whip and strike the one nearest you and say, "You are at fault. Things are not as they should."

Look only to yourself to light the candle of love in the midst thereof, and see how this body of love may be multiplied for you and for me by your own presence, which is so needed.

I have a chart and a course for those to follow who would be ministers of life—washing the feet not only of the pilgrims but of the competitors of the Word, washing the understanding and bringing that understanding of each one to the necessary point of self-revelation.

What Is the Next Step?

Now then, as I stand before you, I ask you to contemplate not past achievement, not even the glorious celebration for which we have gathered, but always to remember that in the turning of the worlds one must know the next step, and it must carefully be considered. What is the next step?

Let us sacrifice for it. Let us sharpen our virtues. Let us soften the rough places. Let us respond to the call of another's heart in the intimate way that that one will never know except that a new day has appeared and now all things are possible because there is joy and communion and understanding of hearts. For this understanding, I am with you.

The Love of Mother

The ascended masters are not beggars, and yet in the name of Jesus and Kuthumi, beloved Magda[8] pleaded for the publication of the teachings of the Mother on habit.[9] These have been delivered by dedicated hearts, and therefore you may take with you this wondrous teaching, which I trust will make plain all that I have tried to communicate to you in love this day on habit—the teachings from the seminar of the Mother of the World dedicated from the heart of the messenger to the taking down of the sons and daughters of God from the cross.[10]

Is this not the office of the Mother to which our Mother has dedicated her life—that you might be taken down from the cross?

Who will take you down but the Mother of Love, the Mother who fills all universes from the beginning and the ending in the heart of Mother Mary and each one who so embodies that flame?

Each and every one in all octaves needs the love of Mother. But when you know the Mother, you will know that her love is also wisdom in action, teaching you by love how to always be more of yourself—greater dominion, expanding the sphere, seeing more of God's universe all inside of you! This is the love of which I speak, the love that presses on and pushes you, as Mary too beckoned Christ at the marriage of Cana in Galilee.[11]

Understand the resistance to the forward step. It must be there because there is a creative tension in all life! And therefore a summoning of the will to break through the resistance will give you that thrust for precipitation that you need, my beloved.

No new work was ever wrought
Without the gathering of momentum
And its precision release!
Nothing was ever born or framed or fashioned,
Nothing ever took form or could stand the test of time
And the beating of the elements
Without that sense of thrust,
That destined purpose of the moving of the hand
And the will and the tongue and the eye,
All in consonance for the leap that flies
And the single thrust of the eye of God.

Self-Sacrificing Love

Into the eye of God, into the eye of life, life beckons. And the fifth ray, as the handmaid of love—as Pallas Athena[12] embracing the Maha Chohan, as I, with the emerald-green lining in my cape as the sign of the love of truth—these two rays as one perform a mighty action for the deliverance of worlds.

Lest I weary you in words, I conclude my message. For I too must go forth to work a work of love this day and lay my sacrifice upon the altar. For God will not receive me tomorrow as I am today. He demands that I too come up higher.

And when my chelas see me move up to the higher rock, they also make their swift sacrifice and climb with me. For they desire not to lose me, nor I them. And therefore we are grateful for the flame of self-sacrificing love that finds us each day made more in the image of his Christ, whom we adore!

August 27, 1982

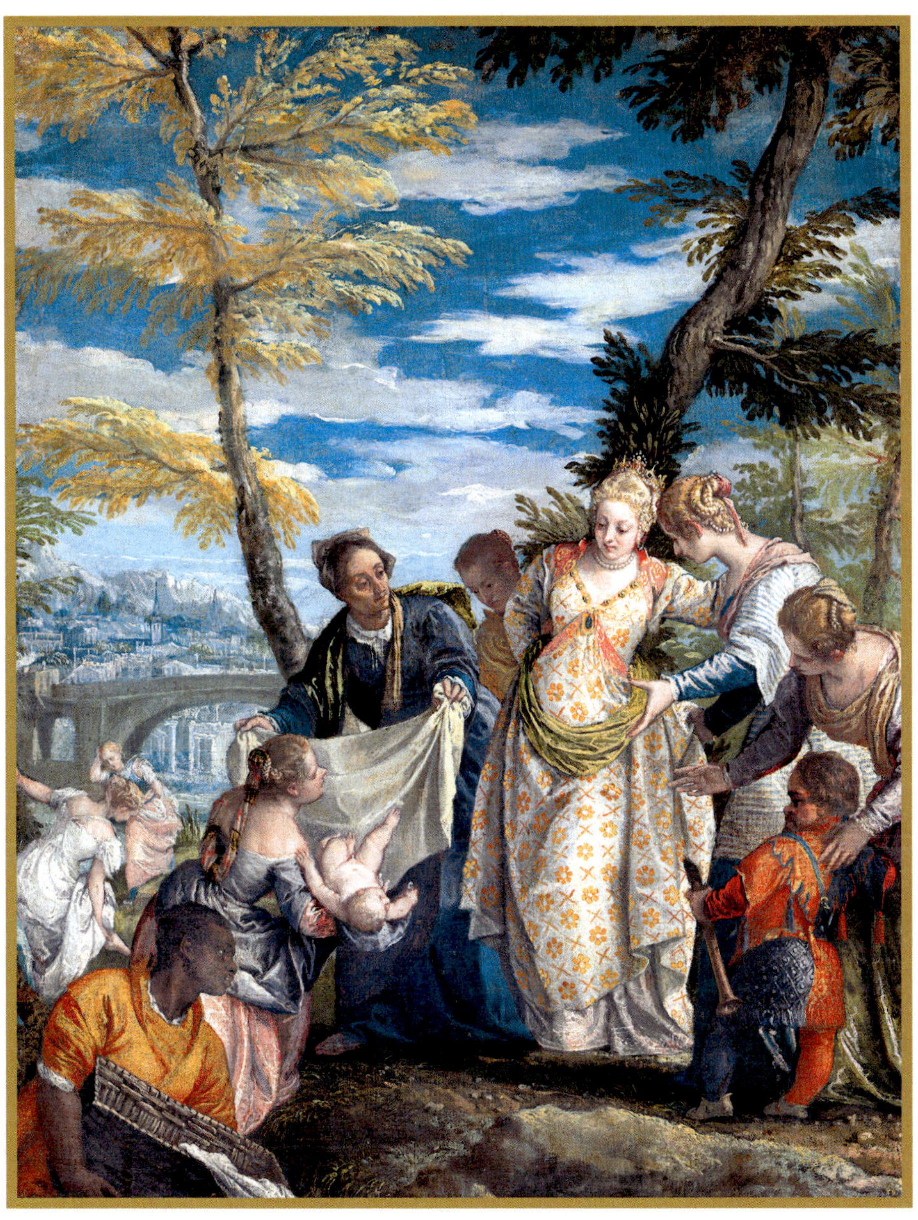

The Finding of Moses, c. 1581–82

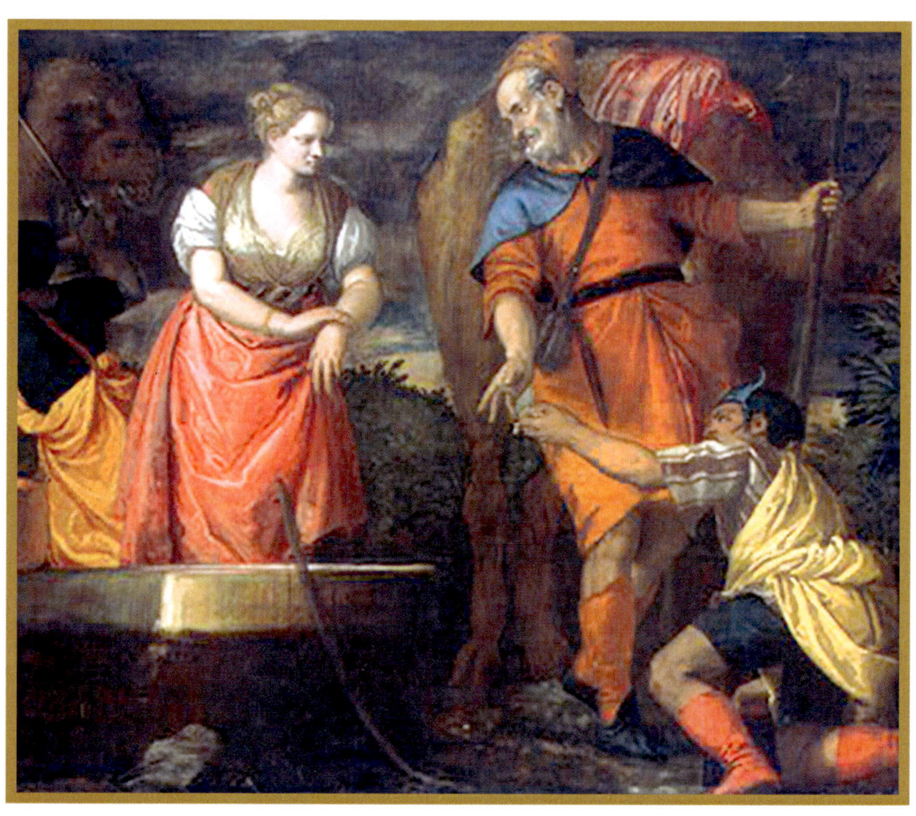

Rebecca at the Well (detail), c. 1582–88

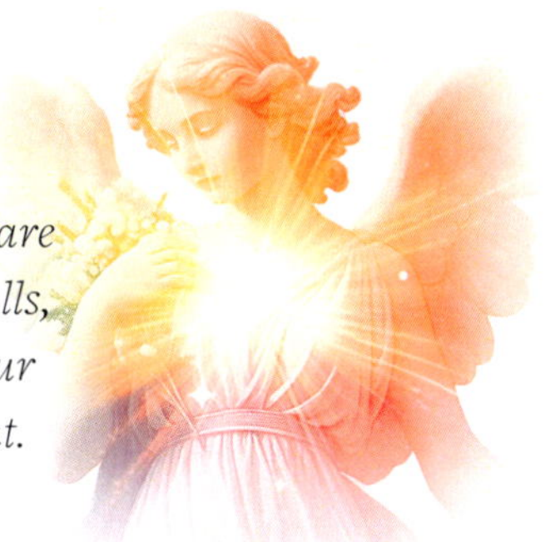

You are living artists of a living art. Whether you are repairing automobiles or machinery, whether you prepare the food or keep the records with the Keepers of the Scrolls, every act is a work of art. Every act is released from your soul as a release of energy that forms an engram of light.

CHAPTER 16

THE ART OF LOVE

Good evening, my beloved. Good evening, ladies and gentlemen.

I come as the representative of the third ray and I am sent, for many angels and councils of light have said, "Go, beloved Paul, and teach. Teach the members of our bands who must draw the line physically of the meaning of thy office and thy love."

This evening I come, and I come also to salute a certain disciple of mine. I come, then, to bring the eternal antidote for fear and for terror that begets terrorism as an organ or organization of fear, if that were possible.

Terrorism, you see, is an ideology as well as a collective of individuals who have not the internal integration of love. Therefore, I consider the word "organization" questionable in their regard. But the bonds that bind them are not the bonds of love. They are cords of fear and hatred. And thus there is a tight bond wherever there is hatred, and this you also understand.

While the world contemplates its fears and arranges itself around and in and under its fears, long ago the word was spoken: "Perfect love casts out fear."[1] Love is an all-consuming fire that does dispel all that fears. For fear is based on the fear to be, the fear of existence, the fear of taking a single step in life, and the distorted preference not to *be* rather than face the *challenge* of living itself.

Beloved hearts, I will tell you why men's hearts fail them for fear[2] and why fear prevents action when it comes to the consideration of absolute Evil, as you have been discussing this evening.[3]

The Courage to Challenge Antichrist

Consider, then, that only the love of Christ can beget the courage to challenge Antichrist. When you hold your beloved child in your arms, the gift of God to you, your love is so great that you are also ready to address that which attacks the child—whether as disease or a villain or an accident or anything that would limit the development of that child.

You have seen some parents, however, who have not contained this love and therefore have not had the pure regard for their children. They have not loved enough to be willing to face that which is directed against that child. And therefore the children go unprotected and they suffer loss and serious setbacks in life.

Caring enough, therefore, caring ultimately as the perfect love of Christ, must become the sign and the mark of true leadership. The leaders of nations who love the Christ in their people become the true shepherds who lay down their life for their people—laying it down not in death but in the living sacrifice of service, of penetration and probing and going after that which threatens the community, the national security, and the internalization of the Word by every citizen.

The Spirit of the Christ Image

I AM Paul the Venetian. I paint on canvas on the ethers. I etch in crystal. I sculpt. I mold the clay. I fashion all things physical and many substances not known to you in the higher octaves. To what purpose? To the purpose of showing forth an evermore revealing and exquisite image of the Christ—the Christ appearing in children, in people from every walk of life.

I remember when Norman Rockwell[4] came to me at inner levels to study in my etheric retreat, and I remember as I counseled him to show the Christ in the American people in everyday scenes of humor, humility, wonder, togetherness, heroism. All these have been treasured, remembered, and valued highly because something of the spirit of the Christ image that is become an image of America came through his work.

He was a unique artist, one devoted to the inherent qualities and identity of the individual. As his perception of the Christ was, so was his painting the capturing of unique moments. You might examine that work to find in each painting what is the glimmer, however great or faint, of some aspect of the individual reaching for the Higher Self.

Modern Art

Is it any wonder that we deplore the chaotic and abstract art that has no point of unity? It also portrays a certain barrenness and absence of that point of light in the individual. One can see anarchy by an absence of dimension—an absence of harmony or focalization in modern art.

Modern art enters the subconscious. Accordingly, whether or not the artist is influenced by marijuana or other substances, art portrayed in fabric design, wall coverings, or clothing style becomes a matrix capable or incapable of carrying some measure of Christly proportion. When the people's art and sense of art flounders, then the images of Christ recede. It is rare to find a work of art that is come from the etheric octave in this period. Understand that it is also rare to find the higher consciousness of the etheric octaves.

Where will your leaders learn to deal with the invaders of the minds of the nations? They will learn from the etheric schoolrooms and cities and retreats. How will they get there if they do not contain the crystal that becomes the magnet and a star to follow when the soul goes forth from the body in the hours of sleep?

Unless angels and devotees of light accompany them, they will have no new idea, no means of resolution. Without internal harmony that is the direct child of perfect love, there is no resolution to international terror or the threat of nuclear war.

And while abortion itself seems to me the supreme act of anti-art, it does beget the callousness that year by year has a lessening sensitivity to the art of angels and the art of God that fashioned the perfect image out of which you were sculpted in clay.

The Contemplation of Divine Beauty

Thus, beloved ones, it is necessary in the very midst of the most tense international circumstances to retreat into the contemplation of the divine beauty and the music of the spheres, to remember that the building blocks of creation are sound, that sound forms a pattern that is a divine harmony, and that this divine harmony can be portrayed in architecture, in life, in everyday utensils, such as pottery. The things you use and you surround yourself with become a focus for the flow of attention.

Art is not a subject so often dwelt upon in our discourses, for there are such pressing needs—pressing needs of the hour for the victory for Saint Germain. I bring my ingredient of love in this hour as an offering to the Christ Child, to the one and the beloved whom I have so longed to paint in the ultimate sense and have done so to the best of my ability in the etheric octave.

Let us realize, then, that as love wanes in the earth, so crime increases. Death becomes more frightening and terrible. Cancer itself is evidence of an absence of focalization upon the divine geometry of the internal crystal of the soul and of every living cell.

When children can pour their light into a cup of beauty and the dimensions of mathematics portrayed, the very dimensions themselves, then impressed upon the cells, prevent the aberrations such as a manifestation of cancer or the vulnerability to the attack of the virus.

Geometry Is the Science of God

Geometry is a science explained by Pythagoras and demonstrated by him. It is the science of God, and its formulas are illustrative of the fact of the very energy of life that can be focused in the angle, in the pyramid, in the octagon, in the cell structure, which is also geometric.

Form itself, designed by God, is a protection for the eternal flame. Even the form you wear has a design of the star-fire body intended to be, geometrically speaking, the ultimate protection for the soul. The geometry of the chakras and the beauty of the unfolding of the flower become a model of contemplation that ought to be considered when designing the physical temple.

The poem that is "lovely as a tree,"[5] reflected in these evergreens high in the Himalayas and in the Rocky Mountains of the north, presents an exquisite design that also has a formula whereby life is enhanced and the sacred energies of nature are released. Even the starry bodies and the rays that come to earth to stimulate the very growth of the hairs on your head are eternally and perfectly designed.

Thus, beauty and mathematics, proportion, and the golden ratio serve to enhance the message of the Word itself. And thus we sought and ever seek in our retreat to bring to life the ancient records of akasha of the great souls who have ensouled a living flame. We study the geometry of virtue as it can be seen in the etheric plane. We study the dimensions of the aura and how the vibrations of light and their harmony enable the individual to carry greater and greater light.

The Natural Grace of the Soul

We would transfer to our teachers in our schools here some understanding of the necessity for grace and line and movement, which brings us to the subject—whether of yoga or ballet or the dance or marching—of the natural grace of the soul that ought to be expressed in the body form for the release of fohat, for the release of the sacred fire breath. Patterns of sound and music outpictured become the means for the opening of the heart chakra, the lessening of tension, and therefore the increase of love and appreciation for life.

We come back, then, to the purpose of art to enhance the love of Christ always. The shepherds of the people who contain that pure love will neither lead them astray nor abandon the people in the hour of tragedy or danger.

Thus, when there is the loss of Christ, of the divine spark and the light of the soul, all else suffers and art is no longer true and there is a violation and abuse of science. That which can never lie is mathematics itself. People may attempt to fool one another by the manipulation of statistics, but number itself cannot be denied. And the number one as the Law of the One comes back to the central point of love—the Great Central Sun.

Love One Another

Grave manipulations of genetics have occurred to destroy the divine art of Elohim in the mind of the offspring of God. This process toward limitation, control, and enslavement has been, to the end, to reduce the children of light to a capacity less than necessary to contain that quotient of love that the ascension process demands.

Thus he admonished: "Love one another *as* I have loved you"[6]—in the way that I love *as* Christ, so love one another. The heart of the message of Christ is love, as it is of every true prophet and avatar. How is it, then, reduced by mortals to hatred?

How have they lost the vision and accepted Antichrist in the place of the figure serene upon the hillsides of the world? It is through a process of self-denial, if I may venture an observation—the self-denial of God within.

We understand, of course, the anatomy of evil as pertains to the fallen angels, but it is difficult to discover how any fallen angel could convince a child of God to deny that God flame within. Obviously, it could not come about directly but only with great subtlety and confusion, role reversal, and the conviction that black is white and white is black.

We Are Close to All Who Love

I ask you to pray for the disciples of the seven chohans, who are now disciples actively pursuing the Path, which means to pray for yourselves and all upon earth who, by the virtue of their devotion (which is love) to an art or a field of endeavor, have actually created and compelled the tie to the hearts of the seven chohans.

I ask you to release to the world the dictations of the seven chohans, that these might bring to the world an understanding of a path that can be followed.[7]

We are so very close to the lovers of Christ and of Buddha, the lovers of Krishna[8] and the great law of Moses. We are close to all who love, for the true lovers of God are the true disciples of the Logos. These individuals, as yourselves, need encouragement, need more love, need to feel the warmth of being at home in a cosmos, even on a cold winter's night.

Blessed ones, let us fan the fire of hope and let love be without dissimulation. With all intense love, let us go after those who have the quality to be the vessel, to understand the meaning of the True Self as the Holy Grail, who love enough not only to seek the Grail but to become it, to fill it with light, and then to become the light.

It will take a great deal of love to fulfill the mandate of God, who has said, "I have decided to save the earth."[9] It will take many decisions by many candles on earth, and a love that some have not yet known.

You Are Living Artists of a Living Art

I have come in gratitude and in joy for the Christ Mass and all beauty that has been sent forth from your souls in this year—beauty as deeds of love, beauty as love in every form, love as an art when you do not consider yourselves to be artists or to have time to perfect a skill.

The art of service is a great art. Unbeknownst to you, you are creating an eternal mural of service. And angel artists paint a mural—I will tell you not where—showing the episodes of this community of lightbearers and the day-to-day overcomings.

Many preparations are being made for your homecoming and your rejoicing at last to understand all that has transpired at all levels. These are master artists who have determined that the sons of the best of men should not go down unrecorded in the murals of heaven but they should indeed rise up and in their own victory perceive that victory as a lesson to those who will one day be the students of the art that they have lived. For you are living artists of a living art.

Whether you are repairing automobiles or machinery, whether you prepare the food or keep the records with the Keepers of the Scrolls,[10] every act is a work of art. Every act is released from your soul as a release of energy that forms an engram of light, impressing upon the etheric octave geometric snowflake forms, roses and violets, or, unfortunately, when done without grace or love, jagged forms of modern art that you would decry in a museum, yet, alas, also manifest in the lower levels of the aura as work done without grace and joy and freedom.

Service in life without freedom creates a record of art that is gray and dissonant. This is why even those who produce films always see a dim light as being present in Communist countries. Films about the Soviet Union or Eastern Europe seem to have that quality of absence of light, absence of dimension and even reality. It is the weight of oppression of the people who in their service are missing the seventh ray as a part of that artwork.

Believe me, beloved hearts, much grace proceeds from the most humble of servants. Therefore you can realize that every movement in life, every thought and feeling is producing on the ethers either a magnificent design of virtue or something less, which by the grace of God is also erased as you invoke the violet flame.

Being co-creators with God, you therefore show all too quickly in the area surrounding you what is the nature of your work. These signs are read by elemental life and the angels, and there are crowds of angels around some and a total absence around the Scrooge characters portrayed on a yearly basis.

Thus, entertaining angels unawares[11] is no mere entertainment, for these become a part of a personal battalion, even as elementals enter formation following the very points of light of the divine geometry of the flow of light in your aura.

Thus, all of heaven bears witness to the auric emanations of the servants of God. Obviously, therefore, those who are the devotees of the chohans can be known around the world by the light of the aura and the harmony of the artwork that their daily service is creating.

The True Mystery of Love

I ask, then, that you might be comforted in the embrace of love this night and that the love of God—through the divine art outpictured in all of nature and all of cosmos—might come for an inner realization of your soul as to the true mystery of love in the innermost parts of your being—love as the cohesive force that enables you to be who and what you are, the heart to beat, and all systems to be functioning.

What ordains it? What maintains it? What seals you as a separate consciousness now able to hear my word and to follow the word into the vastness of your own eternal Self? It is love—universal love everywhere. May you capture it, cradle it, know it, follow it.

May love be the determining factor of your decisions, not fear. May love dissolve the hatred of the enemy, the enemies of the light and of America. May love be such a force of the ruby ray that all assignments may be fulfilled and not one child of light on earth be found wanting for the true message of the path of Christhood.

I Extend to You an Acceleration of the Heart Chakra

I come to sponsor the dissemination of the Word and, in the name of Maitreya, I draw the solar ring around the publications of The Summit Lighthouse—those in print, those about to be in print, those in etheric octaves waiting to be released.

I call forth the tube of light and the mighty pillars of Alpha and Omega, Elohim of God, Helios and Vesta, the God and Goddess Meru, and the messengers of the Sun and all others who support this endeavor, most especially my comrades serving with me in the offices of the chohans and all capable assistants in our departments, as well as the World Teachers, who are so intent in contacting their own.

I, Paul, here with you in this hour, now extend to you from my heart and from the heart of the threefold flame anchored in the Washington Monument[12] an increase of the love plume, an acceleration of the heart chakra—love for the balance of wisdom and power, love for an understanding of the goal of thy life perfectly fulfilled, love for the dissolving now of ignorance and density that prevents thy perfect expression of the Christ image.

Blessed be you.

Blessed be you in light and in victory and in oneness and in the self-expression of the magnificent God-free being that you are.

Blessed be your heart.

Blessed be your threefold flame.

Blessed be your love forever as God's love.

With the sign of the cross of the ruby ray, I place my magnet in this heart to draw by love loving hearts of the universal One for the victory of our mission.

I will see you in the Heart of the Inner Retreat and in the heart of Helios.[13] For I am there, keeping the flame of the divine art of evolutions, civilizations, a Christic path of initiation and of worlds unborn.

I AM grateful for your holy offering of love in this hour.

December 29, 1983

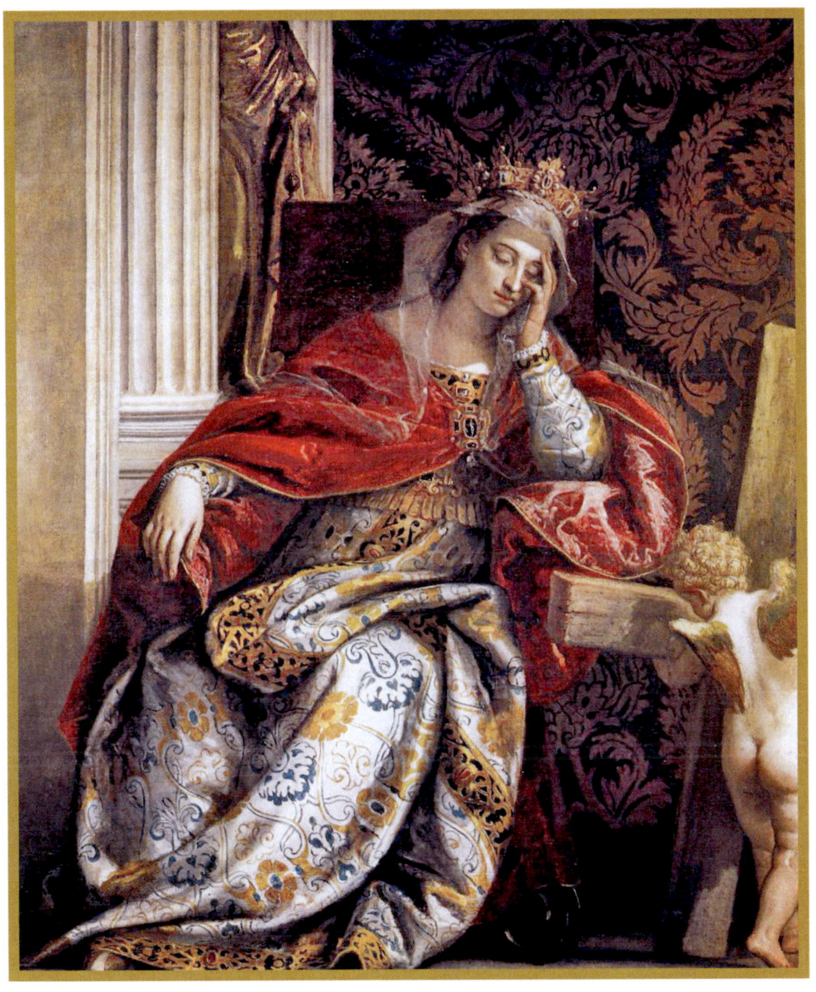

The Vision of Saint Helena, 1580

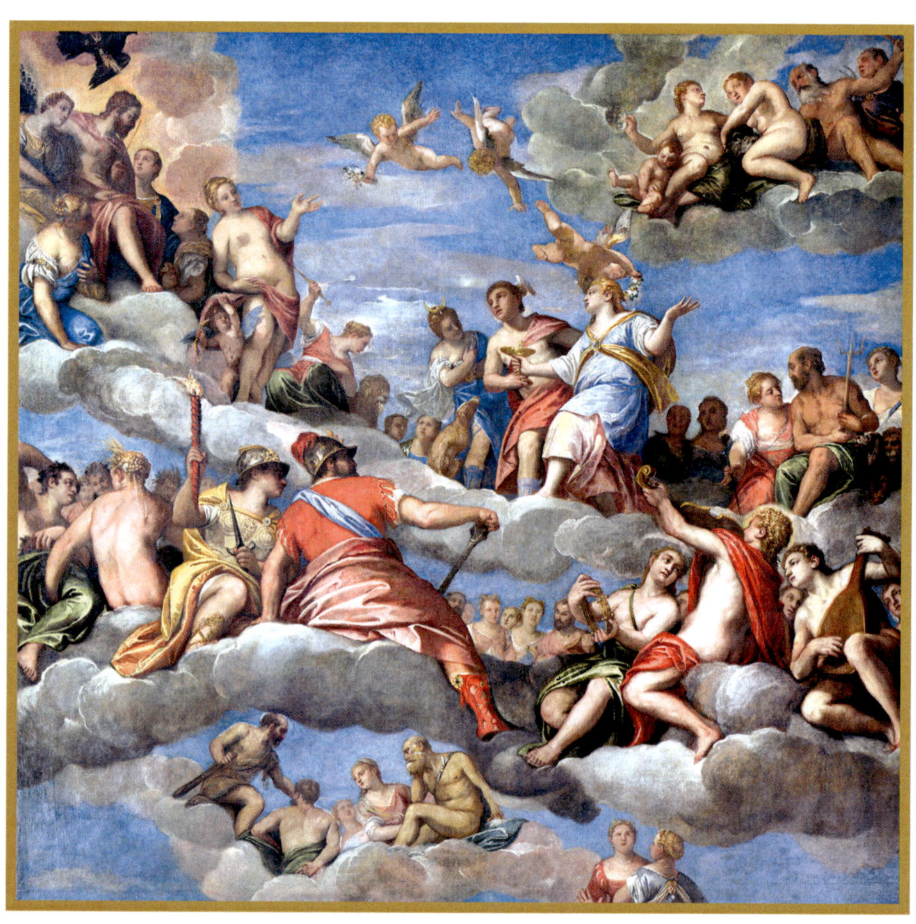

The Coronation of Hebe, c. 1580–89

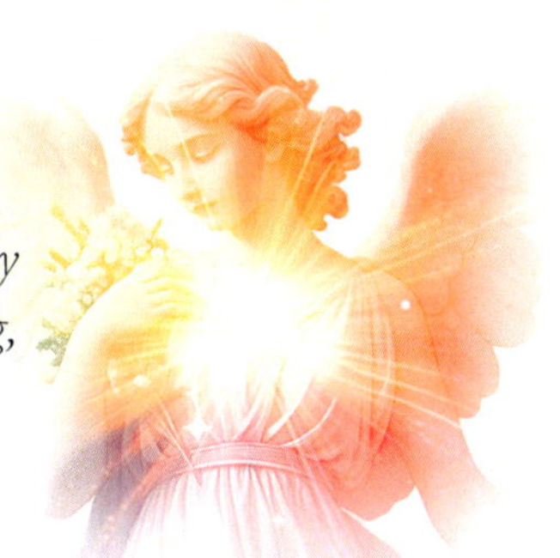

As you trust in God, so God must be able to trust in you and to trust that the light that is given will be held steady for adoring, for joy, for creating, for giving, for building, for tearing down, for laying foundation, and for the raising up of the temple of man.

Beloved Hilarion and Paul the Venetian

CHAPTER 17

The Seven Chakras Must Blossom

Hail, thou Lady of Love, thou starry Mother, Regent, Divine Mother of Sanat Kumara!

Come forth, thou who hast sponsored thy sons in a visitation of light to earth. Come forth, blessed Mother of Love, now to quicken in these souls the memory of the Ancient of Days and of the journey to earth, as many came from distant planetary homes to rescue the children of light of earth who had lost their way.*

So I call you, hearts of light who have gathered here, that you might remember now a half a million years ago, two million, and still consider that thy spirit fiery, which does attend the Mother's travail in giving birth to the light in this earth, therefore doth know that in thy beginning so in thy ending, the Mother of Love is the key to the unfoldment of the star of greatness in thee.

I AM, then, Hilarion, called to be spokesman for that light. O beloved, hear that call. For I am one who answered, yet I must be compelled to answer by the call itself, by the One Sent.

Witness, then, the living Word in that Jesus, who is yet before you tarrying in his ascended master light body in this place, that you might

*See chapter 20, p. 275, n. 9.

absorb truly the ascension currents for thine own ritual in the ascent. Truly, the soul ascending, beloved, must tarry in the houses of the chakras, thereby slaying those forces of darkness that would enter there to displace her divine place in the lotus seat, in the petaled throne.

Thus, beloved, the sounding of the Word is for the filling of the cup of the chakras. What will'st thou do when the cups be filled? I shall tell thee, beloved. Empty the cups by giving to drink to those who hunger and thirst after the Law,[1] whereby in its right use they might also gain fairly a share of light that is their just portion from on high.

I AM Hilarion, come to bestow gifts of healing by first quickening. O ye who would be instruments, know then the law of truth, know the law of vision, know the science of the immaculate concept, know compassion, know the caring, know the transfer of light to the body itself.

Thus, I would speak to you of the need of the hour. You have heard of the call to be mediators;[2] and so he called me.[3] And so I saw from the inner teaching of the mystery, truly of the ineffable, beloved, the necessity and the Mother of that necessity, the Divine Mother of Love who would reach her own through my heart. O beloved, I saw that the truth would not live unless each one in his succession would become the chalice, would become the cup from which all might drink.

You Need a Divine Calling That Will Galvanize All of Your Forces

It is an hour, then, when many thirst. Where are the cups of the Divine Mother? Where are the cups that will catch not only her ascension light but her tears shed in this hour for the burden that is come upon her own?

I plead, then, the cause of the Divine Mother in the name of her Son Jesus. I plead that cause not alone for the children of the Sun or for the gratification of the Mother and the Divine Son. *Hear me, beloved.* I plead it for you and because of you. Because you need it, beloved! You need an avocation, a divine calling that will galvanize all of your forces because you perceive the need and because the Divine Mother of Love has entered your heart and you desire to fill another's need.

Blessed ones, it is said that if one is hungry and naked and in want of "all these things," he cannot perceive and fill the need of another while being about the business of satisfying his own and his family's needs. Beloved, this is true at a certain level, and thus Saint Germain and many of the masters have sponsored a civilization where, if the personal needs of each life are being met, the soul should be free to nourish the spiritual needs of many.

Unfortunately, and as you know, people have become drunk with materialism, desiring and requiring more and more, and therefore are never satiated but filled with their own wants, having little compassion for the basic spiritual as well as physical needs of others.

Blessed hearts, let it not be said of you that there ever was neglect to perceive the need of a lonely, burdened, or pained heart, and to supply that need. Therefore are you nourished. Therefore do I bring to you the mantle of the fifth ray.

This Cape Is Given to See What You Will Make of It

Blessed ones, it is a simple cape that my angels bear. Why do you suppose I have brought them bearing capes? Is it because one is deserving or has attainment or that all do? I have not even regarded levels of attainment this night, beloved, but what I have regarded is the great need of the Divine Mother for her own.

Therefore this cape is reversible. For did you know that the pink cape of Paul the Venetian is lined in emerald green and that my own emerald-green cape is lined with the rose of the third ray? Therefore, you see, we are juxtaposed together, each one with our inner and outer love for that Divine Mother as she does appear in Mary, Kuan Yin, Lady Venus, Portia, Pallas Athena.

You think these names be of Greek mythology? I tell you, beloved, Greek mythology has copied them from the very ancient ones, the divine manifestations that antedated all of the wars and rivalries of the good and bad gods.

Thus understand, precious hearts, that this cape is given to see what you will make of it—a simple cape, fastened at the neck, worn on either side.

Now, if you desire to master the five secret rays by the power of the rose cross and the third ray of Paul the Venetian, wear the rose within and the green without. And then it shall be that without, the mastery of the seven shall be by the portal of truth, truly the third- and all-seeing eye.

If you desire to pursue a course of the mastery of the five secret rays by the fullness of the power of the emerald ray, so let it be reversed and let the rose be on the outer. For divine love radiating from you in all directions will be found to seal within you an inner path of mastery of five points of the heart, even by the Buddha's love, even by the majesty of the fifth ray.

Blessed ones, now you know the secret of the pink rose and the bud appearing and the green stalk. Now you also know that the seven chakras must blossom.

Thus, beloved, at the conclusion of our address to you, angels will place these upon you that you might make of them what you will, that you might wield them and use them. For a cloak may become a mantle by endowment with light.* Thus, let it be charged *by you* this time, as we give you something of ourselves and you add to it your own momentum. Thus, from the moment these capes descend upon you, beloved, each one is instantaneously different by your vibration, by the individualization of the God flame that you bring to it.

Thus, the cape is for your comfort and for the understanding that the path of truth is to comfort all life. Do not judge, then, the condition or the karma of the one you comfort, but know that life is locked inside that one—life that is light and God and soul waiting liberation, perhaps by your hand.

Blessed ones, if you never extend the hand, how will you ever know when God is ready to bless life through you?

If you never give the cup of cold water of Christ's teaching, how will you ever know if the Holy Spirit may speak through you?

It is in doing that God does act through you. Thus, in a time of quiescence, absence of activity does signify a garnering of light in chakras as fiery coils become a fire infolding itself and thus there is

*the Christ consciousness amplified through the seven chakras

intensity built within these centers that shall be unleashed in a time of activity and movement.

I Have Come to Touch Those Who Have Descended from the Central Sun with Sanat Kumara

Now, beloved, I must touch those in all of North America who are the original seed of Sanat Kumara. I must touch and quicken them, for some have come to occupy their place who are not worthy. Let the unworthy servant be removed and let the new plant be planted in that pot and in that earth.

Thus the blossoming continues, hearts unfold, hearts of gold set a standard. And until the Christ standard be set, how can the Christ appear? Therefore, understand the flowers that hold a matrix by fragrance, color, and presence. And that matrix sets a standard, and all must reach it if they would pluck that flower.

So it is, beloved, as the mediators in the earth proclaim by example a Christ standard, that these mediators may also embody the divine standard, the banner of Maitreya, which banner he holds in this hour as the banner of the Divine Mother. Let the Son of God embrace his Mother and thereby let the Mother appear through him.

> *O thou Buddhas, all devotees of the Divine Mother, I, Hilarion, call forth out of the causal body of the Divine Mother truly the science of healing, that in this earth a quickening and an acceleration of the spin and a straightening of axis might be so that all might have restored an ancient memory of the science of wholeness.*
>
> *Sanat Kumara, thou great physician having all remedies, so now transfer morsels of wholeness to these thine own. Saint Germain, let thy elixir of youth, regeneration, and resurrection become, then, accessible to those who will make the call and understand the requirements of the path of eternality lived and experienced and embodied on earth.*
>
> *O currents of eternal life, I, Hilarion, come now for the charging of these chakras and these lifestreams. I send the ray by*

my angels, by my messenger, now to the crown and the base for the establishment of a pillar of fire midst the Dark Cycle of Cancer. Therefore, let the crown and the base chakras so establish the equanimity, the balance, the polarity of being, that these souls might reach for the Polestar of Being in the mighty I AM Presence.

Now let there be the quickening of the heart. For Alpha, for Omega, present now, do quicken. *Now* let there be the touching of the third eye of each one. *Now* let there be the touching of the soul.

Awake, thou that sleepest![4] *Awake,* O soul! Rise now from thy bed, even thy bed of straw in the seat-of-the-soul chakra. Come forth now. Be quickened and live! Come forth now by the quickening power of the fifth ray. Come forth now!

Lo, I AM Hilarion. And I am quickening now even the desiring unto God, even the awakening unto the desiring to be God in manifestation, to know and be the divine mystery, to know and be the divine Word, to know and be the Buddha where I AM. So I am therefore quickening that desiring, that this desiring might be all of thy speaking and thy intoning of the Word.

So let the seven chakras—now let them sound a ringing! Now let them sound a tone! Now let the ineffable be unheard but be sounded in other octaves.

Lo, I have come to touch those who have descended from the Central Sun with Sanat Kumara. *Lo,* I do it here. For in this place some have lost the way and will find it again.

For I say it, and so it is said by the I AM THAT I AM in the mystery of the Ineffable One: *Lo, I AM.* And I AM THAT I AM in the petals of the thousand-petaled rose that does unfold.

Lo, I AM THAT I AM. I AM, then, in the heart of the living Word, and out of that Word do proceed lifestreams who are the ascended masters.

We the lords of the seven rays salute thee this night, thou who art preparing, then, *thou who art preparing, then,* the way of the ascension, the way of the deathless solar body. So, I anoint thee also with that oil of light.

And so the oil of light, the single drop, is placed in the crown chakra of those who require that blessing in this hour, for their inner preparation is just. And therefore I AM come. And the few receive it, for it does require the ascended master as well as the spoken Word.

Therefore know that all who are to ascend in this life are called to keep the flame in order that they might receive the initiation out of the flame that they keep, which is the flame of life. And that life in me and that life resonating through the life flame of the messenger does allow you to receive in the physical octave this blessing, beloved. Therefore, each one shall know it. And so long as the messenger is in embodiment, so long shall the initiation be possible at the physical level.

Therefore let the Christ Self of each one—for whom each one does become in time the spokesman and the mouthpiece—raise up, raise up and quicken now the chakras! Raise them now and quicken them! Raise them now and quicken them! Raise them now and quicken them!

So I seal you in the lotus of the heart.
So I seal you in the twelve-petaled lotus of the heart.
O thou light! O thou light! O thou light!
Be sealed now in the fire of the heart.

I AM Hilarion, come, then, for the initiation of you, each and every one, to receive from your Lord, your Holy Christ Self, gifts of healing, gifts of healing, gifts of healing. As the chiming of a bell, so shall they descend. So I foretell it. Prepare the way, O my soul, for the angels of healing would enter thy house and teach thee their way.

[Meditation music is played.]

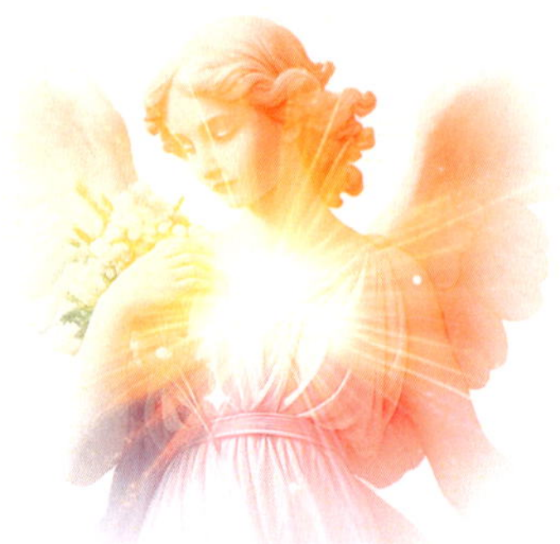

Beloved Paul the Venetian

LOVE'S MYSTERY

Into the fire of the heart is a piercing ruby ray! So, beloved, I come, the initiate of the Holy Spirit, bearing unto your heart a quickening light that is for love's victory in *your* day.

Blessed hearts, we are ascending by increments. We have fulfilled the ascension, fully fused in the I AM THAT I AM. But the ascent, beloved, as an increase in God-awareness, is a never-ending process and thus there is no sky to heaven—no ceiling but only a bliss that does intensify as though new vistas were to appear. Do not, then, consider anything that is beyond in the Infinite as having any ending or any limit or any final end or goal.

For the moment, strive to reach the fruit of the tree that requires even a stretch of the arm and a tippy-toeing to reach and perhaps even a jump itself. Reaching, then, for the fruit of the master that does wait thy call and his call (and both answers) is a way to establish a co-measurement with lesser goals and reachable stars along the cosmic highway.

Intensify, then, thy adoring and self-giving and discover always that the mystery of love unfolds as a magnet drawing unto oneself a light increasing that is given only when love and love's pursuit is for the goal of a self-control and self-mastery, that the power of love be never squandered or lost or abused or trifled with.

So, beloved, understand the meaning of trust when considering the love ray and all that it does portend for the fullness of thy

God-realization. Know, then, that trust is the word that must be received. As you trust in God, so God must be able to trust in you and to trust that the light that is given will be held steady for adoring, for joy, for creating, for giving, for building, for tearing down, for laying foundation, and for the raising up of the temple of man. This temple built without hands is laid stone upon stone by love, and the chief cornerstone is love.

Now understand how all rays of God have a mystery of love and an initiation of love. I come concerning the love that perceives the needs of a nation, the needs of a planet. I come to give you a love that is an enlightenment, for wisdom is truly the other side of love.

I come, then, that the rose side of the cape may be an emanation, a magnet attracting the highest initiates of cosmos to bring to this North America, so consecrated by our Lord Jesus to the path of the ascension,[5] the very best teachers for those who will come to understand the path of the ascension as the very reason for the mission of Jesus; teachers who will teach the soul to return to the Source, to the beginning, in this the ending and the fulfillment of her cycles. For this cause did the Ancient of Days send forth this Son of God.

Now, then, be grateful that the lost teaching is restored and the mystery partially unveiled. For you see, beloved, it is not spoken or written but left as a blank on the page for the soul to fill in. And this knowing may come only from the experiencing. But I tell you, beloved, it will come to those who see the Christ in one another, who minister and clothe and nourish and care for all who are in need.

Let the Lightbearers Take Their Stand to Defend Freedom

The practical necessities of physical life include the protection of life, the defense of life, the drawing of the circle of fire that life might live free of disease and death. There are many needs to be met beyond those of which most think when thinking in these terms. Beloved, there is a need for the ultimate sealing by sacred fire of all who are the children of God on earth from all those things that may be coming upon this earth.

Let love and the bliss of love not blind you, then, to the dangers and the dangerous forces of anti-love, which by a misapplied free will would array themselves against this place, this nation, this path.

Why, then, do the heathen, who are the fallen angels, rage?

Why do they imagine a vain thing?[6]

It is because "it is the last time"[7] and they would devour the light of the lightbearers who will ascend if but given the hours, the weeks, and the months and the years to realize the inner mystery as themselves. It is the hope and prayer of the ascended hosts that this opportunity shall not be cut short—nor for yourselves, nor for others yet to take embodiment and who are also already here.

Blessed ones, the opportunity for each citizen of cosmos, of earth and these states to place the capstone on the pyramid of individual life is indeed here. It is the hour when the Master Mason, having laid the foundation, may now put in place the capstone of life. To this end was this nation founded. To this end was the earth claimed for the lightbearers.

Let the lightbearers take their stand to defend freedom as a flame, as life in every heart, and allow no encroachment in any octave to come forth to snuff out one of these little ones! The lords of the seven rays are deeply concerned that all citizens of the earth come to a quickened awareness that by the flame of peace and the sword of peace, so must war and the hordes of war be turned back. Therefore, today begin a path of the assimilation of light by the simple decree. Rejoice and accelerate as you can.

Capes Are Dropped upon Your Shoulders

I AM Paul the Venetian. And in this split second and moment that must be noted by correct time,* these capes are dropped upon your shoulders. They are for you, beloved, a protection, a reality, a sign.

Let each one feel it, then, as a comfort of the Divine Mother delivered by two of her Sons and their angels. Let each one understand mysteries to be told.

---

*11:18 p.m. CDT

Awake then! *Awake* then! Pray God the mystery be known on the morrow with the dawn.

I, Paul, Brother of light, defender of Mother Liberty my own, place within you a seed. And this seed of light is a seed of gnosis. And according as the light is applied within the chakra where it is sealed (varying for each one), so shall it dissolve and give of itself and create the awareness that you are able to contain. Let each one so desiring it now pursue light in all chakras, lest the one skipped might be one where I have buried a precious seed:

It is self-knowledge of thyself, a gift from the Maha Chohan.

[The master gives intonations for 27 seconds.]

Let gifts of the Spirit beget gifts of the Spirit and gratitude. Let the mantra of the Mother's devotees be "I AM gratitude in action."

Lo, we are come. Lo, we are determined that this giant City Foursquare shall bear fruit. So long as there is effort and love, comfort and truth, it shall be done.

AUM

May 29, 1987

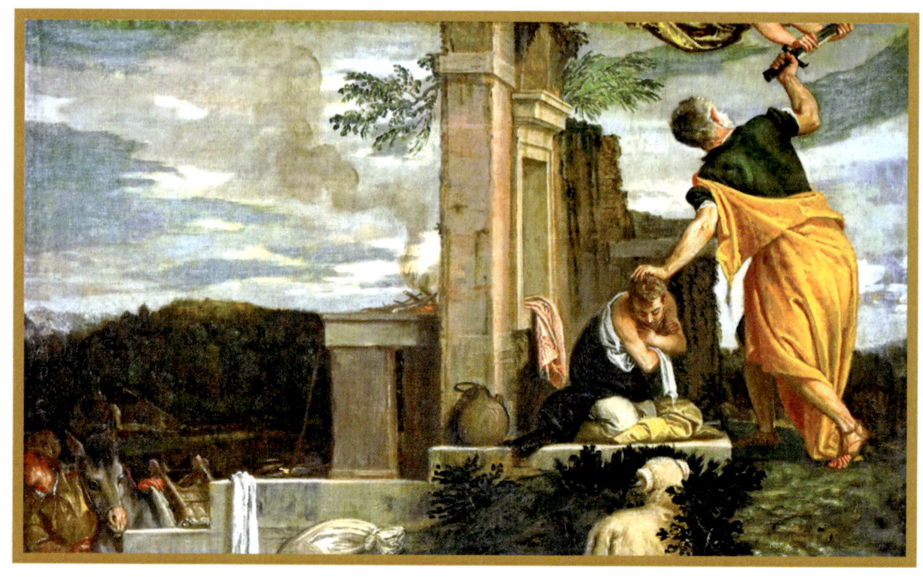

The Sacrifice of Isaac, c. 1580–88

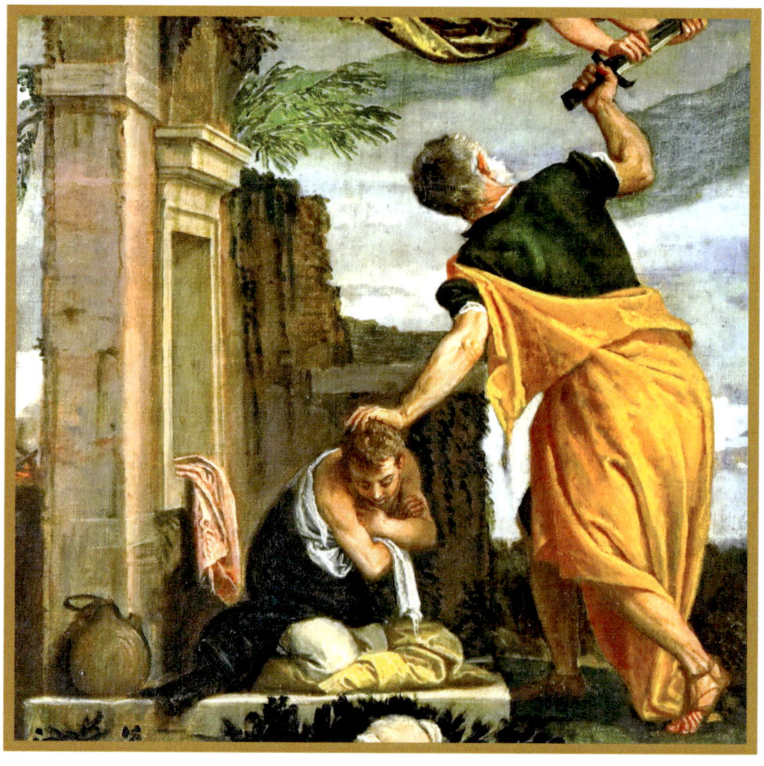

The heart knoweth all things, readeth all things, understandeth all things. Let the understanding of the heart unfold and let the soul rise to her lawful mentor, even the Christ within.

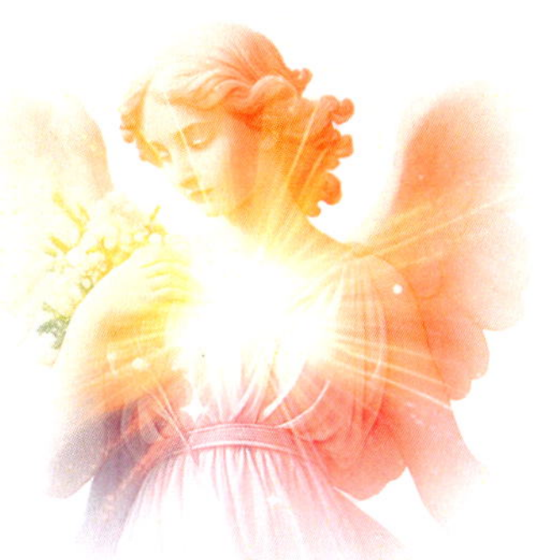

CHAPTER 18

The Initiation of Hearts

Fire for the Realignment of Worlds

Out of the ineffable Word I come, O beloved, as Lord of the Third Ray, your own Paul the Venetian.

I come, then, for the initiation of hearts and heart chakras unto the unfoldment of divine love to all hearts of this state who must accelerate in the development of the discernment of the heart. For the heart knoweth all things, readeth all things, understandeth all things. Let the understanding of the heart unfold and let the soul rise to her lawful mentor, even the Christ within.

My angels of love surround you. They surround each and every lightbearer, every child, man, and woman throughout this state of California. For I, Paul, do come to minister unto those burdened by those tremblings in the earth of karma and the weight of misqualification in this state and from ancient records.

Thus, how bright is the light of the day. Yet those who listen, those who hear and hear angel voices and heed the inner call know that all is not well, and therefore the rumblings of prophecies and predictions of earthquake and cataclysm must surely affect the inner psyche as well as the beings of nature who tend this garden of God.

Now, then, beloved, for the anchoring of pillars of fire in the earth, I commend you to the call of the Divine Mother to rise to meet your destiny in this age. I commend you to the violet flame whereby the light of the heart does simply increase and increase as the flower unfolds its petals and the rose of light of the heart sheds its fragrance to all who are in distress, all who are dying, and those who have not lived in the light, for they knew not how.

The Denial of the Mother of Ancient Lemuria

For want of teachers and those who care, some are lost. And for want of caring for the Law, many self-extinguish the flame. And in the denial of the Divine Mother of ancient Lemuria, there has come to pass a civilization bereft of the intimate knowledge of being the vessel of the Mother and thereby coming unto the love of the Buddha, even the one who unfolds the light of eternal Christos.

Wherefore, then, do we deliver our Word? It is that flood tides of love might descend upon a people reincarnated from the Motherland, here once again to resolute* karma and situations of ancient history.

Blessed ones, be not caught, then, in those places that must receive a purging light and a washing of the waters by the Word.[1] Be mindful to entertain angels of God.[2] Be mindful to establish the inner fount of peace as a means of receiving the Divine Presence and these angels who have always ministered unto the servants of God to take them where they ought to be, perhaps where they desire not to go.

Nevertheless, the Holy Spirit, which is of my ray and bands, must pick you up and take you to other places and sometimes to other times, past and future, that you might establish the coordinates of your own understanding of a prophecy that is written in the rock and in the marrow of your bones and in the very waters of the seas themselves.

I Come for the Healing of Hearts

I call, then, unto those who have heard the call already and are responding by answering with their own call, and I come to you, opening my heart for the healing of hearts. For the heart chakra of this state must needs be expanded that there might evolve fruition and a light.

Let the children of Mu come of age.[3] Let them understand what it means to be sons of God in a time when few accept the responsibility of shepherding.

**resolute* (verb): to express a resolution for *(Merriam-Webster's Unabridged)*

I come also with a ruby fire for the purging of corruption in the government of this state. I come with a purging light that compels the light to rise for the restoration of the divine memory. For with the loss of light there is also the loss of memory. And on the Tablets of *Mem,*[4] with which you were familiar on Lemuria, are the recordings of ancient lifetimes when you, beloved, possessed an extraordinary light.

But for vast numbers of those settled in this state in this time, it was the compromise of the heart and the heart chakra that allowed them to lose that light and therefore to descend in an apartness, a separation first from the Mother and then from her Son, from the universal light and then from one another, being divided, then, by fallen ones, angels who waged the wars of the gods unto the utter destruction of the inner temples of light.*

You Stand on the Pinnacle of a Choice

These fallen ones have come again, beloved, to destroy the temples and the devotees of Tibet. And who has raised the hand to say, "Thus far and no farther!" to those Communist hordes who have denied the culture of the Mother in the gentle ones of Tibet who have carried forward the ancient wisdom?

I tell you, it was not the government of this nation or the West. Blessed hearts, it is a crime against humanity when hordes who are undeveloped are given the freedom in the name of Aquarius to snuff out the candle that has been lit upon the altars of the ancients for hundreds and thousands of years.

Will the candle go out in your heart, in the hearts of the people of Lemuria on this side of the fire ring?

It is a decision that the individual must make by free will to keep the flame of life and to know that in the science of the spoken Word (which you have so gently and powerfully exercised this evening) is the means to raise up the Mother light† to draw forth the light of the Father from the I AM Presence, to experience that union of both [the Mother light and the light of the Father] in the temple as an increase of the fire of the heart that shall consume the ancient karma of the

*the inner sanctum of Lemurian temples where the Divine Mother was worshipped
†the sacred fire from the base-of-the-spine chakra

compromise of the heart—ultimately that fire, that threefold flame expanding, returning to you the consciousness of God you once knew.

Though I read the records of akasha in a moment of each one gathered here and all former citizens of Lemuria living in California, I shall not read them in detail in my dictation but only tell you, beloved, that the axiom is so true—that those who neglect a self-knowledge of their history are doomed to repeat that history. Thus, you stand in a moment on the pinnacle of a choice: to move upward in the spiral of being to transcend oneself all the way back to the days of Lemuria and enter the high road of reunion with God, else to repeat the former cycles and go down again.

The Sacredness of Life within You

Blessed hearts, the Great White Brotherhood is compelled to send forth the messenger to reach its own with the knowledge of *choices,* for you have earned the right to know, to be loved, and to yourself love as God loves every part of life. You have a right to learn and walk the way of self-givingness, which the adepts of ancient Lemuria did in the last days of that continent as they gathered their disciples and transferred the flames of the temples to mountain fastnesses.[5]

Know, beloved, that what is in the earth as karma must be transmuted, for the earth cries out in agony for the weight of infamy of the fallen ones, even within this state alone, and, yea, the entire planet: "How long, how long, O LORD?"[6]

Thus do the beings of the earth and the fire and the waters and the air cry out unto God, "How long must we bear the infamy of rebellious spirits who wander about perverting the life force in little children and in their bodies?"

Thus, it is, beloved, that the sacredness of life within you must needs be acknowledged. God is in you! Revere that light, that consciousness, that Being, and understand that unless life be revered and some pull away from the ease of the pleasure cult, the ease of squandering the light of the chakras, you will know once again the cataclysms of the past. All prediction may be turned back by the violet flame. Some may be but mitigated.

I Release the Fire for the Realignment of Worlds

Let us hasten to higher consciousness. As the watchman of the night climbs to his tower to see that all is well or that it is not, so may you rise to higher planes of your being and see through the mind of Christ in you what is your destiny and what is earth's destiny, that you might chart a course to be in planet Earth a pillar of fire—*a pillar of fire*. Thus are the adepts of love and of the third-ray initiates of the Holy Spirit and of the priesthood of the Order of Melchizedek.[7] Thus do we know the ruby fire that is a love so intense as to bring judgment upon the forces of anti-love that abuse the light of the heart.

May you run to the Immaculate Heart of Mother Mary, to the Sacred Heart of Jesus, and to the purple fiery heart of Saint Germain, and therefrom receive the engrafted Word.[8] *This,* this is Cosmic Christ illumination! This is the transfer from the great masters to you directly through your own Christ Self, who is high priest at the altar of your being, of that fire so needed for you to *know* and to *sense* and to *be* who, what, and where you ought to be in this age.

I release now the fire for the realignment of worlds. Come Home, my beloved, to the heart of everlasting love. So may it be that you discover Reality, and in the process know the Teacher, the twin flame, and the beloved God.

My angels touch you and love you in this hour. They have known you for a foreverness. May you greet them as long, almost lost friends from higher octaves, who salute you now with the embrace of other worlds. Heaven is so close—closer yet, heaven's love.

My coming, then, is established as angels of the third ray throughout the city have established focuses for transmutation and the righting of this government for the benefit of all people.

In the flame of your heart, I remain a teacher of love who loves you unto the heights of love's mastery.

Be at peace, beloved, but keep the flame. Do not fail to keep the flame of love burning. So is the dawn of the New Age through the flame of love.

February 16, 1988

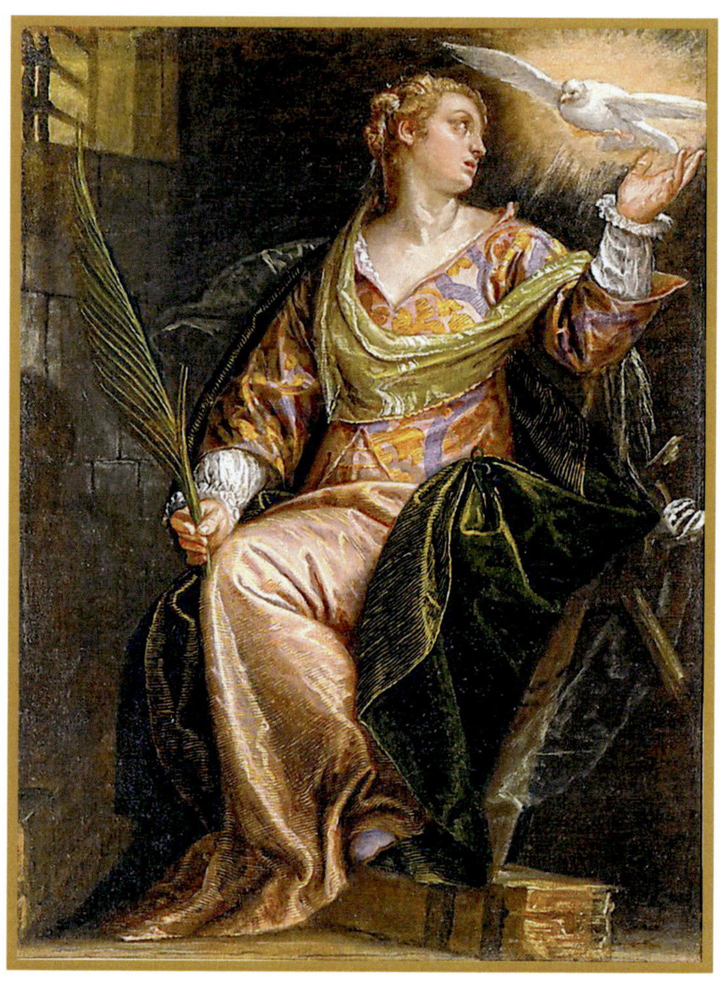

Saint Catherine of Alexandria in Prison, c. 1585

I take you through these rays by an appreciation of the heart . . . the sensitivity, the profound love. For only love enables you to pass through the walls of the crystal ruby ray that is indeed the lining of the caves of the Dhyani Buddhas, caves of light.

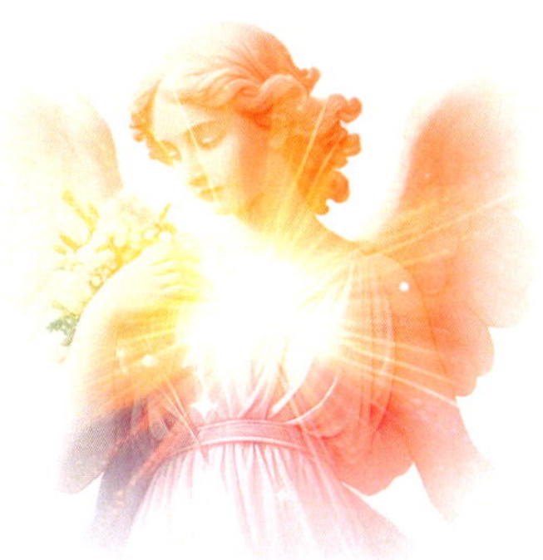

CHAPTER 19

An Appreciation of the Heart

Discipleship under the Third Ray unto the Ruby Ray Buddha

It is the hour of the melting of the elements with the fervent heat[1] of the divine love of the Buddha of the Ruby Ray[2] and all manifestations, replications, of the Five Dhyani Buddhas.[3]

I come to you this hour escorting your soul from the place of the Divine Mother to the secret chamber of the heart, the eight-petaled chakra. Let us steal inside and abide.

Om Om Om Mani Padme Hum [chanted 35 times]*

Om Vairochana Om   Om Vairochana Om   Om Vairochana Om

Beloved of my heart, I address you this evening on the line of the cosmic clock of my Cosmic Mother, the Goddess of Liberty, the seven o'clock line of the flame of God-gratitude, which does release the power of the eighth-ray chakra for the multiplication of the five secret rays.

Thus, I take you through these rays by an appreciation of the heart—*the appreciation of the heart*—the sensitivity, the profound love. For only love enables you to pass through the walls of the crystal ruby ray that is indeed the lining of the caves of the Dhyani Buddhas, caves of light. Thus the buddhic path of Saint Germain is also revealed.

*Seed syllables and mantras were sounded by the master with the congregation joining in.

A Ministration of Love

The Maha Chohan has called me for a ministration of love whereby you might pursue a discipleship under the third ray unto the ruby ray Buddha.

Aim [chanted 16 times]

Maim [chanted 6 times]

Om Ah Hum Vajra Guru Padma Siddhi Hum [chanted 56 times]

The ideal purpose of my coming is the use of the emerald crystal to direct to your hearts, and specifically to the eight petals of the eight-petaled chakra, that wavelength of the emerald ray, beloved, whereby there is established the forcefield for the precipitation of the chalice for the Buddha of the heart. Thus, as you continue the mantra, the mantra of Padma Sambhava,[4] so I shall extend now that action.

Some of you know that I use the emerald stone as well as the emerald cape and the emerald lining of the rose cape. Therefore, beloved, be receptive to the action of this fifth ray that does unlock, petal by petal, the means whereby the door shall be opened to you unto the chambers of the Five Dhyani Buddhas. By the love of the beings of the third ray, so receive this action.*

Om Ah Hum Vajra Guru Padma Siddhi Hum [chanted 59 times]

Ribbons of emerald light punctuate the Eightfold Path etched in the petals of the heart.

Now, beloved, my mentor and Guru, the Maha Chohan, does take this wondrous occasion of divine alchemy to serve to you the communion of the Holy Spirit, the Alpha and the Omega of cloven tongues of the Holy Spirit. Thus, out of the universal light body of the Holy Spirit that is the attainment of this Lord there is transmitted to you a communion that is essential if you would seriously pursue the path of the five secret rays as a means to the mastery of the power of the three-times-three, the balanced threefold flame, and the initiations of the half hours of the Dhyani Buddhas.[5]

---

*While the assembly of lightbearers gave the mantra of Padma Sambhava with Paul the Venetian, the messenger faced the congregation from different points on the altar as she held up Saint Germain's emerald crystal in her right hand.

Oh, Kuan Yin is so near as the Mother flame of this Communion, beloved, as the Mother representative of these Buddhas, even as the Lord the Maha Chohan does minister to you now through our servants. Therefore, let the wine and the bread be brought before the altar, for our Lord the Maha Chohan desires to consecrate it.

I AM Alpha and Omega in the white-fire core of being. [repeated 19 times]

July 4, 1988

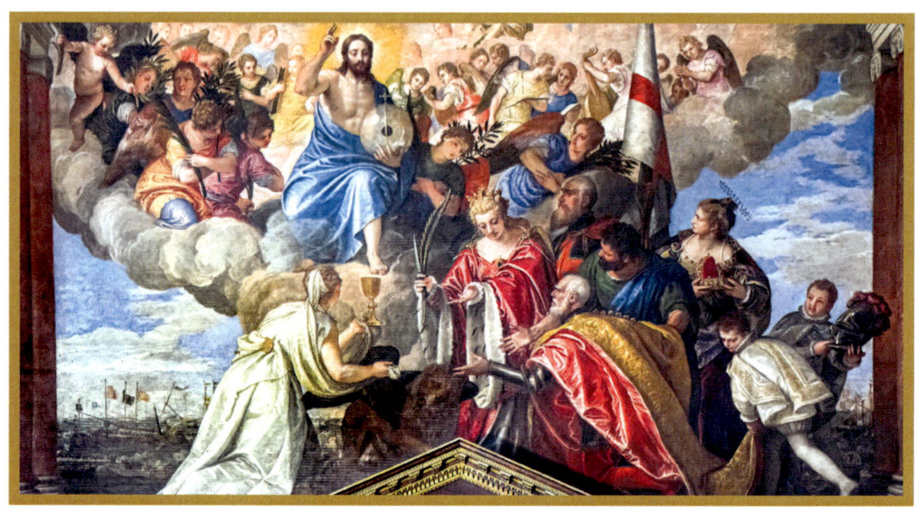

Votive Portrait of Doge Sebastiano Venier, c. 1581–82

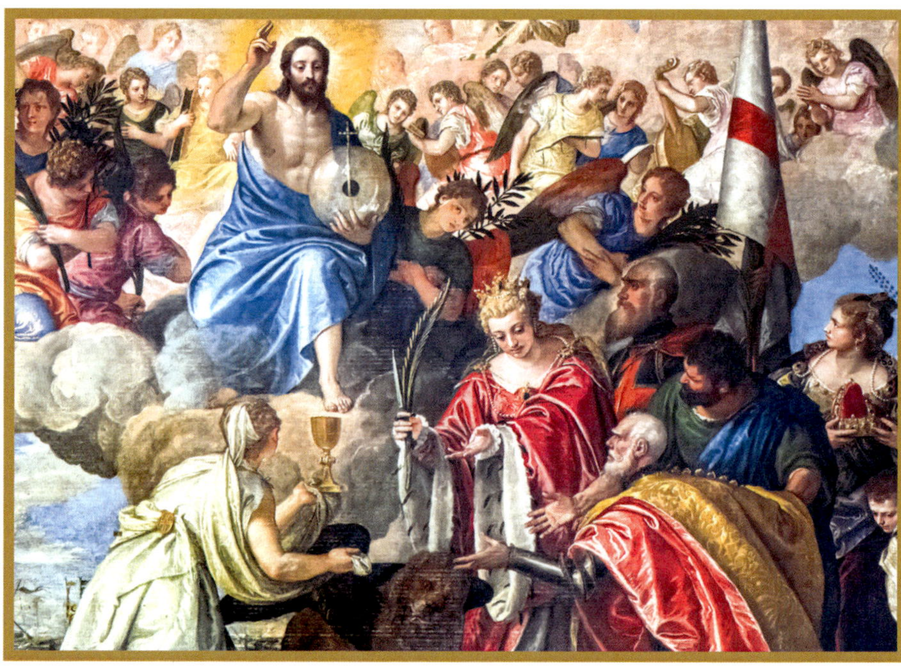

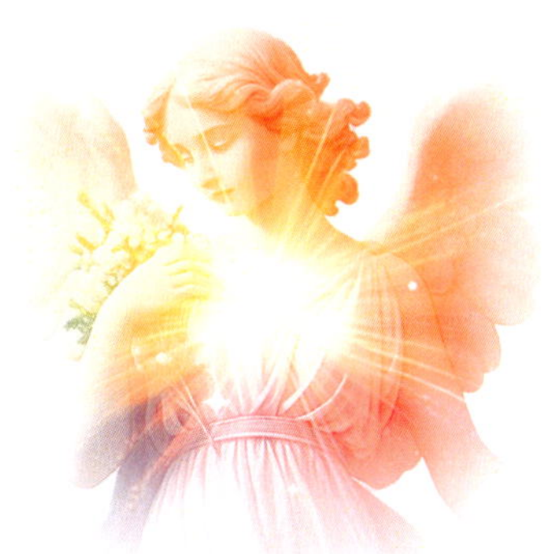

Let love lead you and guide you to the depths and heights of being, to the fulfillment of holy purpose, to the completion of the rounds in this century.

CHAPTER 20

Love: The Age-Old Solution

I AM the Resurrection and the Life of the Spirit of My Lord and Saviour in My Heart This Day

[Throughout the dictation, the congregation held candles lit from the flame on the altar. The candlelight vigil continued through the dictation of Gautama Buddha, which followed.]

Shafts of divine love descend. And within and upon them, behold angels of the living flame of love!

Love must be the cure in this opening of the New Year, with new opportunity. Therefore, at the focus of the threefold flame in the obelisk in Washington, D.C.,[1] in the heart of the Temple of the Sun over Manhattan[2]—wherever there is the living flame of love on the altars of the retreats of the Brotherhood throughout the earth—there love is magnified, magnified by holy angels and saints above and those who gather at the throne of Sanat Kumara.

I AM your brother Paul the Venetian. So I have come with the solution, the age-old solution to all divisions, dichotomies, and all that divides one from another or the members of the individual. And that solution is Love.

Let love, then, be the dividing of the way of Light and Darkness, for the two cannot coexist. Let your invocation of love, O my beloved, be for the drawing forth of the flame of the Holy Spirit through the Lord the Maha Chohan—yes, love in government, love in the economy, love that is in such an intensity of concentration in your heart that it can truly break the stranglehold of the money beast upon the nations and of greed itself.

Oh, such love, beloved! It is of the heart of Christ in you. And it is the love that can indeed heal many flaws, many cleavages in the earth. Contemplate love! Defend love! And begin to depend on the great power of love for the resolution of many things.

Oh, I would that you would spend a full sixty minutes in giving the decrees of divine love[3] so that you might sense not only the power of love but all that is arrayed against the love that is God's and that God releases through the newborn babe and in your hearts in love for one another, in love for the things of God and the ways of God and the path of God.

Many do not embrace this path of love's devotion because of the challenges of evil spirits who come to destroy love by all manner of amplification of elements in the psyche and the mind. And therefore, to be a master on the path of love is to be whole, is to seal one's aura, is to expand the heart and be fearless before any force of Antichrist that seeks to tear the child, the mature one from the infinite flow of divine love, from the manifestation of that Christhood, which is love.

So, my beloved, love goes abegging in the world and has many substitutes. But the love of which I speak is a love that you may keep if you are willing to give all of yourself to it and, as one has said, to not be offended by the assailants of love. The greater the love in your aura, the greater the protection you need.

Let Art Be for Healing

I bid you, then, come to my fount of love as you follow the meditations within the "Sacred Ritual for Transport and Holy Work,"[4] that you might arrive [on inner levels] at the Washington Monument [while you sleep], the gathering place of devotees who pronounce the Ashram rituals[5] and go forth at night for the healing of souls and for the defense of the little ones.

Yes, love is pressing in upon the nations. And what do you think the effect will be?

I tell you, it is the treading of the winepress. Yes, beloved, love is the element of God that forces out the anger of anti-love, and therefore love wreaks havoc in the earth.

Know, then, precious hearts, that love is truly the initiation that I offer. And I give love in my vast school, where devotees come and use the medium of art to paint that which is within, that which is the beautiful, that which is the pain and the record, and of course to perfect the masterpiece that each one of you is working on—the drawing of yourself made in the image and likeness of your Holy Christ Self.

Therefore, let art be for healing—every form of art that is lawful. Let the art of the spoken Word, the word of mantra, of profound devotion, also be for the healing of the heart.

Anger Is Death to the Soul on the Path

The expression of the soul through the movement of the trained eye and hand, this, then, brings satisfaction. There is art that is drama and music. There is so much that can be offered to people of all ages, whether in sculpture or the art of design or the art of creating all things that adorn the homes, the walls, the hangings, architecture itself. Art, beloved, allows the great cube, the white cube of self, to take on dimension, quality, and a foundation for the soul's rising.

Do not neglect this form, then.

Do not neglect the art of moving with angels, commanding legions, and directing forces of love for healing.

Do not neglect the art of entering in to a level slightly beyond the physical where you find nature spirits—sylphs and gnomes, undines of the waters, fiery salamanders.

Do not neglect the art of using the magnet of love of the Central Sun to magnetize these workers in the vineyard of the Father-Mother God and in your own gardens—to magnetize them back to the centeredness of being whereby under your tutelage and that of the ascended masters they may earn a threefold flame and thereby have eternal life.[6]

Lo, the gift of the resurrection has been given unto them by the Saviour.[7] Now teach them the mantra of the Saviour's love: *"I AM the resurrection and the life of the Spirit of my Lord and Saviour in my heart this day!"*

You would do well to also give this mantra that is given for elementals. For you must remember: by anger released you can in a moment easily snuff out the flame of the candle that you have nurtured in the heart.

Thus, beloved, atone this night for all outbursts of condemnation and anger that you have had, even through the Christmas season, throughout the years, the decades of this life. This is the hour to come to terms with this, beloved. For that anger is death to the soul on the Path, and it must be consumed.

Let Love Light Your Way Each Day

I hold in my hand, therefore, the torch of the Goddess of Liberty. And in this hour, the fire is the rose-pink and ruby-ray flame in swirls and undulations of love's great power. Love's great power comes to you, then, as my angels and the angels of my mother, the Goddess of Liberty, come to you now.

Receive this love fire for the consuming of those levels of anger, which if they are not consumed, which if you do not make the resolution in this hour, will surely remove you from the opportunity for the ascension in this life.

Go not the way of the angry generation! Go not the way of the fallen angels, who have not love and substitute for it their intellectual prowess, a brilliance that is dull by comparison to the sheen of the wings of the tiniest angel you might discover.

Blessed hearts, the angry ones are out to tear you from your love tryst in God. Do not allow it! Let love for you be a humbling experience, that you might be endowed with love.

You are potentially the chalice of the Holy Grail. Let the outline of the grail that I draw upon you in all dimensions this night be, then, as a hologram for that grail that you fill in.

Yes, beloved, I fill the chalice with love and I say, drink ye all of it!

Let love lead you and guide you to the depths and heights of being, to the fulfillment of holy purpose, to the completion of the rounds in this century.

Think, now. Seven years and the door of this century shall close. What will you have to say for those seven years? What shall the new day bring and the conclusion of the year 2002?[8]

Yes, beloved, cycles are moving swiftly onward. Those who do not have a hold on the torch of love—yes, mighty love—may not see the way of the soul's perfecting.

Let love light your way each day! And remember the one who originally kindled love in the earth, your Lord Sanat Kumara, who came bringing not only the physical fire again but the spiritual fire that none had retained.[9] Oh, think of this, beloved, and be grateful for the Flame behind the flame that you hold!

Love Will Not Leave You as It Has Found You

Now then, know that I speak to you under the disciplines of the Holy Spirit. This is a year to intensify that strictness with yourself whereby the power of love may come to you and not leave you again.

How long, how long has it been since you have held the torch of love in your hand? How long has it been since Liberty could trust you to hold that torch?

Love will try you and pummel you, sift you, grind you to powder.[10] But, beloved, love will not leave you as it has found you but will pour you into love's own mold, the pattern of the loving, adorable Christ. Oh yes, beloved, love is the highest and most difficult calling. Love flees so quickly in a moment's indiscretion.

Let love, then, come. Let it come to the nations! Let the people of love in the heart of the earth know that upon them depends the victory of the violet flame and the resolution of the money systems. These are not as they should be, and the manipulations and the hoarding take from the people that which is theirs.

How is it that that which is your own can be taken from you by those who have no light at all? It is because you have first allowed the light to go out. It is because you have first compromised love and therefore you do not have the magnet of divine love that could draw to you instantaneously all the love of the cosmos because the love of God is in you. Like attracts like, and love brings to you every good and perfect gift, the meeting of all of your needs.[11]

Oh, I say, tend the flame of love! I do not hear you call to me often nor sing to me. I seem to be one of the neglected chohans. It is because you are busy fighting your battles and winning your battles and engaging with the hosts of the LORD.

No Battle Is Ever Won without Love

My legions come too! We come with the Buddha of the Ruby Ray and the Dhyani Buddhas. We come in all of the fierceness of ruby fire. We are there, beloved.

You may depict me in the mode of artist, but I am a true knight of the cross. And the numberless numbers who carry the flame of love bear the mighty banner upon which is embroidered in the beautiful rose color the cross pattée.* We come as legions of far-off worlds and knights of old, and we come accompanied by ladies marching in line, keeping the torch of love.

Yes, beloved, no battle is ever won without love. For it is the superior force, which none of those who have left off from the living flame of love of Almighty God can have. They cannot match that flame; therefore they are overcome by it.

Your love is great, for you serve devotionally, tirelessly in defense of a world and many who sleep, who when they shall awake will yet find a world because of you. Because of you they will know a new day and recognize the sun rising in the sign of Aquarius for love's freedom won.

Oh, love, beloved! Oh, love! What is the object of thy love and devotion? Not thy idolatrous self! Nay! The object of thy love is the mighty I AM Presence, the Holy Christ Self, and all who so embody that living Presence on earth and in heaven.

Love goes forth and connects with the Christ Self of each one, that the Christ Self might give that love—nurturing, nourishing, training,

*cross pattée: a type of Christian cross with arms that are narrow at the center and often flared in a curve or straight line shape to be broader at the perimeter. The form appears very early in medieval art.

disciplining, raising up, showing the way by comfort, teaching the lessons of the Holy Spirit. Yes, love, beloved, is always an active force. It is God in action *in you,* nourishing life *in all.*

Let, therefore, the love of God pass through you. Open yourself now, as angels of the flame of love pass the love flame through you. Open yourself, beloved, that the flame might consume much that you have tried to bear to the altar but could not. You could not let go for want of something to replace it. Let love displace and then fill in the pockets of those conditions that are no longer a part of you, no longer necessary, that are divisive indeed.

Visualize, then, the pink rose in the heart as you receive now the fire of love as you are able. This is the assistance you will need as you descend each night for thirty-three consecutive nights down the spiral staircase[12] for the exorcism of compartments of consciousness by the living flame of love.

Oh, such a gift of the Maha Chohan! Receive it now.

[30-second pause]

How gentle is love's caressing of each and every part of the four lower bodies. The caressing flames of love are healing rays. Sometimes you see me wear my cape with the emerald on the outside, but tonight I wear the rose pink on the outside and the emerald within. And I come, as always, for love's healing. [14-second pause]

Love Is Indeed the Key!

Now there is a mighty procession through the Inner Retreat on the etheric octave, close to the physical plane, of all the students who study at my retreat. They come looking like those of many centuries ago who marched with banners in the name of the living Christ. These are artists and artisans of the Spirit, and you are counted among them. And you rejoice to have those hours when you may spend time in their company refining—refining the image of self that you might give to others a higher image and therefore knowledge of their own Christhood.

There is a reason that they are processioning through. They have come to the Retreat of the Divine Mother.[13] They have come to the New Jerusalem. There is, beloved, a gathering of many on each of the rays and the secret rays. And as they gather, so there is a grand meeting this night in that retreat. And when you have finished your journey to the obelisk and your ministering unto the needs of souls, you may also join that convocation.

You may wonder how you can accomplish so many things in a single night. But, beloved, you are in your etheric body. Yes, beloved, you can accomplish all things, including the exorcism of the compartments of being.

This is a night of transition and the passing of torches. This is a night, beloved, for love. Thus, I seal you in all the love that I have brought with my angels, and you have a brand new opportunity to conquer yourself, your temper and temperament, by love. Do it, beloved. For it will hasten all things, including that which you have written about to the Lords of Karma.[14]

Love is indeed the key! So take the key, beloved. One day it shall turn in the keyhole and open the door of the great heart of the Lord God. Prepare thyself, for the time is nigh.

December 31, 1992

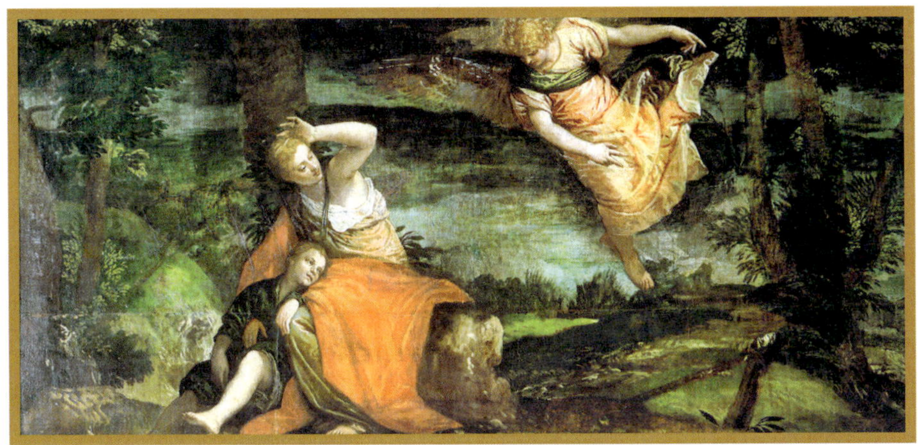

The Angel Appears to Hagar in the Desert, c. 1585

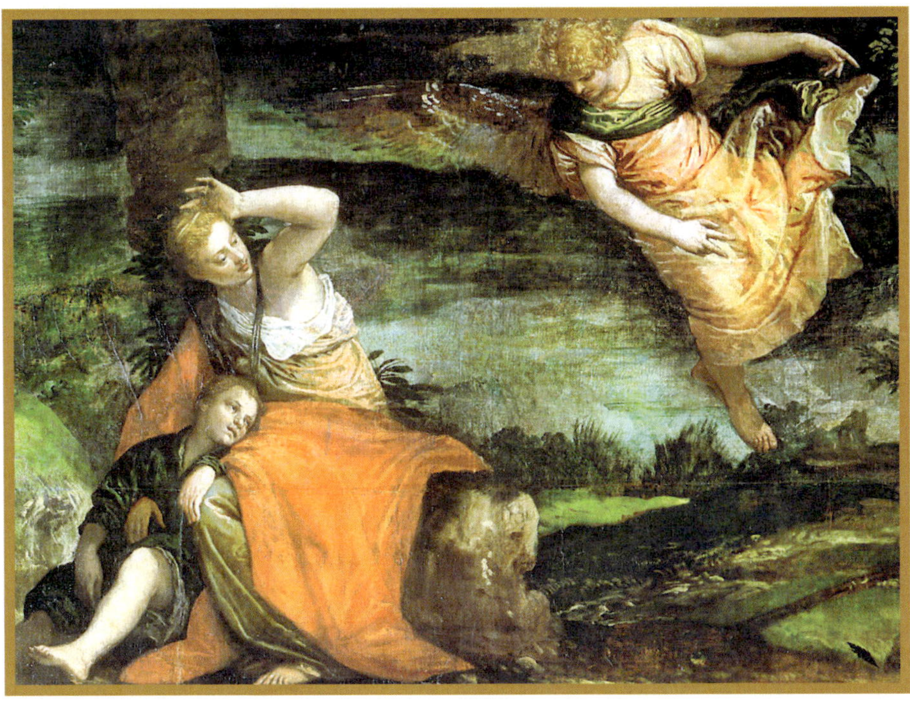

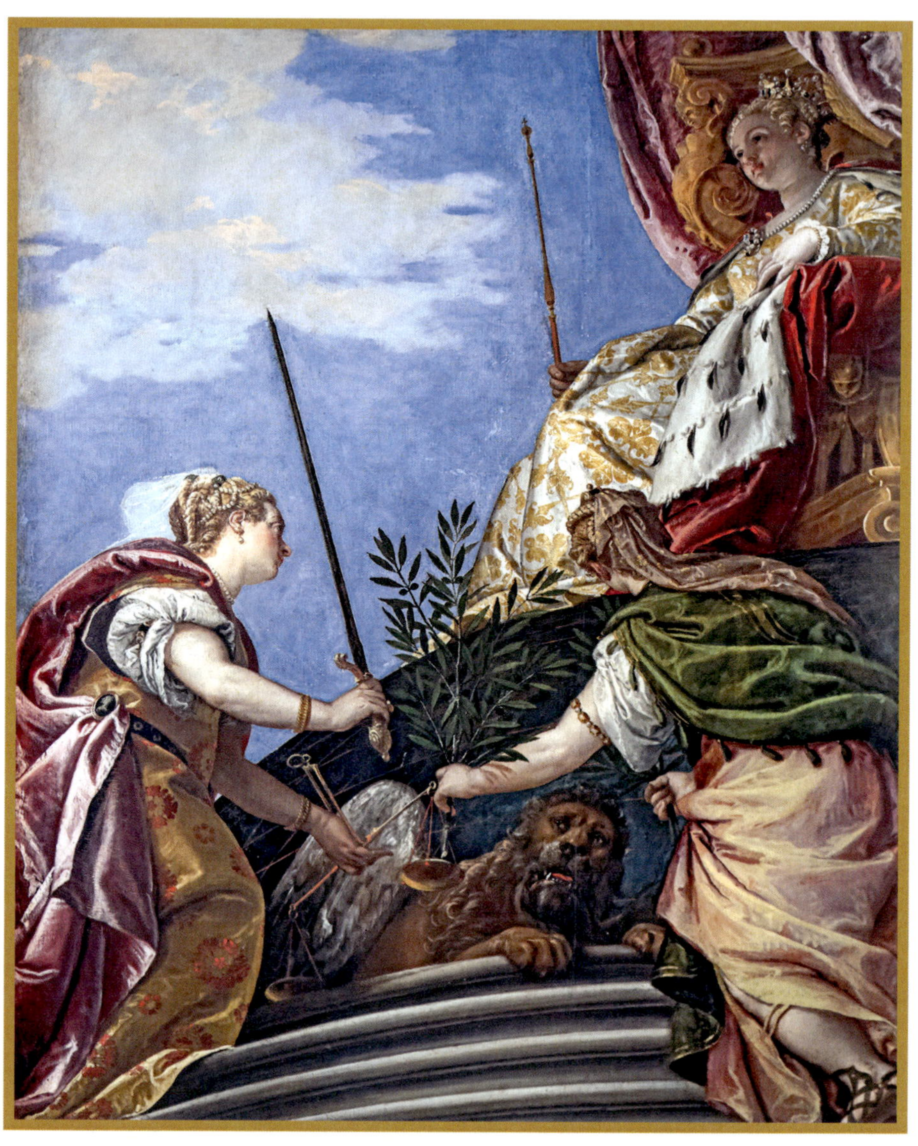

Venice Enthroned between Justice and Peace, c. 1575–77

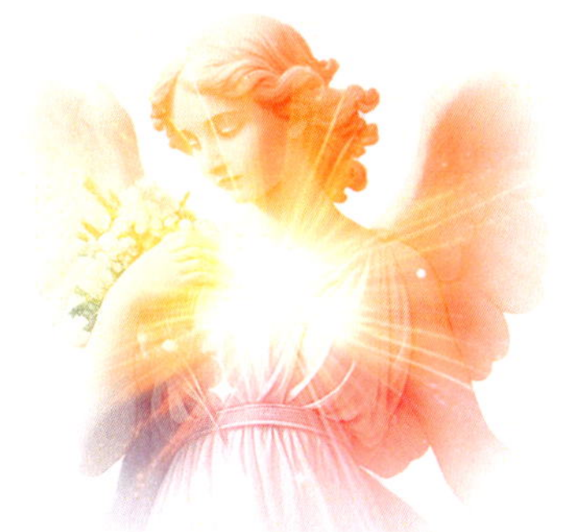

Study, then, at the inner retreats and bring forth, for children to feast their eyes on, the symmetry, the beauty, the luster of divine art.

CHAPTER 21

The Love of God Is the Divine Solution

I Make a Plea for Chalices of Love

Chelas of the third ray of God's love, I am honored to be called by the Darjeeling Council to speak to you with our Lord the Maha Chohan for the opening of Freedom 1993.[1]

Blessed ones, truly the love of God *is* the divine solution. Truly the love of God begins with your loving of your own soul and spirit, your own Christ Presence and all that is real about you.

Love is truly cloven tongues of fire that divide in you the Real from the unreal. You can love the Real. You can cast the unreal into the violet flame. And that energy liberated can return to you so that every part of your manifestation can be in the geometry of divine love.

At all periods of history when nations and empires have passed through straits such as you now face, it has been those who have carried the flame of love who have been willing to make major sacrifices for their civilization. When these have come forward, beloved, they have borne a fire of love that has overcome all else. I speak of a love that is enlightened, that is wise, that is knowledgeable in the things of God and in the things of this world.

Who Is the Doer within You But God?

How you admire the prophets of old! How they understood the political equations of their times! And according to all the information they had access to, they would report the untoward conditions of the times to the I AM Presence. Then they would lend their heart and ear to the Lord God, and the archangels would prophesy through them. And as the mouthpiece of God, the prophets would deliver to the princes, kings, leaders, and people of Israel and Judah that which the Lord God commanded them to do.

Those commands often went unheeded, and as a consequence Israel and Judah ultimately were led captive into exile in Assyria and Babylon. And the lost tribes, save for a remnant, were scattered abroad in the earth and have not yet known or understood the true communion of the Holy Spirit whereby they might also make their mark in this age.

Therefore there did come a time when the people left off listening to their God, and their councils decided that God was no longer talking to man and that man's problems and deliberations were in fact no business of God's. Then came the ridicule of those who communed with God, to whom God had spoken. For God has not ceased to speak to his own throughout all ages. Failure to commune with God or to make excuses why man should not commune with God is the work of fallen angels and of the Devil himself.

God has freely communed with imperfect men and women. I remind you of this. Moses was not perfect. He had slain the Egyptian taskmaster[2] and yet God appeared to him. He was called. He was chosen to be the instrument of the deliverance of the people of God.

I repeat, then, what the Maha Chohan has said. Your sense of your being not prepared, not ready, not having enough attainment is in fact a lie, because who is the doer within you but God, but the living soul and the living Spirit? Thus to postpone a work of the Lord in this decade can be ultimately fatal to you and those whom you love.

We Speak the Truth because You Have Come for the Truth

I never speak to incite fear or doubt or anxiety, though it may sound so to some because the leaders in Church and State today would tremble before they should tell the people what truly is coming upon the earth and what is happening in this nation alone, let alone the nations abroad. They fear to tell the people all that they know.

Well, when the ascended masters speak, they speak to those who have come prepared to hear the truth, to hear what is reality, for they are no longer content to avoid all confrontation by dwelling in illusion and surfeiting themselves, whether in television or partying or drugs, et cetera, et cetera.

We speak the truth because you have come for the truth. And the truth is that problems do not just go away! Problems continue like viruses and diseases. They mushroom around the planet. And therefore someone, somewhere, must stand up in the wood, by his cabin or wherever he may be, on his farm or in his skyscraper, and simply say:

> *Thus far and no farther! I will stand for truth and defend truth with all that I AM, God willing and God with me, so that this darkness might be set aside and the light solution can come forth!*

Art Should Represent the Next Level of Ideas, Creativity, and Invention

As you know, I preside not only over the arts but over music, sculpture, and even drama. But much that we see as art and music today in the popular culture causes the scrambling of the inner engrams of the blueprints of past golden-age civilizations and etheric cities and retreats, where there is a pristine manifestation of the geometry of being and where the likeness of the inner patterns is brought forth in magnificent works of art.

Art ought to be a representation of the potential of each and every one—what man can do, what man can become, what he can aspire to! Art should represent the next level of ideas, creativity, and invention, instead of the degradations of the depressed, the chaotic, those who do not have an integrating fire, for they long ago snuffed it out. To call chaos art is to be asleep to the fact that chaos in any discipline, whether it be science or art, must lead to the chaos of the mind and the chaos of civilization.

Let those of you who have the least talent in art, who may not be trained but who have that sense of balance and that attunement with beauty, meditate upon the inner realms of light. Ask to be taken to the university of the Spirit that is the Temple of the Sun over New York City, presided over by the Goddess of Liberty. Ask to be taken to the Château de Liberté, my retreat on the Rhône River in southern France.

Go there, beloved. Go there and attend classes that you might bring forth into the physical, in your waking hours, that which you have seen of the etheric octave, of the golden cities of light and of the spiritual temples, and even of the records of the heyday of Atlantis and Lemuria.

Study, then, at the inner retreats and bring forth, for children to feast their eyes on, the symmetry, the beauty, the luster of divine art. Conduct the experiments that we conduct in our retreat, and bring forth the same inventions that we have produced from those experiments—inventions that have not been reinvented on earth since the days of Atlantis.

Blessed hearts, it is of utmost concern to us who work with the All-Seeing Eye of God that we are seeing the inner sight of children being ruined because they are constantly bombarded with chaotic images, chaotic sounds, chaotic everything in their environment, including the outrageous misuse of guns among children.

Beauty, then, is for the calming of the soul, true music for the upliftment of the spirit. And even the body itself will conform to new patterns, especially when the diet is also corrected. Blessed ones, where there is no longer beauty to gaze upon, how shall mothers who are pregnant look upon pure designs and translate these to the molecules of substance?

Love as the Key to the Turning of Worlds

I make a plea for chalices of love! Chalices of love come in art and drama, architecture, and sculpture and in all of the many avenues that are open to you in design, even in the presentation of the masters' teachings as you set them forth in books and periodicals.

But my work goes far beyond art, beloved. I enter the art of politics. I enter the art of economics as a student and a teacher of the economists of the nations, in cooperation with the Darjeeling Council. I am therefore here to tell you that unless the consciousness of the people is raised to a new understanding of the availability of the power of God to work change, you will see civilization, at best, remain at this level or, at worst, continue its downward spiral.

Let all ye who gather here know that the universal Christ—call him what you will, call him Krishna—who is apportioned unto you in your Holy Christ Self, is able to lead you in the right direction whereby you may not only fulfill your divine plan and gain a greater mastery than you now have but balance your karma because you see love as the key to the turning of worlds and the turning of this civilization.

I leave you, then, to ponder all of this as you now come forward to receive Holy Communion, administered to you by the Maha Chohan himself.

I seal you in the matrix of love and in the beauty of your soul. And I invite you to our retreats that you might bring back the keys—the very keys that will turn around the decadence in some corners of this civilization.

For the victory of earth and for the healing of your four lower bodies, for the healing of broken hearts and for the healing of the mind, I am come. And I seal you with a pink rose superimposed upon the golden cross that I place upon you and before you.

The Blessing of Holy Communion by the Maha Chohan

O Holy Spirit of God, I, the Maha Chohan, send forth this light as cloven tongues of fire. So this bread and this wine receive the blessing of the Holy Spirit.

Partake, then, of the Body of Christ and the Blood of Christ and know that transformation of the human becoming the divine.

So let it be done. Let it be done in the name of the Four and Twenty Elders, the Solar Logoi, and all of the cosmic councils who hold session in this hour. For the hierarchy of light gather to assist in determining the fate of issues at hand, and they set themselves to the task of the upliftment of humanity through the kindling of those hearts whose fire can ignite the many.

In the purest love of God, I, the Maha Chohan, receive you, and I receive you in the name of the bride of the Holy Spirit, the holy Mary, Mother of Jesus. May you sing to my bride as you come forward to receive Holy Communion.

[Congregation sings hymns to the Blessed Mother during the ritual of Holy Communion.]

June 25, 1993

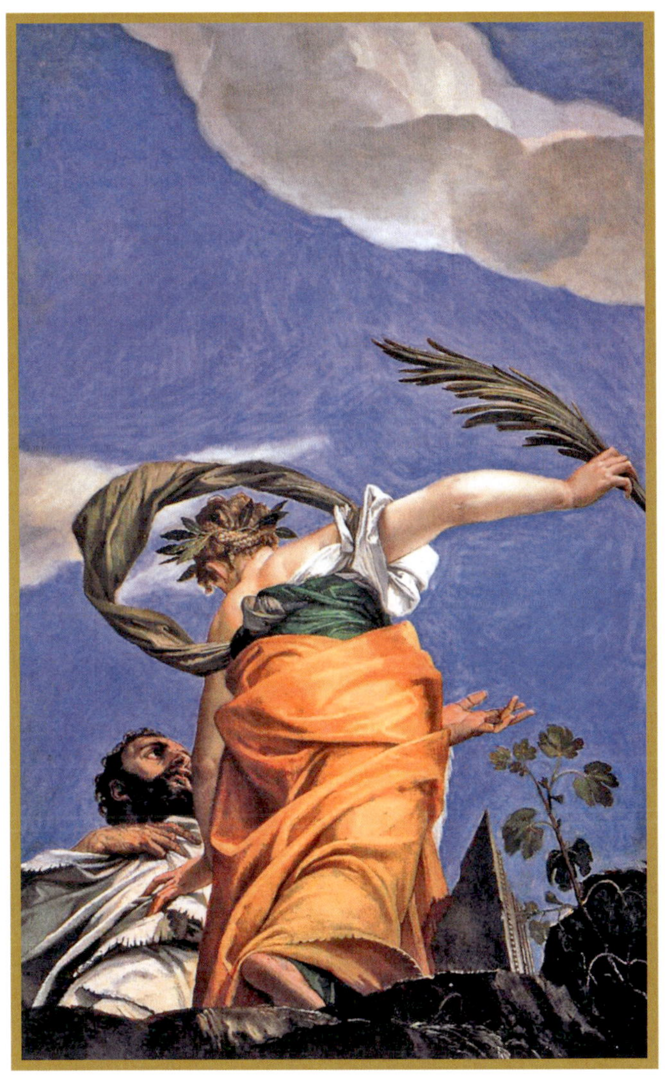

The Triumph of Virtue over Vice, c. 1554–56

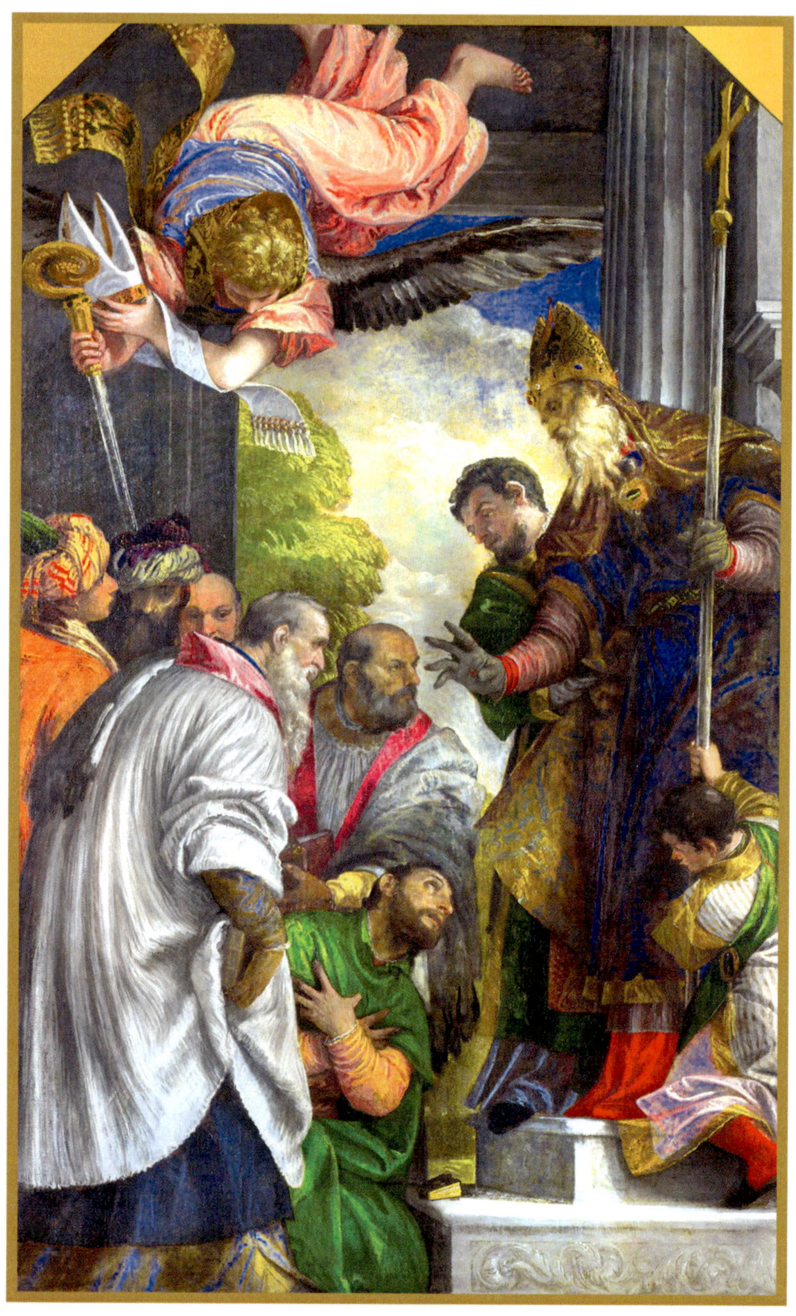

The Consecration of Saint Nicholas, 1562

*I call you to take measured cups of love—
yes, measured cups of love—and give them to those
who can assimilate your love as an elixir.*

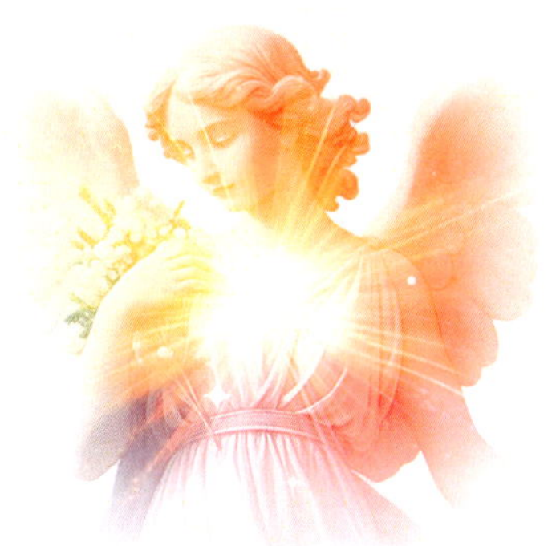

CHAPTER 22

Love Is the Great Challenge

"'Comfort Ye, Comfort Ye My People,' Saith Your God"

Heightened awareness, discernment of spirits, discrimination—it is well to ponder these.

I understand the disciplines of love in every field. Love is the great challenge, for love can be dissipated when it has no chalice. Be chalices of love and know the disciplines of the disciples of the Lord Sanat Kumara.

Understand love's underpinnings in the fields of art, design, theater, architecture, engineering, and so many endeavors. Love embraces them all. For without the element of love, nothing will stick together. You cannot even take clay and cause it to stick except by the ingredient of love.

Love, then, exists at many levels. There are basic levels of human love, and then there are levels of all-transcending, self-transcendent love, love that is sacrificial—love that is so all-consuming that in its presence one desires to surrender and to surrender again to the arms of love as cherubim raise one up into exalted levels of being.

Love is surrender unto one's calling, unto one's God, unto one's principles. And as one surrenders unto these, one transcends them and enters the Word itself that is made flesh in every son and daughter of God.

There is love that never gives up, will never say die, will stick with you through and through, through thick and thin. There is love that is beauty, love that is precision in the design of the human body or the design of a temple or in the light and harmony of paintings, such as those I executed. Without the works of art that have portrayed and kept to the fore even the image of God in every world religion, there should not be understanding.

When You See through the Third Eye, See with Love

Love embraces the All-Seeing Eye of God. Therefore, when you see through the third eye, see with love. Cast not the beacon of the third eye upon this or that one without shedding petals of love upon the scene. For as you qualify your third eye, beloved, so shall you create. And if you create that which is not of love, you shall have a long, long journey to uncreate that which you did fail to create in love.

Love is bringing to life those who have been burdened, who experience death and dying even while they are living. Love, beloved, contains all that science need ever know in the way of healing.

Yet so many are not ready for healing. Their chalices are filled with fear and anger, as they have resentment for those who did this or that. Not only is this state of consciousness without love but it is also self-destructive and ultimately destructive of the very functioning of the cells of the human body. Therefore, I call you to take measured cups of love—yes, measured cups of love—and give them to those who can assimilate your love as an elixir.

Understand this, beloved. All great teachers of wisdom have taught that one must not cast one's pearls before the swinish elements of the human consciousness. For these pearls are made by God. They are seeds of light. The pearl represents the sphere of the soul.

So love is a disciplined pathway. And as you know, the day when the ray of divine love intensifies on earth is Monday. And you have noted that it is often a day of chaos and confusion and sometimes of little accomplishment. This is because the forces of death and hell are virulent in their thrust against love. For love is the fire of creation, the fire of invention, the fire of the elevation of the soul! Love is the reuniting of twin flames, formed out of a single fiery ovoid in the Beginning with God in the Great Central Sun.

Resolve All Things with Love

Love is the fulfillment of every law. And when you bow to the Law and are obedient to the Law, love becomes your fortress—fortifying you, sealing you, protecting you. Make no mistake, beloved. Love is the all-power of God to accomplish all things.

Love thyself. Love thy soul. Do not allow schisms within! Go deep, deep into the unconscious and saturate, saturate, saturate again and again with love's fires along with the violet fire of freedom's love.

If you do not love yourself because you have been condemned by parents or others, then, beloved, that condemnation will become self-condemnation and it will follow you and follow you and follow you like a plague. And if you do not watch out, it will become a plague in your body and in your house.

Resolve all things with love. Pray to be immersed in the fires and the waters and the fragrances of the love of Elohim, Elohim. Yes, beloved, if you have not been loved, then love ten thousand-times-ten thousand again and again, loving and loving and loving as you serve to set yourself and all life free. Take note of how regiments of demons and darkness would tear you from your first and best love, would tear you from kindness, from carefulness, from tarrying awhile with your brother or sister to comfort, to "'Comfort ye, comfort ye my people,' saith your God."[1]

Love is dispersed and parted where there is war, where there is resentment, where there are those who will never forgive and never forget. This nonforgiving and nonforgetting is, in reality, a dark disease in the earth. And as you see nation warring against nation around the globe, remember that where the love fire of the heart has been extinguished by harshness, by the blackness of the plague of nonlove—there, beloved, *there, beloved,* is the need for the reigniting of the flame.

How did the flame go out, the very flame that God placed on the altar of being?

It was snuffed out oh so easily by that blackness of the plague of nonforgiveness.

So in those areas where the tempter does come to unseat you, you must be in control. You must be in God-control of your vibration, how you think and feel about everyone you know and the millions whom you do not know who are spiritually bankrupt, for their love fires are gone out.

Blessed ones, you cannot love and hate simultaneously. You cannot have love and hate in your heart simultaneously. I say to you, as the messenger has said long ago, when you are angry you have made both a conscious decision to be angry and a conscious decision to forsake love. Anger does not just happen because you are out of control. You have been out of control for many, many lifetimes because you have allowed that anger, that out-of-control state to overpower you.

Tend the Fire of the Love of the Heart, for Aquarius Is an Age of Love

If you choose to be love, to have love, and to be in the Sacred Heart of Padma Sambhava, of Jesus Christ, of Lord Maitreya, of Lord Gautama Buddha, of Sanat Kumara—yes, if you choose to be in the heart of their love, then you must also make the choice to not be in the gall of bitterness, not to allow your wrath to be kindled, not to entertain aggression, aggravation, argumentation, accusation, et cetera. You make the choice, beloved. Tend the fire of the love of the heart. This is my call to you, for Aquarius is an age of love.

How shall love be outplayed? How indeed, beloved, when there is such a great greed in the hearts of men for money? How indeed, when decisions are made by nations and peoples solely on the basis of money and the money beast?

Beware the money beast! Beware how it insinuates itself into your soul when you have not taken your stand against the poison of avarice or envy or greed.

All things are God's. All things shall return to God. The temple you wear is not yours; it is God's. Therefore, do not covet. Do not covet. You may not be aware that you covet the wealth or the blessedness of another, but, blessed ones, most people do have a layer of untransmuted covetousness that says, "Why can't I have all of this and all of that that my neighbor has?"

Covetousness will eat away at your heart. It will eat away at the very marrow of your bones. It will make you sick. What good is the Path if you forget that you already have all of God inside of you?

So, beloved, seek early to pluck out the black threads of the plague of nonlove. Pluck them out of the psyche! Pluck them out of your mind! Whatever else you do, get rid of them! Let this year be a year of such love and loving that love will be the melting of all hardness of heart nation by nation.

When You Choose Love, There Is the Dividing of the Way

Legions of cherubim of God surround you. Oh, be taken to the retreats this night! Come to the retreat of the Royal Teton in your finer bodies. Come to the retreat of the Goddess of Liberty over New York City. Come, beloved, and study. Allow us to show you the great glory of the reality you have already encapsulated in your being and have therefore become, and allow us to show you the dark shafts that have entered the precincts of your soul, which must be consumed by your sendings of the violet flame to the very core of your being.

Indeed, let love be the dividing of the way. Choose love! Choose love and keep love. When you choose love, there is the dividing of the way. For you can no longer know communion with anyone who yet embodies the forces of anti-love.

Show the Christhood that you are becoming. Show it by love. In this manner, I say, be healed! Be healed of all thy diseases. Be ready chalices for self-transcendence.

In the living fires of the resurrection flame, I wrap you in the swaddling garment of the Divine Mother. And the swaddling garment she places around you in this hour is the garment of love and the love fires of the violet flame.

Therefore, I ask you to join me now in sealing my dictation by singing the decree Saint Germain has dictated. It is a worded chalice into which you pour your love of Saint Germain and his violet flame. Thus the seventh ray shall seal your day of eternal rest and of love in action.

I invite our beloved choir to lead you in singing "Violet Fire, I Love Thee!"

Now visualize the violet flame sweeping up through you, curling up from beneath, from the very center of the earth to the center of the Great Central Sun. See the flames dancing, leaping, rejoicing!

The violet flame is a singing flame of the Holy Spirit. Know that it is the source of alchemy, your own alchemical transformation whereby you shall absolutely conquer the forces that you have aptly called the Martian perversions of the Alpha flame.

[The Church Universal and Triumphant choir leads the congregation in singing song 804, "Violet Fire, I Love Thee!," in Church Universal and Triumphant's *Book of Hymns and Songs.*]

Violet Fire, I Love Thee!

by Saint Germain

1. Violet fire, I love thee!
Come, strengthen right desire
With Mercy's flame enfold me
All guilt and blame retire.

Blaze through me now!
Blaze through me now!
Blaze through me now!

Refrain: Come, violet fire!
Descend into my form!
Thy consecrated purity
Bringing cosmic ecstasy
Making me to be like thee—
Adorn my being now!

2. Harmonize my members
My body fill with light
My perfect image render
In beauty I delight!

Penetrate through!
Penetrate through!
Penetrate through!

3. Descending drops of Mercy
Like gentle summer rain
Melt all hardened substance
Dissolve my inner pain!

In I AM name!
In I AM name!
In I AM name!

4. Collapse my human ego
Momentums of the years
My burdens I relinquish
Surrender all my fears!

Assume me now!
Assume me now!
Assume me now!

5. By consecrated wafer
Christ-essence flows through me
Thy Body and thy Blood
Transforms me, I AM free!

Subsume me now!
Subsume me now!
Subsume me now!

6. In thy mighty crucible
By holy alchemy
My soul is now transmuted
Desiring only thee!

Crystallize here!
Crystallize here!
Crystallize here!

7. I AM bonded to my Christ Self
On fire with His love
My mind affixed forever on
God's Presence there above.

Flow unto me!
Flow unto me!
Flow unto me!

8. Commanding Buddhic peace
Envelop all my soul
My consciousness expanding
To reach the highest goal.

Manifest here!
Manifest here!
Manifest here!

December 30, 1994

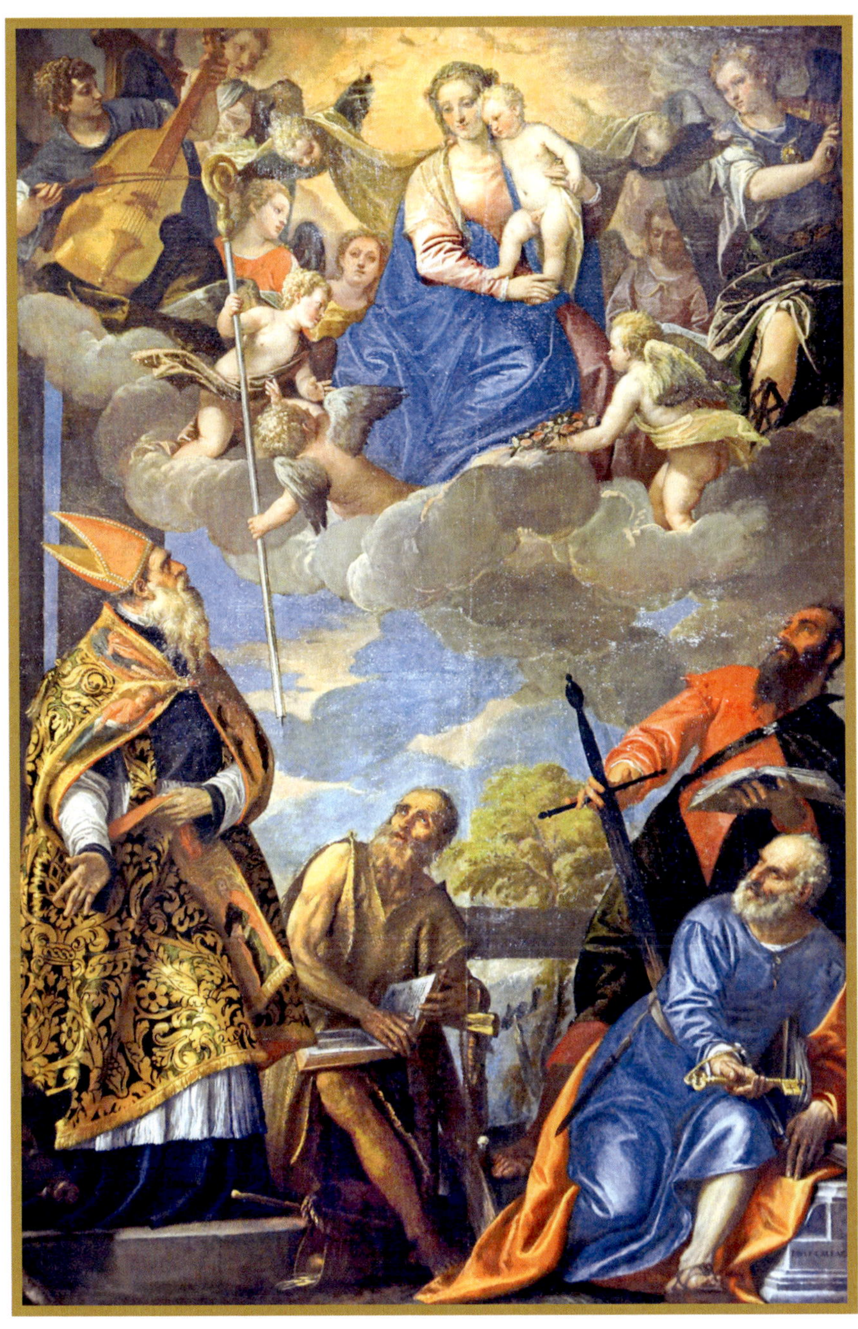

The Virgin and Child Appearing to Saint Anthony, Saint Paul the Hermit, Saint Paul and Saint Peter, c. 1580–90

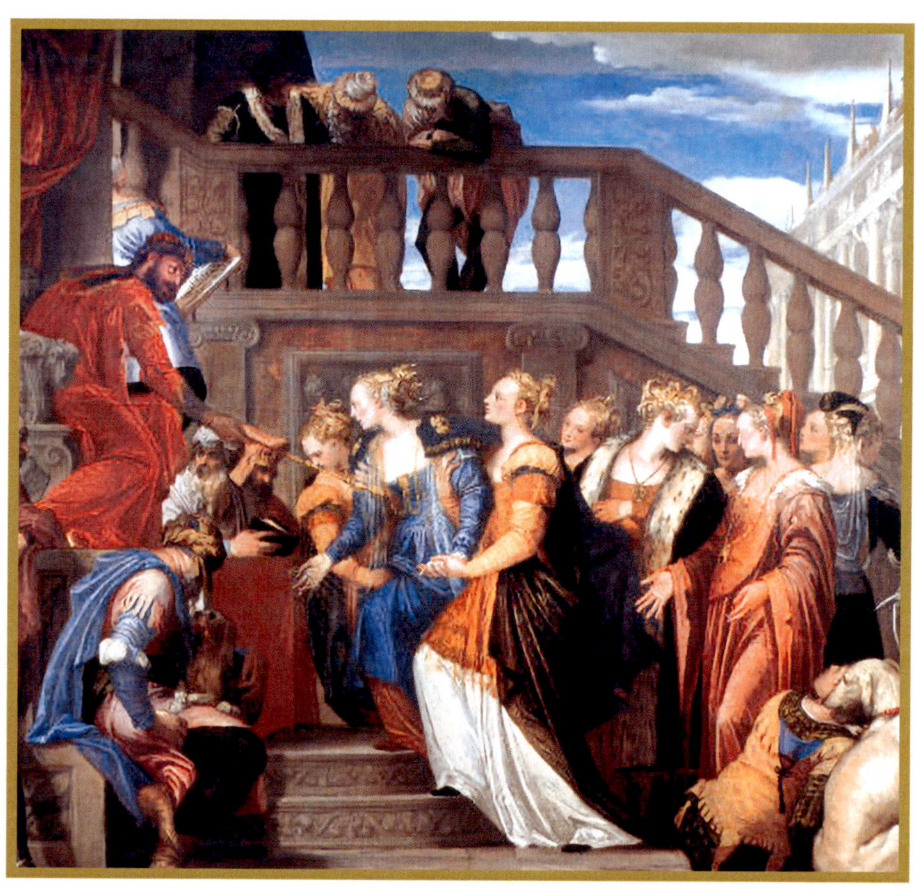

Esther before Ahasuerus (detail), c. 1555

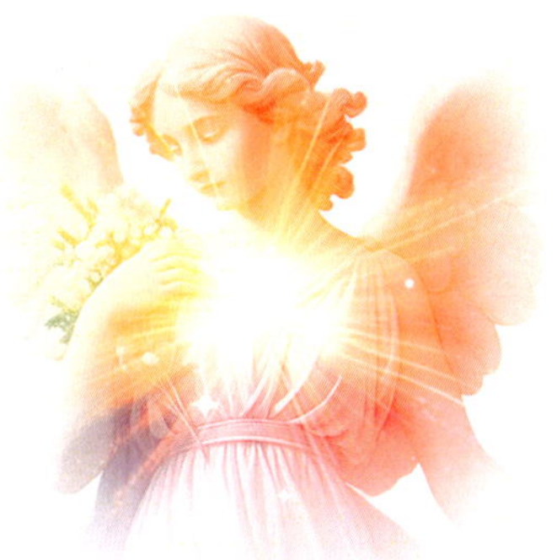

It is interesting that the flag of the United States... bears the white and the red. So these "ribbons of interconnecting glory" in Old Glory, representing the thirteen original states, are a reminder to all initiates that the white fire and ruby ray are the ultimate keys to their God-mastery.

CHAPTER 23

Walk in the Flame of Divine Love

A Remembering of Responsibilities

Most special friends of God, why has our Lord the Maha Chohan thus spoken?*

It is because divine love is the greatest power in the universe, and therefore the application of divine love by the devotee of love requires the utmost discipline.

Each of the seven chohans, as well as their Lord, the Maha Chohan, opens to you a path of discipline that corresponds to the ray and chakra that that one represents.

You understand the precision of the white fire to be the foundation of architecture and the engineering feats that have been accomplished in ancient and modern civilizations. When the love fire intensifies from the powerful petal pink to the deep ruby and then is combined with this white fire of the Divine Mother, you have an energy that can transform worlds. But these twin powers, beloved—the ruby ray and the white fire of the Divine Mother—are the ones upon which most chelas stumble.

Thus, I would recommend that you take up the *Love Meditations*[1] recorded by the messenger and her devoted staff. These prayers,

*The Maha Chohan delivered a dictation just prior to this dictation by Paul the Venetian.

affirmations, and love songs are for the healing of the heart.

I have requested that the messenger create audio recordings of these meditations so that wherever you are you can enter the deep penetrating love and the fiery devotion you feel for God when you join in giving the calls and singing the songs. Beloved, as you give your loving devotion to God by this means, God sends his loving devotion to you with the message that he who would embody love for a world must overcome all forces of anti-love.

And I tell you, the forces of anti-love have established their strongholds across the galaxies. They have turned their backs upon Almighty God and therefore they wander about seeking what souls they may devour,[2] stealing genes and other genetic material from human life. These forces also create poisoned arrows of anti-love.

Wherever love is extolled and embodied, it is always under fierce attack. And so, many people in the earth know profound sorrow, for though they have loved deeply, they are not able to hold steady the cup of divine love. And, alas, the forces of anti-love dash the cup from their lips before they can quaff love's elixir.

The White Fire and the Ruby Ray Are the Ultimate Keys to God-Mastery

If you would know the Maha Chohan as I know him, you must immediately go after the forces that would deny divine love and the white fire of the Divine Mother that is sealed in your base-of-the-spine chakra, strengthening you and transforming you day by day in preparation for your ascension.

As you raise up the sacred fire from the base to the crown chakra in your daily meditations and dynamic decrees, remember that you also activate this Kundalini fire by following the path of the ruby ray cross under the Buddha of the Ruby Ray. This path is won through your daily sacrifice, surrender, selflessness, and service. And it requires that you embrace the Divine Mother and offer her your devotion on behalf of all humanity as well as on behalf of those close to you whom she has entrusted to your care.

If you are victorious on this path, the day and the hour of your ascension will come when the sacred fire shall rise on your spinal altar with an intensity so great as to almost overwhelm you. Your I AM Presence and Holy Christ Self shall then draw you up into the arms of everlasting love and you shall make the transition from mortality to immortality.

And you shall hear the words of the Father: "Well done, thou good and faithful servant: thou hast been faithful over a few things, I will make thee ruler over many things.[3] Rise to the levels of the kingdom of God and let others follow in your wake!"

So the white fire, beloved! So the white fire is the fire of the Creation. All worlds are born through the white fire, yet not without the complement of divine love.

It is interesting that the flag of the United States (as well as the flags of many other nations) bears the white and the red. So these "ribbons of interconnecting glory" in Old Glory, representing the thirteen original states, are a reminder to all initiates that the white fire and ruby ray are the ultimate keys to their God-mastery.

You Are Retraining the Mind, the Heart, the Soul, and the Spirit

Now, beloved, while you are enjoying yourselves, protected as you are in this encampment in the wilderness, you are reinforced by the messenger and one another and angels who keep their vigil in the Western Shamballa. Therefore take this opportunity to work with the white fire and the bija mantras to the Divine Mother. You may be surprised by what empowerment she may transfer to you through your diligent practice.

Also take the opportunity during this conference to give the decrees of the third ray, the love ray, and to work with your invocations to the hierarchy of the ruby ray. As you do so, be mindful that you will encounter opposition from the fallen angels. Observe how they cunningly wage war against divine love in all its forms. You see, the fallen angels must defeat love (as well as the white fire of the Divine Mother), for if they do not, they themselves will crumble and fall apart.

The Heart of the Inner Retreat is a good place to experiment with the science of the spoken Word. Begin with the "Violet Fire and Tube of Light Decree," calls to Archangel Michael for protection, the "Heart, Head, and Hand Decrees," and the violet flame for personal and planetary transmutation.*

Having established this strong foundation, see what it is like to walk in the flame of divine love that you then invoke, braiding it with white fire. This begin to know, for it is the work of the adepts. It is what you are taught in the retreats of the ascended masters as your soul is escorted there out of the body night after night.

Why is so much schooling necessary? Because you are retraining the mind, the heart, the soul, and the spirit, which have been trained in the wayward ways of generations of earth's civilization.

We are preparing you to enter the universities of the Spirit in golden-age civilizations that exist in the etheric octave. Here you will learn how to meet the standards of the adepts so that when you return from the retreats and take up your daily responsibilities, you can contribute to the raising of the planetary consciousness. Thus when you are called by us, you may be chosen to be an example for others who would walk in your footsteps.

Two Choices

Being a devotee of God and determining to achieve a higher level of soul evolution in this life than you did in your last life is a worthy goal. So is balancing 100 percent of your karma. With the latter in mind, you have two choices: (1) to take your ascension when you have balanced 100 percent of your karma and then move on to service in higher octaves, or (2) to take the bodhisattva vow to remain with earth's evolutions until they are free.[4]

If your intent is to remain in embodiment only until you have balanced your karma and obeyed Jesus' injunction to preach the kingdom to the lost sheep (i.e., souls) of the house of Israel, to heal the sick, cleanse the lepers, raise the dead and cast out devils,[5] your choice is number one.

If you take the bodhisattva vow, you may choose to tarry with

*See pp. 238–48 for these decrees.

mankind as an unascended master or, like the bodhisattva Kuan Yin, to serve mankind as an ascended master. Either way, your choice is number two.

If you would remain and be the bodhisattva, then know what rejoicing shall be unto you on your path of victory as you infuse earth's evolutions with your spirit of victory! Beloved, does not your soul yearn to be able to nurture the millions because you have submitted yourself to spiritual disciplines lifetime after lifetime and dedicated your temple to be the temple of God? [Congregation responds, "Yes!"]

Do you not suffer when you find yourself unable to save a loved one who suddenly, seemingly without warning, passes from the screen of life? [Congregation responds, "Yes!"]

So, beloved, this can change. All of this can change.

Please review your list of priorities daily. Ask yourself: "What is my first priority, second, third, fourth, and fifth?" Those that are first and second one day might be fourth and fifth the next day.

If You Would Apprentice Yourselves under Me

I am the Chela of the Maha Chohan, in training to receive his mantle when he moves on to higher service. This promotion may be a long time in coming, for Alpha and Omega do not desire to change the seats of the chohans and other ascended masters who have held key positions in the hierarchy of the Great White Brotherhood during the Piscean age. For so many chelas on earth depend upon us in the configurations in which we are positioned.

Now then, beloved, if you would apprentice yourselves under me, choosing me as one of the two chohans in addition to El Morya, who will teach you and guide you on your path,[6] I will then transmit to you what is appropriate for me to give you from the teachings of the Maha Chohan that he has given me on my soul journey with him through the ages.

I will call for reinforcements of cherubim of God to assist you, but the path of the third ray is not an easy one. It is one which, as our Lord has said, must be of a remembering—a remembering of God daily, a remembering of responsibilities.[7]

The Maha Chohan, his presence over me now and over you, transmits first a light, then a consciousness, then an individualized program of study for each one whom it shall please to take up the course our Lord offers him.

Caring Leads You to Secure the Love Essences of the Angels

In addition, our Lord takes you on a methodical walk with God. It is a lesson in caring for each soul in a unique and personal way. And that caring leads you to secure the love essences of the angels that you may impart—indeed the love essences, the love essences—so many essences of love!

Are not the flower remedies[8] the essences of love that have come through the floral offerings of the angels and elementals who render a service of healing to receptive souls under the direction of the archangels and the hierarchs of the elements themselves?

Yes, so many essences of God in the flame of divine love!

When all of your adoration to God and your giving and receiving of love has filled your cup, realize that there is yet an infinite number of beautiful ways in which you can express divine love and human love at all levels to all evolutions.

Oh, how the world needs love!

Oh, how *you* need love! Is it not why you are here?

You come to the fount of love. You come to the fount of white fire. You feel the love fire of your heart and you trust—you trust in the love of God.

Speak to Our Lord the Maha Chohan

Now from within the precincts of your heart and mind, speak to our Lord the Maha Chohan. Pour into his cup your sorrows, your cares, your fears, your tremblings in the night. He has a great chalice. He will receive all that you would entrust to him and he will show you how to pass your burdens into the flame of the Holy Spirit.

[Congregation prays.]

Beloved, great, great healing can come to you through your daily prayers to the Maha Chohan. Through your prayers, you have strengthened the "prayer loop" from your heart to his. See this loop as the love tie that binds you together as one.

Know that at any hour or moment of the day or night you may call to the Maha Chohan and he will answer you. He will receive you and extend to you comfort and consolation, healing, divine direction, and, above all, enlightenment.

Come, Holy Spirit, enlighten me! Let this be a mantra that you turn to when making decisions. For the Maha Chohan will always fill your worded chalice with the wisdom of his enlightenment. Give this mantra now with the messenger.

[Congregation joins the messenger in giving the mantra:]

Come, Holy Spirit, enlighten me!
Come, Holy Spirit, enlighten me!
Come, Holy Spirit, enlighten me!
Come, Holy Spirit, enlighten me!
Come, Holy Spirit, enlighten me!
Come, Holy Spirit, enlighten me!

June 26, 1995

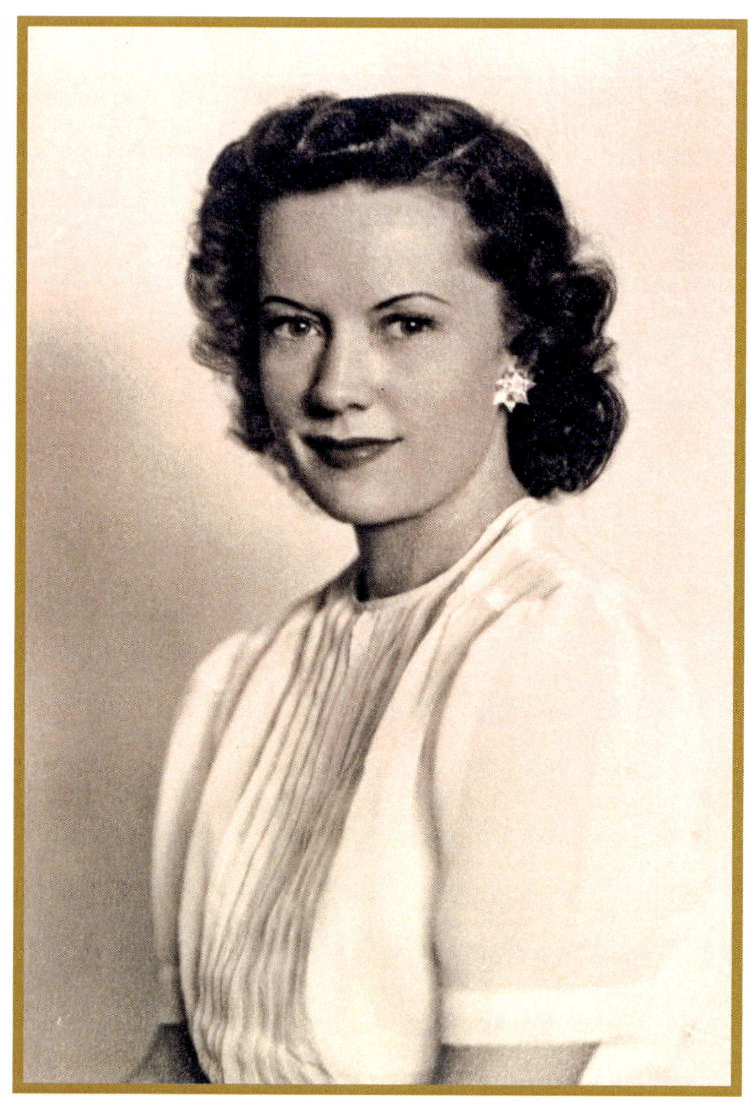

Ruth Hawkins

So, beloved, when the child has that sense of inner majesty, of empowerment, when the child has the inner sense that he or she is connected with God, you can see this in the child.

CHAPTER 24

Gain the Immortality of Your Soul

Nurse Your Inner Child to Wholeness and Divine Being

Ladies and gentlemen, it gives me great joy to introduce to you my beloved ascended twin flame, the lady master Ruth Hawkins.[1]

[34-second standing ovation]

My Beloved stands to the messenger's right as I stand to her left. I describe to you now the glorious robe marking this entry into the heaven-world and stepping down to this octave through the presence of the messenger. This garment is almost undescribable, having layers and layers of filigree of such fine golden substance woven in white.

My Beloved fulfills the beauty of all lifetimes for me, and I am grateful for her perseverance as she has worked through her karma and many challenges, many activities in this and former lives, her soul desiring each hour and each day to find that eternal reunion with God and with me.

Therefore please be seated now.

The burdens of the earth are our concern, and especially the burdens of our youth. We ask you to call daily to Rex and Nada and Bob and Pearl that you might summon through them their legions of light.[2] They have armies of youth, beloved, who may cover the earth and bring many souls of the youth to that point of understanding their I AM Presence and Holy Christ Self, of understanding ascension's walk from these levels of darkness in the earth to the brightest light that could ever be known or experienced.

Dedication to the Youth and to the Inner Child

So, beloved, if you desire to see the earth continue, know that all depends upon the youth—how you are moving with them, educating them, caring for the very littlest ones, directing those who have been severely burned, who have been put down and whose identities must be healed.

Therefore when we come with the third ray, we also come with a ray of healing. This healing action and this pink fire that comes from the love of God—*this* is truly the means of transmutation, of elevating the souls of the children and bringing all to the awareness that they, too, can walk and talk with the Holy Christ Self and the I AM Presence.

This conference is dedicated to the youth of the world and to children of all ages. It is dedicated to the soul of each one on earth and to that fragmented soul as well as to the inner child. Understand, beloved, that many mighty works may be done for the people of earth, but if love does not blossom in the children it will not blossom in the adult. This you well understand.

Lose yourself in an all-consuming fire to bless, to heal, to elevate, to bring to that point of Christhood all souls of light in this world. Pray for them as your predecessors have prayed, as my beloved Ruth did pray for the children of the world. So many souls have come through this activity who have made their ascension because they have dedicated their prayers and their dynamic decrees, which they have given hours and hours by the day. So they have dedicated this to the blossoming and flowering of the youth.

The Higher the Soul, the More Is Required of Parents

There are many who are teachers in the schoolhouses of the world who do not know how to connect the child with his or her inner teacher. That inner teacher, as you know, is the Holy Christ Self. And within the Within is the Holy Buddha Self.

So, beloved, when the child has that sense of inner majesty, of empowerment, when the child has the inner sense that he or she is connected with God, you can see this in the child. The child is self-assured, is determined, is joyous, is happy, is interested in investigating life, in trying on everything and anything that is new and wonderful. And as the years go by and the depth of the wisdom of the soul of the Holy Child comes to fruition, you will see that even in this community, as in places throughout the earth, there are souls who have arisen who are mighty, who are high indeed and who will bring to the earth a tremendous gift.

Remember, beloved, the higher the soul, the more is required of parents to keep their harmony, to give their decrees for the child and rise into new dimensions of being. This do, beloved. For in this octave and in this world, all truly does depend on what does become of the children.

What will become of your inner child? Will you nurse that child to wholeness and divine being and such a sense and presence of victory and wholeness that in your very body and life and movement and action that inner soul, that inner presence, so having been made whole through your care, is now able to lead tribes and nations and peoples from here around the world?

Let the little child lead them. Let the little child lead them. Let your child of the heart lead you and yet understand that you are also parent to a soul and that that soul is not yet immortal. Gaining the immortality of one's soul is the most priceless, *priceless* effort that you must make—the effort to know that wholeness, to know that oneness, and finally to see that one's soul shall return to the realms immortal and to that soul's immortality.

You are about to celebrate the ritual of wholeness. You are about to celebrate soul retrieval as the messenger guides you.[3] This soul retrieval at this Christmastide and New Year conference is also tied to the action of the love ray.

The Lack of Mercy in the Earth Is a Tragedy

So we come, beloved. So you have understood and have seen how the fallen angels move against the lightbearers, mock them, strike them, whip them, bring them to their knees. O beloved, the lack of mercy in the earth is a tragedy. Consider how there is no mercy in some of the nations of the Far East, no mercy upon their very own people, slavery being rampant in the earth, with child labor being used.

How can there be such a discrepancy between one such as the beloved Kuan Yin, the Mother of the East, and the outpicturing of those individuals with their hardness of heart who have no thought for the children, no thought for those of all ages, yet use them in building their domain, their armies, their tanks, their weapons.

This, then, must be understood by all. All of you know that the destruction of Maldek came about by the warring of factions until the warfare became so great and science so advanced that that planet—now the asteroid belt between Mars and Jupiter—that planet itself was totally blown up.[4] These evolutions who are the warring factors, and other warring factors of other planetary systems, have come to earth to corrupt those who are of the light.

This corruption, beloved, is something that must be exorcised from the planet—*yes,* the corruption of those who do not resolve their issues in their religious leaders such as the Buddha, the Christ. So, beloved, these very ones have reincarnated again and again and have been called laggards because they have lagged behind their evolutions everywhere that they have gone, because they are ultimately materialists and have no desire to enter the kingdom of God but rather to amass wealth and comfort and to carry on and on and on.[5]

You, then, see that among them there is a mockery of the Word. You also see and understand how these fallen ones affect the attitudes of education, of higher learning, the uses and misuses of technology when this comes to allowing children to see things on television that they ought not to see at such an early age. Violence is everywhere, and there is that presence in the motion-picture industry such that each successive film must carry greater and greater violence. Thus children come to believe that it is all right to kill, to maim, to harm, to destroy.

We Count on Keepers of the Flame and Lightbearers

Civilization and life are becoming more and more chaotic. We are counting on Keepers of the Fame and lightbearers throughout the world to turn this around, beloved, else you will find a type of individual, a type of people on earth that you cannot even imagine, those whose souls have been so marred because they are without the love of one or both parents that they, then, have that hardness that is difficult to undo, whether in therapy or whether in the churches.

I call all these things to your attention. I know that many of you know all that I have said. I have come to place emphasis on those points that I have made so that you will understand that there are legions of light serving with Rex and Nada and Bob and Pearl and that you must ask to be taken with their legions every night for some portion of that period of sleep, that you might help the youth of the world.

Having so said, I turn you over now to my beloved twin flame, who will speak to you.

December 30, 1996

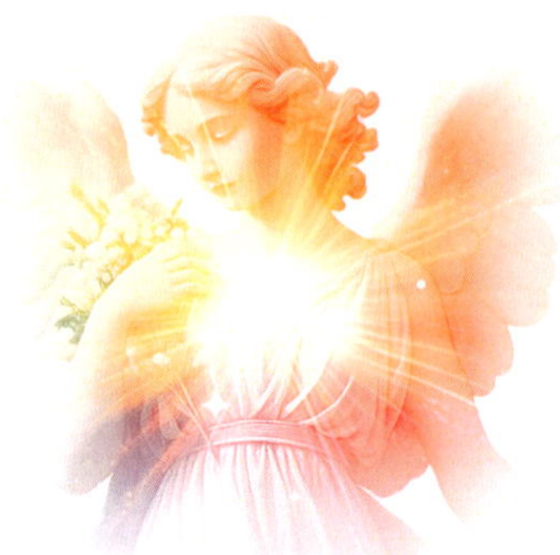

Beloved Lady Master Ruth Hawkins

Bring to Wholeness the Soul That Is Yet Mortal

Call for the Fragments of Your Soul to Be Returned

Beloved Mother and beloved friends, I rejoice to be with you in this moment. I have waited long, *very* long, beloved, to reach this moment when I might stand, as an ascended being and in my robes of immortality, to speak to you of God's call to me long, long ago, which I also answered.

I speak to you, beloved, of art and art itself in so many forms and manifestations. I have pursued art over many, many lifetimes, and in doing this I have perfected my own soul. I have been able to draw back to myself the fragments of the soul. And I understand that you are now engaged in this, and I am grateful that our Mother has introduced this and does lead for you the soul retrieval exercises at quarterly conferences.

Know, then, and understand, beloved, that the fragmenting of the soul bears warning and a sign. If the soul becomes fragmented, it is because the soul has been abused and the light of the soul has been stolen. Your own carnal mind may steal the light of your soul. Far worse, the fallen angels and the laggards may come to steal components of the soul.

Once these components of the soul are no longer tied to the soul, they may float beyond in octaves and in levels that are dark that may consist of millions of miles across the galaxies. Once the soul and the body of the soul has been tampered with and ceases to be whole, then that soul, she* is vulnerable.

Call Daily for the Great Central Sun Magnet

You, then, have come to this meeting today to call for the fragments of your soul to be returned to you. I know that the messenger has made it clear to you that in order to hold on to the soul and to bring the fragments back to the soul, you must have a very strong heart chakra—a very strong chakra, a chakra that is greater than the antithesis, that which is the heart of the fallen angels.

So if you have neglected the raising up and the balancing of your threefold flame regularly through many lifetimes, lifetime after lifetime, then at the moment when you desire to magnetize back to you all of these soul fragments, you find that the magnet of your heart is not strong enough to hold on to those fragments. And once the soul retrieval is concluded, then you find that those fragments begin to wander again or they may be stolen.

I would suggest, then, that on a daily basis you call to God for the Great Central Sun Magnet to be superimposed upon your heart chakra.† And thereby, even though your heart chakra is not developed nor is the Great Central Sun Magnet developed where you are, that magnet will be placed over your heart and will hold intact the fragments of soul that you have called back through many prayers and mantras and decrees in these rituals of soul retrieval. So you see, beloved, this in itself is a great dispensation—to know that you may have that Central Sun Magnet over the heart flame, over the threefold flame, protecting, protecting the fragments of being.

As you do this, then, and you call home the sheep from your pastures, from far-off worlds, when all are together and all components of wholeness are sealed, then and only then can the soul enter into the path of becoming one with the Holy Christ Self. So, you see,

*The soul of man and woman is feminine in relation to the masculine, or spirit, portion of being. The soul is therefore often referred to as "she" or "her."

†The Great Central Sun Magnet is the white-fire core of the Great Central Sun. To invoke the action of the Great Central Sun Magnet, see the decree on p. 247.

there are steps and stages of development that must not be missed. When you miss some of those stages, then unwittingly you have skipped steps that will be costly to you.

Guard the Harmony of Being

I recommend, then, that you realize that once you have placed upon your heart chakra a replica, a small replica of the Great Central Sun Magnet—once it is placed by your Holy Christ Self, the I AM Presence and the Solar Logoi, who control that magnet—you, then, must maintain your harmony. For if you break your harmony once you have established the magnet over the heart, then you see, beloved, you have a schism and a discord in your world, which means you have a rent or a tear in your garment. This may start the process all over again of the fragments of the soul drifting to the farthest corners of the universe and you in your Christ Self having to go forth to bring them home or to rely on the messenger to make this powerful call for you.

So I give you one more reason why it is important to guard the harmony. Guard the harmony of being. Do not be ruffled. Do not be moved. Recognize that God is your champion, your I AM Presence is your champion, your Holy Christ Self is your champion, the messenger is your champion. And many angels and saints and ascended beings and the entire Spirit of the Great White Brotherhood are also your champions.

So, beloved, you cannot make it to the octaves of light, of permanent being and immortality if indeed you do not bring to wholeness that soul that is yet in the state of mortality. And she is there because this is the place to which she has fallen.

The Great Love of Ascended Twin Flames

Now I think I have made myself clear, as I wonder if on this my first occasion of speaking to you I have truly conveyed to you my deep desiring. My deep desiring, beloved, is to share with you the great love of twin flames, especially of ascended twin flames.

Ascended twin flames who occupy the same fiery ovoid may move through the universes in all dimensions and octaves carrying, as it were, a sphere (and the spheres of the causal body, as these spheres have been developed over centuries), a great sphere of being that allows twin flames and ourselves specifically to reach untold millions of souls that are in different dimensions of being, different systems.

The universes are far flung, beloved. We are grateful to be stationed in New York City at the Temple of the Sun, for there so many of different races and backgrounds make their way through that city and then throughout the nation. So each soul that comes representing a different evolution of a different time, a different root race, makes one individual or thousands of that same root race have special qualities, a special service to offer. And then again this is multiplied by the tremendous creativity that everyone has, though many have not touched, in the secret chamber of the heart.

Love and Live in the Secret Chamber of the Heart

Those of you who are artists of one kind or another understand that the greatest art of all is the art of loving and living in the secret chamber of the heart with your Holy Christ Self. When you are able to do this, you know that you are moving closer and closer to your ascension. Let nothing stop you, beloved, for you are not a point of eternity until you are immortal.

With all of my heart's love I tell you that no matter what the challenge, no matter how great the pain, no matter what it takes to overcome the sinister force and to beat down the demons of the night, go for it. Do it. You can have not only your glorious victory in this life but your eternal union with your twin flame, who is either waiting for you in heaven or helping you along on earth.

I am your beloved Ruth. I shall be with you always, for I am a part of your mandala. I seal you in all the love of my heart and I tell you, each one, all things are possible unto those who love.

December 30, 1996

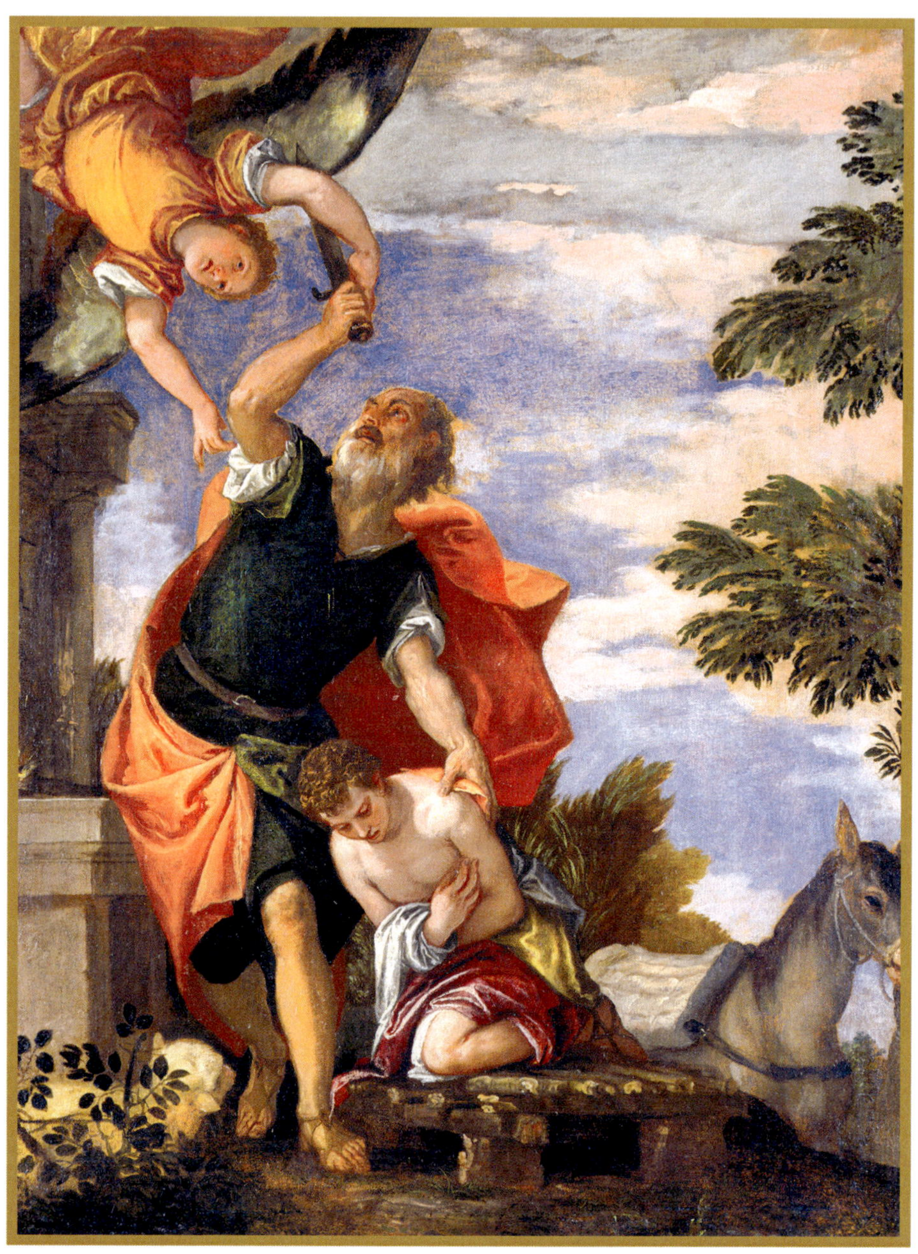

The Sacrifice of Isaac, c. 1586

In the beauty of the presence of every soul of light who has ever been a part of earth's evolutions, we say: Come apart. Intensify. Let the action of your causal body become one in this day and hour with your Holy Christ Self.

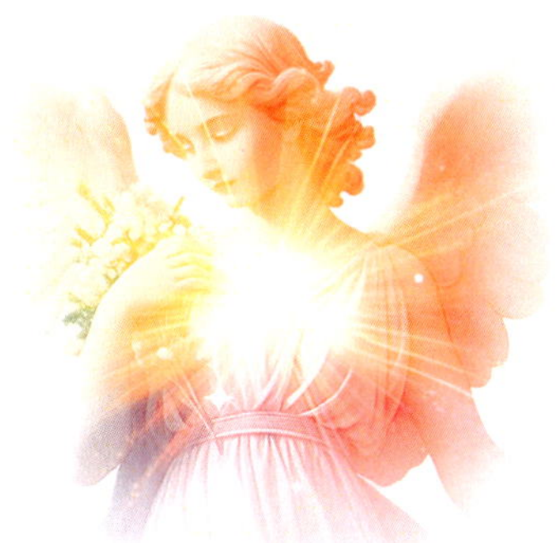

CHAPTER 25

Empowerment through Love

Shafts of white fire descend, touching the heart. Let the heart be the opening of the way. Let the heart now be a point of God-reality manifest here below as Above.

We come as one and as twain. We come for the victory of the God flame here in this very place, throughout this city and state, throughout the world and ultimately throughout the galaxies.

We come, beloved, so that once again you might understand the victory of twin flames. Some of you know me in that path of eternal being, and some of you have realized that your twin flame as well as my own twin flame, Ruth Hawkins, have taken their place among the immortals, the place of inner victory, and they have manifested that victory so that all might see and know that it is possible for you, each one, to make your ascension.

This, then, is our reason for coming as well as your reason for coming, even if you know it not. It is that inner signal of the sacred fire of your heart that brings you here and says to you, "Now is the moment, now is the hour, now is the light of victory."

Therefore, beloved ones, we bring to you now the beloved Ascended Lady Master Ruth Hawkins. Won't you give her a standing ovation.

[50-second standing ovation]

Thank you. Won't you be seated.

A Burden of Light

The messenger has known Ruth Hawkins for many, many decades, from their earliest years of serving together, and she was present on a number of occasions in the final hours of Ruth Hawkins' sojourn on earth. Ruth bore burdens of great, great severity in her final illness. This happened to many devotees of light around the world who desired to balance more karma before they made their ascension. The messenger would speak to Ruth by telephone and comfort her, and the messenger felt that this was a great, great privilege.

Ruth's desire to win her ascension enabled her to follow a path of strict oneness with her twin flame, and her great victory came about because she determined to master a certain style of art and she placed that art upon canvas for all to see.

In this moment, then, you have the opportunity to feel the presence of her heart, to know the expansion of her light and to be aware that you, too, can make your ascension in this life.

So much has been given to you, especially the gift of the violet flame, that I say to you all, even as the messenger has said frequently: Strive and continue to strive for the highest calling in God, for the highest manifestation of your calling in life.

Know, then, that when twin flames come together there is a tremendous energy and a tremendous manifestation, as that wholeness is almost the equivalent of a central sun whose two halves have come together, nevermore to be apart. Recognize that it is not this person or that person who makes the difference in your life, but it is the one and only person who is your twin flame.

Therefore, since we have come to this city, may you know that for many, many years to come, you may enter in to the presence of the Goddess of Liberty and her retreat over Manhattan. May you know the great love of the people of New York. May you know the great love of many ascended masters. And may you realize that whatever calling you are prepared to accept, that very calling can bring you to the moment of absolute God-victory.

Fanaticism Can Be Deadly

Now I would speak to you, beloved, of the condition of the economy and also of fanaticism, which the messenger has spoken about. If anyone engages in fanaticism, that one will not be a part of the Great White Brotherhood. And what a sorry state it will be if fanaticism destroys that individual.

Thus, let love be the fulfilling of the Law, especially the deep love that comes into your chakras once every year on Valentine's Day. Your chakras are filled with light, filled with love, filled with the energy of the cosmos. So, then, remember that on this weekend there is a moment of the opening whereby souls of light might take their ascension because of such great service by love.

The Wonder of God's Love in You

I am in your midst and I tell you how great is the wonder of God's love, how great is the wonder of the love that is in each chakra in your four lower bodies. Cherish this experience, beloved. And through this cherishment, truly realize that everything that is not of love passes from the screen of life and is no more.

But all those who gather together in the flame of love come for the reigniting of worlds, the reigniting of chakras, and the reigniting of the mind of God. This mind of God is not only in Christ Jesus but it is also in Lord Maitreya, in the power of Gautama Buddha and the presence of Sanat Kumara. Let this understanding go deep within you, and let the love of our twin flames be the fire of the golden cross paving the way to your eternal victory.

You are aware of a number of souls who have taken their ascension. They also are present now. And they have come, beloved, to remind you that you have the ability to accelerate and to make your ascension in this life.

Beloved hearts, if you move with those who do not seek the ascension in this life, you may be taken down by them. So watch and pray, beloved, that you are not unduly influenced by those who do not have the liberating, spiraling energy that goes back to the Great Central Sun and carries you there with it.

Empowerment through Love

Beloved hears, this day of love is a day of empowerment. Seek and find this empowerment through love. Seek to slay the aggressors who are not of charity.

In this moment, then, of the great victory of love, take the opportunity to let your heart become one with my heart and with the heart of beloved Ruth Hawkins and Chamuel and Charity.

Thus, I send white fire to each of you, to each of your chakras, as in silent prayer we send forth the emanations of our manifestation in the heart of the earth. [19-second pause]

Beloved Chamuel and Charity enter now the precincts of your being. Let fanaticism be cast into the sacred fire of God. Let angelic hosts descend upon you one and all.

May your inner being be transformed. May your solar plexus now become a shield of intense fire so that you might know the immensity of all that God will give you through Heros and Amora and all beings of the third ray.

Accept this, beloved. Accept it. Accept the universal manifestation of divine love. Accept it and know that God will continually, *continually* blaze forth his love ray upon you. And if you sustain this love ray, beloved, and if all on earth sustain it, then perhaps we shall entertain a perpetual Valentine's Day—not only for one day of the year but for every day of the year—that love might blossom and many souls might be the givers of gifts of love to all life.

In the beauty of the presence of every soul of light who has ever been a part of earth's evolutions, we say: Come apart. Intensify. Let the action of your causal body become one in this day and hour with your Holy Christ Self.

May you know this eternal oneness. For one day your lower self will become one with your Higher Self, eternally one with the great spheres of your causal body. Therefore I ask you, beloved, to come into that point of absolute God-harmony that is a facet of divine love.

Love Fulfills the Law in Your Life

Therefore, I call forth your causal body. Receive it. Receive Maitreya. Receive the messenger. And know, beloved, that wherever you are, wherever you go, if you make the call, love will be the fulfilling of the Law in your life.

To this end I seal you. And in the cosmic cross of white fire, I seal now one cross with three crosses. Thus you see how close you can come to scraping the ceiling of heaven unto your victory.

This is your joy. This is the joy of Jesus. This is the joy that Jesus holds for you.

Let us, then, sing to our Lord "Arise Shine, for Thy Light Is Come!" For this is truth: Your light is come. Your ascension draws nigh. So let it be.

[Congregation sings song 547, "Arise Shine, for Thy Light Is Come," in Church Universal and Triumphant's *Book of Hymns and Songs.*]

February 14, 1998

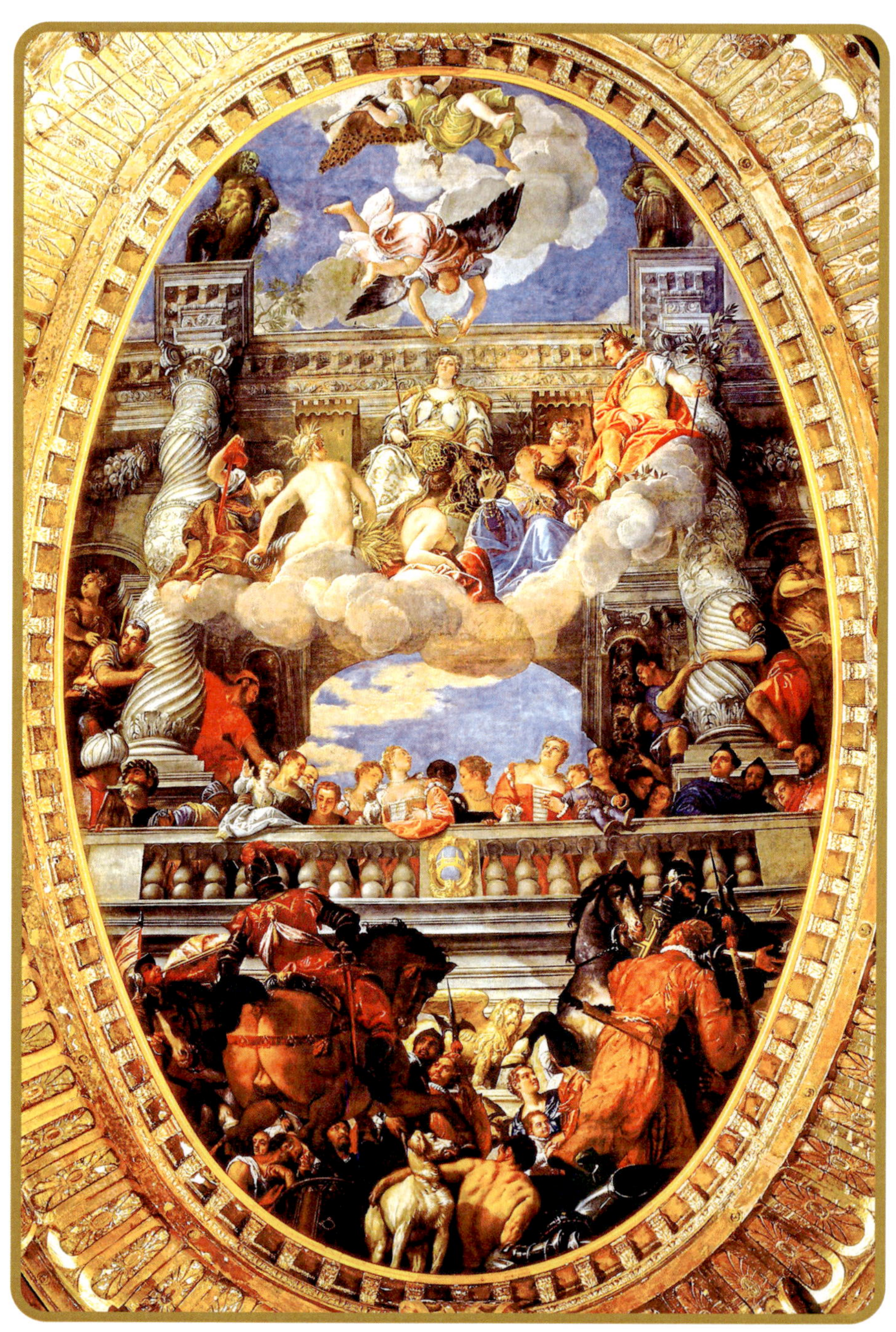

The Triumph of Venice, c. 1585

What for the Path, if not to assist the way of a brother, a sister? What for the Path, if not to raise up an entire evolution?

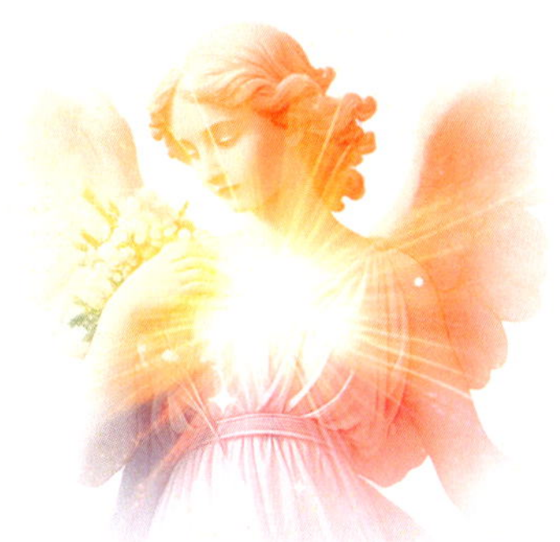

CHAPTER 26

The Call of Serapis

Most gracious children of the Sun, Serapis Bey has called and I have answered and so have you. And we have come to meet in the dot of the center of the circle within and without the square. And within that dot, behold, I AM there, you are there, and we are one.

We have come to begin the rising spiral of being whereby ascended adepts call chelas near and far, for we would set a flame and a fire here in the heart of San Francisco. We come to ignite an ancient spark within the souls of devotees who have lived and served here within these seven hills, which were the seven temples of the seven Holy Kumaras.[1] We come in the service of the Mother light, guarded for aeons by the Goddess of Purity.[2]

You have seen the dissipation of mass elements of human karma in the recent earthquake,[3] all of this in preparation for the release of a greater light. For certain elements of the human consciousness were required by cosmic law to be dissipated before we could release those initiations to any and all who would respond to the call of Serapis.

Understand, then, that when mankind themselves do not dissipate their human karma (by ignorance and for want of the use of the violet flame), then it is elemental life who, themselves bearers of the cross of planetary karma, must expiate in physical conditions those ancient discords that prevent the race from accelerating to the higher place of God consciousness toward which you aspire.

Because you aspire to that place, you have come. And because we aspire to lead you there, we have come. And therefore the Brotherhood welcomes you in the flame of love to service, to sacrifice, to surrender, and the path of selflessness.

There Is a Price for Eternity

Is there a price for eternity? Indeed, there is. It is the price of the exchange of the lesser self for the Greater Self. And who do you think it is, my beloved, who gets the greater bargain? Why, of course it is the soul who comes, who must surrender that which appears to be the only thing that it can surrender. But in reality, the thing surrendered is not the Real Self but the temporary portion, the temporary self. Thereby in having that self to give, one can receive the initiation of the descent of the Higher Self.

Is there any other path? Is there any other goal? Believe it not. For some have offered an easier way, the way of indulgence or formulas or this or that mantra as being the all and the end and the everything of life. Well, my beloved, if it were so, then many, many would have joined the ranks of the candidates for the ascension at the Temple of Luxor. But as a matter of fact, they have not.

And therefore the many byways offered today, coming with the allure of making life easier and exalting the outer personality, have detoured souls of light to endless, endless labyrinthian passages. But all this must end.

When does it end? It ends when the individual soul declares, "*Enough!* I have had enough! I will find my freedom and I will find it lawfully, lovingly, God's way—the way of the eternal Logos, the way that the doves have flown, the way that the stars glow."

O my beloved, yes, there are innocent sheep trapped in the false teachings, but there are also many who are also the goats who enjoy the false teachings because they enjoy the perpetuation of unreality. Therefore this is the question you must ask yourself: "Do I desire to know the truth even when the truth hurts? Or do I desire to continue hearing only what the lesser self desires to hear?" By and by, the real souls of God tire of the half-baked half-truths. By and by, the souls who are real come to the door of Luxor.

The Love of Serapis

My brother Serapis and El Morya have called upon me to speak to you, for they would give to you through me the essence of love that is the true heart of the initiations of Luxor—though many there have been who have denied that there is any love in Serapis or in the brothers of his retreat because of the appearance of sternness. Indeed, they are one-pointed and sure-footed. Indeed, they know the Way and its pitfalls, and they must uphold a light of discipline for the purest light, the whitest way on the great white way.

I am come to assure you that the core of that teaching is nevertheless love—a love that loves your soul far more than you know (and far more, indeed, than your carnal mind), a love that does not pamper but compels you by the most immense compassion to risc to thc Greater Self even when fear assails and demons and discarnates berail you, the soul, rising with Christ upon that cross.

Do you think that any soul is exempt from the path of the cross? Nay. If it were so, he would have told you. But he said that the cross must be borne. It must be taken up.[4] It is a cross of light. Remember that the burden is light.[5] The appearance is of burden, but that burden is light. When you carry light as light is given to you by the hierarch of Luxor, know that that light is for a purpose and not for the glorying of yourself but for the mission. It is for the bearing of personal and planetary karma.

Wherever there is a vortex of light, as the person of the Word, there the darkness goes to be transmuted. For even the darkness is God misqualified. It is his energy misqualified that longs to be realigned with the Word. Where there is light, there is a vortex of transmutation. When you draw forth light in your meditation, then you must know the path of preparedness to deal with the darkness that is exposed within the subconscious of the self, within previous incarnations, and within the planetary collective unconscious.

What for the Path, if not to assist the way of a brother, a sister? What for the Path, if not to raise up an entire evolution?

A Path of Joy

We are the real and the living Brotherhood of light and we show you a path of joy. It is not a path of sorrow or deprivation, save for those who are not of the light in the first instance. For them the Path is drudgery. They soon weary of it and they are no more. But the soul of light who knows who he is and why he is born seeks the way out, not for selfish reasons but because by love he senses the plight of a humanity that by God must be enlightened in this age if it is ever to be enlightened! And by God, it must be enlightened by those of you who have taken embodiment determined to effect change.

Why, some of you have recently spent other lifetimes squandering energy, and you have come before the Lords of Karma and you have seen Serapis Bey and me and Morya and you have said, "Let me go back. Let me now take up my life in earnestness and contribute something of worth, for I have spent, lo, this and other lifetimes here and there. And now with the vision of inner levels, let me go forth. Let me go forth with a light to lighten my way and the way of others." And you have pleaded with Serapis Bey himself to contact you in this your present incarnation and to not leave you bereft of the memory of the Ancient of Days.

Dare to Be Different

Therefore we come to touch your heart with love and to tell you that if you would do something about your present plight and that of this planet, then you must dare to be different than you were when you entered this forcefield. For could you change the earth when you entered the hall this night?

I say to you, beloved, that if you could not, then is it not obvious that something must change? Is it the Brotherhood of Luxor, or is it perhaps your own soul's understanding of life itself? Changes come, and by those changes you rise in new dimensions of your own Selfhood. And by the gradual process of love, you come to know more expedient methods for contacting the multitudes of souls who are waiting to be fed.

Would you become a shepherd, feeding the sheep on the hillsides who know not the way to go? Is this not the real longing of yourself, rather than to follow the fashions of the times and this or that interesting book or show or even some new teacher offering some new way of rearranging energy, perhaps?

Well, we are not content merely to rearrange energy. We come to challenge energy to rise. And the matrix of the rising of the flame in you is ascension's flame, ascension's pyramid.

My beloved, the Brotherhood of Luxor knocks on the door of the heart of the chelas of any and all gurus and those who have not yet entered the path of chelaship. Our purpose in this year 1979 is to work with the World Teachers, Jesus and Kuthumi, to instruct, to initiate, to bless and prepare you who know that you have a more than ordinary mission and a very special life to live in the giving of the Word to souls who need both the teacher and the teaching—souls who need love and someone who cares enough to sit down with them and break the bread of life.

We come, then, in search of those who have vowed recently, before the Lords of Karma, and those who have vowed thousands of years ago to strike a blow for the LORD in the beginning of that Aquarian age. It is an age that can commence a spiral of freedom and lead the earth back to those inner golden ages that once she knew.

It is also an age when, by the absence of free will, children of the light may postpone for untold aeons the coming into the physical octave of that which is destined to be. No psychic predictions can secure for the United States or Russia a victory of light, a breaking down of the engines of war and of manipulation and of the abuses of the people for the gain of money and power and blood.

Your Tie to the Eternal Chain of Hierarchy

Yes, indeed, there are initiates of the left-handed path walking the earth, manipulating the governments and the fates of the people. Indeed, there are initiates of Satan. Mark my word well. Therefore, let the initiates of light come forth and understand that if you would be a match for those fallen ones who have seized their positions of power in your very government, you yourself must learn to increase the light in the sacred centers of being.

You must know that not you but God in you can save a life that is your own and a life that is a planet and a people. You must know that it is by the eternal chain of hierarchy and your tie to it that mighty works are wrought. You must know that when you go forth to challenge those who are the deceivers and destroyers of the people, it will require the extraordinary arm of the hosts of the LORD and of our Brotherhood to effect those changes that are desired.

Well, tell me, then, if in the last decade all of the discussions and all of the demonstrations and all of the wars and all of the grabs for power have netted any light for the children of this earth or any greater vision of freedom. I do not see it. Perhaps you do.

I only see the futility of the outer self by a scientific humanism, by Marxism,[6] by a perverted capitalism, by manipulations of monopolies, national and international. By all of this, I see only the lessening of light in the total civilization side by side with the increase of light in the few who have understood the Path and have pursued it to the best of their ability.

Thus, side by side in this age is the degeneration spiral of death in the midst of those who have gone astray, destroying their sacred centers by chemical means and drugs and pollutants and thereby closing the door to the higher contact. We have seen those souls who have been tempted by the fallen ones to take the initiations of the left-handed path through the drug culture. We have seen these pass through the treacherous waters of the allure of the astral plane, losing hold on reality, the flower of youth passing into some psychic unreality while the demand of the hour is to feed my sheep![7]

Have you not heard the Saviour's cry? And do you not know the allure of the fallen ones, whose promise of salvation is, in reality, unto death—not the mere death of the body but the death of the soul? This is a battle for ultimate survival. And therefore, we come.

The Path of the Ascension by the Initiation of the Ruby Ray

We are gratified that there are so many souls of light in this nation alone who uphold the standard of freedom. Now we would introduce to you the shortest distance between two points outlined in the Great Pyramid. It is the path of the ascension by the initiation of the ruby ray. The ruby ray is the intensity of the blood of Christ, which is the true essence of love in such concentration, as the rose pink of the third ray becomes an intensity that is a sword that is able to divide, as a laser beam, the Real from the unreal and to judge error and the path of error. The path of the ruby ray is being revealed by my father Sanat Kumara, your father and my own.[8]

The path of the ascension is the path of the white light of the body of Christ. The body is the temple. The body is the Word. The body is the teaching. And the body is the Mother, and the Mother light within you is the light of Omega.

Thus by the ruby ray and the white light, the blood and the body, the Alpha, the Omega of being, there is the fusion within you of a path of acceleration that is for the sincere and the determined ones who recognize that they can no longer dally the centuries away, waiting, waiting, procrastinating their own self-mastery. But indeed, the fate of civilization hangs in the balance of the decision of the few.

There are other paths, lesser paths, and slower paths that wind up the mountain, allowing greater passages of time and space between initiations, further incarnations, and of course not the great demands of the self for sacrifice and service. But, my beloved, consider—consider the prolonging of that surgery that must one day come if your soul is to become the fullness of the Christ that is in you. Consider, then: Why not now? Why not remember the ancient vow? Why not?

You say, "Why?" And I say, "Look with me upon the suffering masses. Look upon world hunger and the displacement of persons and the boat people and war, and look upon those fallen ones and their treachery and their cruelty and their torture of human life mercilessly.

Who will call forth the judgment for the binding of those fallen ones? It must come by the science of the Word within you! And it will come when you decide to make your throat chakra the instrument of the seven chohans of the rays, and your heart chakra and your third eye and the crown."

These are gifts of life that we have long ago given to Almighty God. And he has come into those centers and he has worked a work through us whereby many have walked through the door to eternal life. This is the joy of the Path. It is knowing that you become the indispensable link in the chain of universal Being when you love enough to live and to give of yourself so that another self might become the fullness of itself.

Thus, the goal of the Path is your ascension. But the path of the ascension includes all of life. It is the infusion by the light that flows through you of the body of humanity with the light of the living Lord.

I Would Impart the Sacred Fire Breath

My beloved, I embrace you. For I, Paul the Venetian, have stood with the Maha Chohan, with each one of you, as that representative of the Holy Spirit breathed into your nostrils the breath of life in this incarnation. Aye, 'tis the cry of the Manchild! Aye, it is the breath of life that I long to hear!

And now I would impart to you the sacred fire breath of the Holy Spirit, that when you speak the children will listen and the demons will tremble and the gifts of that Spirit might be yours to bind these fallen ones that are, to put it in the vernacular, messing up things on this planet, messing up the cities and the homes and the lives and the souls and the hearts of souls whom I love and know as my brothers and sisters.

I lift the veil for a moment, that you might see me as I AM. For you know me and you know our band. And I AM determined that the decay and rot of a diet that is fed this generation shall no longer block your brains or your chakras, that you shall fast and pray and eliminate those toxins polluting your bodies that make you dense and not able to contact our light or recognize us.

Yes, I come in the name of the Holy Spirit. And I feel in my very being the intensity of the Maha Chohan, the intensity of the challenge of all those purveyors of a synthetic civilization that has served to stand between the children of light and the angelic hosts. Why, angels walk and talk with you today but you do not answer. In olden days, the children answered. The only difference was the absence of pollutants. Do you know that that substance and all of those chemicals in the atmosphere actually cut off the outer senses from the inner senses of the soul?

My beloved, I know you feel that intensity as you look upon the bodies and the faces, so many of them blank and the eyes so burdened with an inner sadness, of people who are truly of the light and yet are so beset by the burdens of this life.

Wake Up and Live for a Greater Cause!

I pray to you in the name of Gautama Buddha. In his name, in the name of the Lord of the World, in the name of Maitreya: Wake up! *Wake up! Wake up* and live for a cause greater than the feeding of your mouth and the clothing of your temple and the enjoyment of paltry gain. *Wake up and see life who needs you and needs your love.*

Be not concerned about this messenger. Be concerned about your own relationship to the Great White Brotherhood. That is what counts. It is the teaching that counts, and it is your application of the teaching. Messengers have come and gone, but it is the Word they bear that lives on. It is the Word that we transfer to you, and we must have a physical messenger and a physical temple. But your relationship with us must be sought and won on your own merit and your own love.

Take, then, the gift freely given and know that in the community of Camelot[9] we have called forth the sangha of the Buddha and the community of Christ and his disciples. We have prepared a home and a school for children and a place for retreat and study. It is our cradle for you to give birth to the Manchild within you. Won't you come as the wise men of old and attend your own birth in this lifetime, the Mother's giving birth within you of the eternal Christ?

We have come to celebrate your own Christ Mass. Welcome, my beloved. I pour forth my love to you and I breathe a breath for that transfer of the Spirit. [The master breathes the holy breath.]

Purusha.

Be sealed in the love of the Brotherhood and your own God Presence.

I love thee, I love but thee,
With a love that shall not die
Till the sun grows cold,
And the stars are old,
And the leaves of the judgment book unfold![10]

Yes, I quote one of your bards to express the intensity of the love of the Brotherhood for our unascended devotees. It shall not die but it shall quicken you to Life.

I touch you with a kiss of peace upon the brow.

August 10, 1979

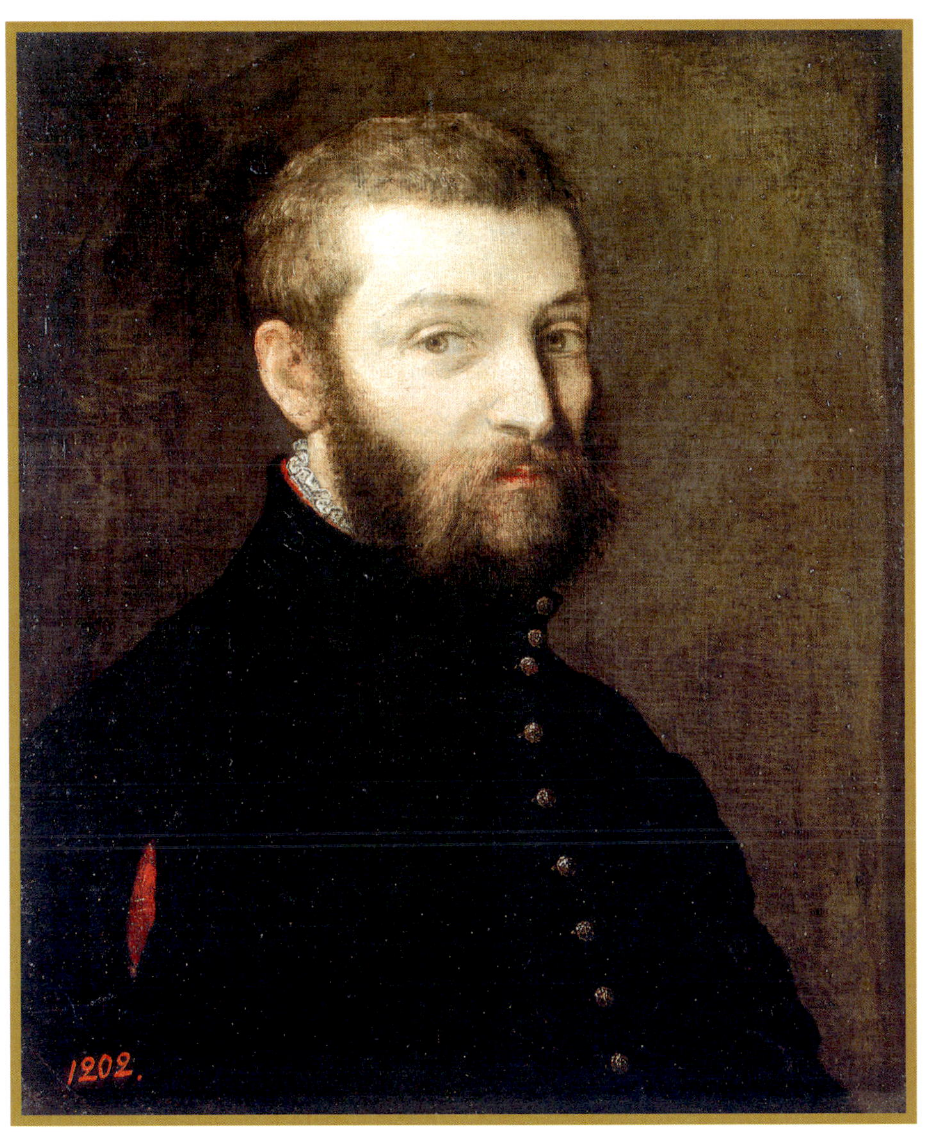

Self-Portrait, c. 1558–63

Prayers, Mantras, and Decrees

Giving prayers, mantras, and decrees, also called the science of the spoken Word, is an opportunity for you to garner more light and to send that light to those you love and to the world. Starting your day by asking for protection anchors the "perfection of light," as described by Paul the Venetian. The first two decrees, "The Violet Fire and Tube of Light Decree" and "Light's Protection," will do just that.

Following these decrees are the "Heart, Head, and Hand Decrees," which are the shortest means to touching every major step we need to take on the path of uniting with our Higher Self and to our soul's ultimate Victory. The next two decrees, also referred to as prayers or mantras, are for the anchoring of the violet flame and to bring light to the elementals, as Paul the Venetian has requested we do. Next are a few more decrees that are sure to enrich your heart and soul.

May this journey of invoking the light be a most joyous one that propels you to your spiritual victory.

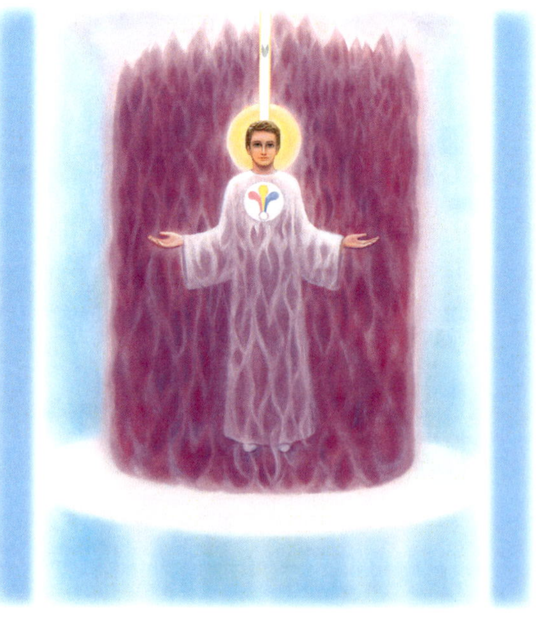

Violet Fire and Tube of Light Decree

by the Ascended Master Saint Germain

O my constant, loving I AM Presence, thou Light of God above me whose radiance forms a circle of fire before me to light my way:

I AM faithfully calling to thee to place a great pillar of Light from my own Mighty I AM God Presence all around me right now today! Keep it intact through every passing moment, manifesting as a shimmering shower of God's beautiful Light through which nothing human can ever pass. Into this beautiful electric circle of divinely charged energy direct a swift upsurge of the violet fire of Freedom's forgiving, transmuting flame!

Cause the ever expanding energy of this flame projected downward into the forcefield of my human energies to completely change every negative condition into the positive polarity of my own Great God Self! Let the magic of its mercy so purify my world with Light that all whom I contact shall always be blessed with the fragrance of violets from God's own heart in memory of the blessed dawning day when all discord—cause, effect, record, and memory—is forever changed into the Victory of Light and the peace of the ascended Jesus Christ.

I AM now constantly accepting the full power and manifestation of this fiat of Light and calling it into instantaneous action by my own God-given free will and the power to accelerate without limit this sacred release of assistance from God's own heart until all men are ascended and God-free in the Light that never, never, never fails!

Light's Protection

In the name of the beloved mighty victorious Presence of God, I AM in me, my very own beloved Holy Christ Self, Holy Christ Selves of all mankind, beloved Archangel Michael, I decree:

1. Light's protection manifest—
   Holy Brotherhood in white,
   Light of God that never fails,
   Keep us in thy perfect sight!

Refrain: I AM, I AM, I AM protection's mighty power,
I AM, I AM, I AM guarded every hour,
I AM, I AM, I AM perfection's mighty shower
Manifest, manifest, manifest!

2. Lord Michael, mighty and true,
   Guard us with thy sword of blue.
   Keep us centered in the Light's
   Blazing armor shining bright!

3. Around us blaze thy sword of faith—
   Mighty power of holy grace,
   I AM invincible protection always
   Pouring from thy dazzling rays!

And in full Faith I consciously accept this manifest, manifest, manifest! (3x) right here and now with full Power, eternally sustained, all-powerfully active, ever expanding, and world enfolding until all are wholly ascended in the Light and free!

Beloved I AM! Beloved I AM! Beloved I AM!

Heart, Head, and Hand Decrees

Violet Fire

Heart

Violet Fire, thou Love divine,
Blaze within this heart of mine!
Thou art Mercy forever true,
Keep me always in tune with you. (3x)

Head

I AM Light, thou Christ in me,
Set my mind forever free;
Violet Fire, forever shine
Deep within this mind of mine.

God who gives my daily bread,
With Violet Fire fill my head
Till thy radiance heavenlike
Makes my mind a mind of Light. (3x)

Hand

I AM the hand of God in action,
Gaining Victory every day;
My pure soul's great satisfaction
Is to walk the Middle Way. (3x)

Tube of Light

Beloved I AM Presence bright,
Round me seal your Tube of Light
From Ascended Master flame
Called forth now in God's own name.
Let it keep my temple free
From all discord sent to me.

I AM calling forth Violet Fire
To blaze and transmute all desire,
Keeping on in Freedom's name
Till I AM one with the Violet Flame. (3x)

Forgiveness

I AM Forgiveness acting here,
Casting out all doubt and fear,
Setting men forever free
With wings of cosmic Victory.

I AM calling in full power
For Forgiveness every hour;
To all life in every place
I flood forth forgiving Grace. (3x)

Supply

I AM free from fear and doubt,
Casting want and misery out,
Knowing now all good Supply
Ever comes from realms on high.

I AM the hand of God's own Fortune
Flooding forth the treasures of Light,
Now receiving full Abundance
To supply each need of Life. (3x)

Perfection

I AM Life of God-Direction
Blaze thy light of Truth in me.
Focus here all God's Perfection,
From all discord set me free.

Make and keep me anchored ever
In the Justice of thy plan–
I AM the Presence of Perfection
Living the Life of God in man! (3x)

Transfiguration

I AM changing all my garments,
Old ones for the bright new day;
With the Sun of Understanding
I AM shining all the way.

I AM Light within, without;
I AM Light is all about.
Fill me, free me, glorify me!
Seal me, heal me, purify me!
Until transfigured they describe me:
I AM shining like the Son,
I AM shining like the Sun! (3x)

Resurrection

I AM the Flame of Resurrection
Blazing God's pure Light through me.
Now I AM raising every atom,
From every shadow I AM free.

I AM the Light of God's full Presence,
I AM living ever free.
Now the flame of Life eternal
Rises up to Victory. (3x)

Ascension

I AM Ascension Light,
Victory flowing free,
All of Good won at last
For all eternity.

I AM Light, all weights are gone.
Into the air I raise;
To all I pour with full God Power
My wondrous song of praise.

All hail! I AM the living Christ,
The ever-loving One.
Ascended now with full God Power,
I AM a blazing Sun! (3x)

And in full Faith . . .

I AM the Violet Flame

In the name of the beloved mighty victorious Presence of God, I AM in me, and my very own beloved Holy Christ Self, I call for the Violet Flame to expand within my heart, infinitely, presently, and forever:

I AM the Violet Flame
  In action in me now
I AM the Violet Flame
  To Light alone I bow
I AM the Violet Flame
  In mighty Cosmic Power
I AM the Light of God
  Shining every hour
I AM the Violet Flame
  Blazing like a sun
I AM God's sacred power
  Freeing every one

And in full Faith...

Set the Elementals Free

In the name of the beloved mighty victorious Presence of God, I AM in me, my very own beloved Holy Christ Self, I decree:

Seal, seal, seal in an ovoid bright
Of the violet fire's clear light
Every elemental, set and keep them free
From all human discord instantly.

1. Beloved I AM (3x)
2. By Christ-command (3x)
3. By God's blue ray (3x)
4. By God's violet ray (3x)
5. By God's love ray (3x)
6. By Hercules' might (3x)
7. By Jesus' Light (3x)
8. By Michael's sword (3x)
9. It's done today, it's done to stay,
   it's done God's way

And in full Faith...

Introit to the Holy Christ Self

In the name of the beloved mighty victorious Presence of God, I AM in me, my very own beloved Holy Christ Self and through the magnetic power of the sacred fire vested within the threefold flame of Love, Wisdom, and Power burning within my heart, I decree:

1. Holy Christ Self above me,
Thou balance of my soul,
Let thy blessed radiance
Descend and make me Whole.

Refrain: Thy Flame within me ever blazes,
Thy Peace about me ever raises,
Thy Love protects and holds me,
Thy dazzling Light enfolds me.
I AM thy threefold radiance,
I AM thy living Presence
Expanding, expanding, expanding now.

2. Holy Christ Flame within me,
Come, expand thy triune Light;
Flood my being with the essence
Of the pink, blue, gold, and white.

3. Holy lifeline to my Presence,
Friend and brother ever dear,
Let me keep thy holy vigil,
Be thyself in action here.

And in full Faith I consciously accept this manifest, manifest, manifest! (3x) right here and now with full Power, eternally sustained, all-powerfully active, ever expanding, and world enfolding until all are wholly ascended in the Light and free!

Beloved I AM! Beloved I AM! Beloved I AM!

Keep My Flame Blazing

In the name of the beloved mighty victorious Presence of God, I AM in me, my very own beloved Holy Christ Self, I decree:

Keep my Flame blazing,
By God's Love raising,
Direct and keep me in my rightful place!

I AM Presence ever near me,
Keep me mindful of thy Grace;
Flame of Christ, ever cheer me,
In me show thy smiling face!

And in full Faith I consciously accept this manifest, manifest, manifest! (3x) right here and now with full Power, eternally sustained, all-powerfully active, ever expanding, and world enfolding until all are wholly ascended in the Light and free!

Beloved I AM! Beloved I AM! Beloved I AM!

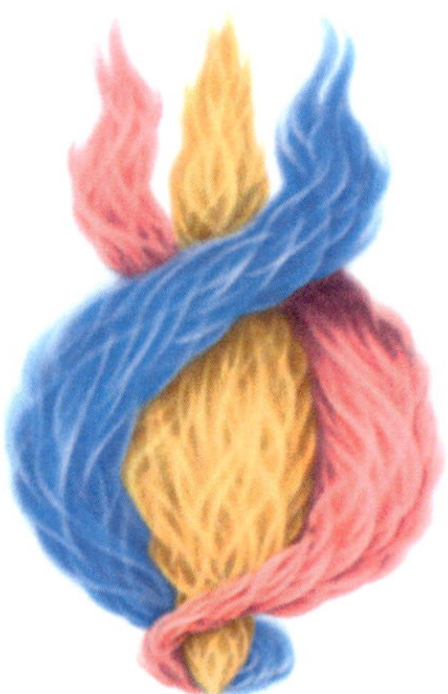

The Threefold Flame

Great Central Sun Magnet Invocation

by Surya and Cuzco

O Lord God Almighty, maker of heaven and earth, I call to thee in the name of the Christed ones, in the name of Jesus the Christ and Mary the Mother, in the name of Saint Germain, and I say:

Seal the arc of contact between my heart and thine own! O Lord God Almighty, seal the arc of the contact! Seal the arc of the contact! And now let flow the coils of Alpha and Omega, the spirals of the Great Central Sun Magnet. And let me receive as I am able, as my chalice is stable and worthy to receive these energies winding about the coil of being, manifesting the magnet of the Sun. O Alpha and Omega, let me be thyself in Mater! Let me be a focus of the magnet of the Great Central Sun!

After you have invoked the magnet in this wise, then you may call to your own God Presence and Christ Self for the implementation of the action of the magnet, saying:

In the name of the Christ within me and my own beloved I AM THAT I AM, in the name of the Holy Spirit and the Flame that blazes upon the altar of my heart, in the name of the sacred fire breath, I call for the action of the Great Central Sun Magnet to demagnetize these planes of Mater of the energy veil. I call for the transmutation of all human karma. I call for the transmutation of the karma of the Dark Cycle by the action of the Great Central Sun Magnet which I AM.

I call for the balancing of life in the four planes of consciousness and in my four lower bodies. I call for the seed of Light that is the blueprint of my Ascension and my Victory. This which I call forth for myself, I call forth for all mankind, the elemental kingdom, and the angelic hosts. And let this invocation be according to the mathematics of the will of God, as Above so below. Let it be sealed in the name of the Father and of the Mother, of the Son and of the Holy Spirit.

I AM My Brother's Keeper

In the name of the beloved mighty victorious Presence of God, I AM in me, my very own beloved Holy Christ Self, I decree:

I AM my brother's keeper.
O God, help me to be
All service and assistance,
Compassion just like Thee!

I AM my brother's keeper.
O Jesus, by thy Flame
Of Resurrection's blessing
Give Comfort in thy name!

I AM my brother's keeper,
O Presence of God so near,
The fullness of thy blessing,
Pure Divinity appears!

I AM my brother's keeper,
The guardian of his Flame;
In quiet power and knowing,
I love him in thy name!

And in full Faith I consciously accept this manifest, manifest, manifest! (3x) right here and now with full Power, eternally sustained, all-powerfully active, ever expanding, and world enfolding until all are wholly ascended in the Light and free!

Beloved I AM! Beloved I AM! Beloved I AM!

An Invitation to Visit Paul the Venetian's Etheric Retreats

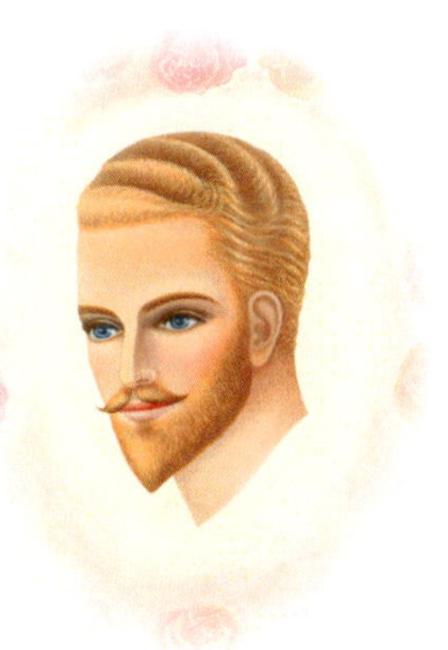

Beloved Paul the Venetian invites you to visit his etheric retreat in the heaven-world while your body sleeps at night. Visiting his retreat is an effective way to learn more about him, deepen your inner relationship with him, and bask in his teachings and the light of the third ray of love, beauty, and art. You may simply give the following prayer, also called "a call," to be taken to either one of the retreats of Paul the Venetian through soul travel, and you will be escorted by archangels and legions of light.

> *In the name of the Christ, my own Real Self, I call to the heart of the I AM Presence and to the angel of the Presence, to Archangel Michael and beloved Kuan Yin, to take me in my soul and in my soul consciousness to the retreat of Paul the Venetian in southern France—or to the university classes currently being held at the Goddess of Liberty's Temple of the Sun—according to the direction of my Holy Christ Self and the Maha Chohan.*
>
> *I ask to receive the instruction of the law of love and to be given the formula for the victory of the love flame within my heart, especially as it pertains to the gift of the discerning of spirits. And I ask that all information necessary to the fulfillment of my divine plan and that of my beloved twin flame be released to my outer waking consciousness as it is required. I thank thee and I accept this done in the full power of the risen Christ. Amen.*

You may adapt this prayer in order to be taken to the retreat of many other ascended masters that you feel drawn to, which are described in the book *The Masters and Their Retreats.* You may also visit AscendedMasterSpiritualRetreats.org for more information and an engaging *Touring Heaven* audio podcast.

In recent eras, few among mankind have entered the retreats and temples of the Great White Brotherhood. The retreats, once physical on the lost continents of Lemuria and Atlantis, were withdrawn to the etheric plane, reachable only by the most advanced initiates. With the dawning of the Aquarian age, however, lightbearers were given the opportunity to enter these retreats—this time by soul travel, apart from the physical body. In the twentieth century, a number of the retreats were opened to unascended students of the masters, and on January 1, 1986, Gautama Buddha announced that the seven chohans of the rays had been granted approval by the Lords of Karma to open "Universities of the Spirit in each of their etheric retreats where they might welcome not dozens or hundreds but thousands and tens of thousands of students who will diligently pursue the path of self-mastery on the seven rays."

The following is a description of Paul the Venetian's magnificent etheric retreat, and a description of The Temple of the Sun, the retreat of the Goddess of Liberty, where Paul the Venetian also teaches classes.

Le Château de Liberté
The Retreat of Paul the Venetian

In the South of France on the river Rhône is a focus of the flame of liberty and the retreat presided over by Paul the Venetian, chohan of the third ray. The description of Paul's retreat contained herein is of the etheric focus, which is congruent with and extends far beyond a physical castle now owned and maintained by a private French family. Much of the physical surroundings resemble the etheric counterpart, however the master rarely manifests in the lower octave. The castle itself contains many great works of art and at certain times during the year it is open to the public, even as the great halls in the

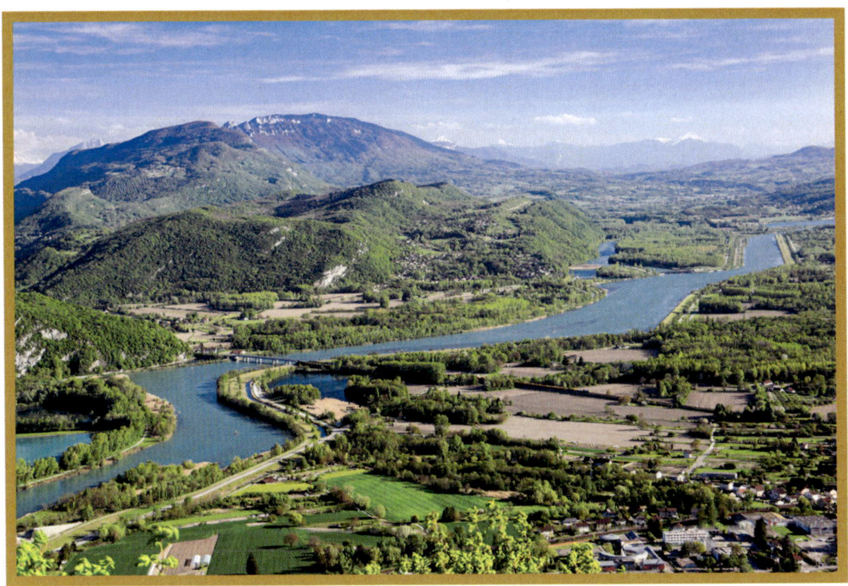

Panoramic view of the river Rhône in rural France

etheric retreat are open to students of the Venetian who come to study art and culture and the true concepts of liberty.

This vast etheric retreat lends itself to the function of gallery, museum, and archives of art and artifacts from many cultures and civilizations. A Versailles of its own splendor, it contains endless classrooms where great works of art of all ages are displayed. Paintings by Paul, his students, and other masters abound. Here workshops for musicians, writers, sculptors, students of voice, as well as crafts of all kinds have been held, and ascended masters of all the rays have introduced new techniques in every field of art.

The art of beauty and the art of liberty are everywhere in evidence. When one is present upon its surrounding landscape, one enjoys the rise and fall of the waters from the marble fountains, the musical trills of the birds of multicolored plumage, the water lilies on the ponds, the beautiful and fragrant roses that bedeck the graceful marble columns, and the magnificent statuary from the many centuries past.

Within the walls one is also exposed to an exhibit of the grandeur of expression in sculpture, painting, and music—the piano, cello, organ, harp, and the caroling of the many voices of the choirs. Those who are accomplished in and are exponents of the fine arts—music, writing, sculpture—frequent the Château as guests to imbibe the radiation of its beauty.

But one sees not only the sculpture of genius and hears the music of the spheres, but also the crude attempts of the hopeful amateurs—the timid endeavors of the beginners who have taken their first cautious steps upon the ladder of attainment. It is easy to enjoy the beauty and the fragrance of the flower once its petals are unfolded, but it is the tender shoot first appearing above ground that needs the nourishment of divine love.

Within the Château walls, therefore, the crudest of expressions have an honored place. For to the least of these aspirants, the ascended master Paul extends his loving care, lest their first attempts be shriveled and the bud fall from the stem. Within the circumference of his consciousness, he welcomes all those sons with motives pure, for he considers each man's heart a "Château de Liberté" within which is enshrined the flame of liberty, pulsating to expand some talent, gift, or grace—the individual facet of the God-intent for each lifestream. He sees each one's potential and esteems it his reason for being to help each one refine his crude expressions into beautiful designs—whether in statesmanship, in education, in the fine arts, in science, in medicine, in ministration, or in the understanding of pure truth.

As host at his retreat, he greets—with the dignity and majesty of an ascended one—all these chelas of his heart. Beyond the entrance to the etheric retreat, they enter an expansive hall where they are held spellbound by the radiation from the canvas on the wall ahead. This is Paul's painting of the Holy Trinity. Its vibrant emanations throughout the entrance chamber inspire in each beholder such reverent awe that he dare not move nor speak for quite some time. The heavenly Father is portrayed by a majestic figure. The likeness of Jesus depicts the Son, and an impressive white dove with a nine-foot wingspan focuses the Holy Spirit. Begun before his ascension and completed thereafter, this great work of art focuses both dimensions of Paul's service to the earth. Beneath the painting Paul inscribed in gold letters, "Perfect love casteth out fear."

As they become accustomed to this exalted state, the students move across the tessellated floor and descend the stairs, passing through the corridor that leads to the auditorium known as the Flame Room. The threefold flame of liberty is in the center of the room, focused within a golden chalice. Within the base of the chalice is a concentration of the crystal fire mist, the white light out of which the threefold flame proceeds. The focus of the flame of liberty was brought by the Goddess of Liberty from the Temple of the Sun just before the sinking of Atlantis, when the physical structure of the Temple of the Sun was destroyed by cataclysmic action.

The radiance from the flame renders the room as bright as the sun. Paintings done by Paul depicting the saints and sages of all times grace the circular walls of the room. Devotees enter the Flame Room to pay their respects to the flame and to briefly absorb its pulsations, which expand as the rhythm of a giant heartbeat. The focus is so intense that they are asked to meditate in other rooms of the retreat provided for that purpose. The entire retreat vibrates to the rhythm of the liberty flame.

The fleur-de-lis design that we see in the retreat is the symbol of the threefold flame. It is no mere coincidence that the crowned heads of France adopted this symbol as their emblem, for the real liberty flame blazed upon their native soil.

For centuries Paul has felt that beauty is a necessary part of the thought and feeling processes of those who desire spiritual progress, who desire to obtain their freedom and the liberty to do the will of God. He feels that one's capacity to appreciate eternal beauty is expanded in accordance with one's adoration to his own God Presence.

The Temple of the Sun
The Retreat of the Goddess of Liberty

While embodied on Atlantis, the Goddess of Liberty erected the Temple of the Sun where Manhattan Island now is. With the sinking of the continent, the physical temple was destroyed, but its etheric counterpart remains a major world center focusing the flames of the twelve hierarchies of the Sun. The temple, which was the West gate of Atlantis, has become the East gate of the New World. It is one of the most important retreats on the planet.

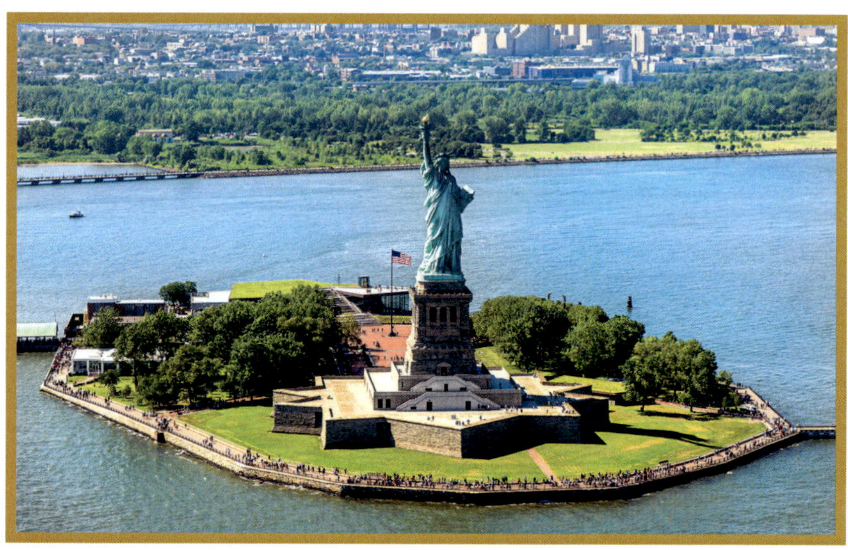

Liberty (Bedloe's) Island in New York Harbor

The central altar of the Temple of the Sun is over the Statue of Liberty on Liberty (Bedloe's) Island in New York Harbor, the spread of the focus extending over Manhattan Island and parts of New Jersey. The temple is a replica of the temple of Helios and Vesta in the sun of our solar system. In the central flame room of the temple, we find the pattern that is reproduced over and over again throughout the universe from the heart of the Great Hub to the Flaming Yod, to the sun of each solar system and each God Star. Every planetary home has a Sun Temple where the central altar is dedicated to the Father-Mother God, the pure white essence of the creative fire of Alpha and Omega, and the twelve surrounding altars are tended by the representatives of the twelve hierarchies of the Sun who focus their flames on behalf of the evolutions of that planet.

Tiers of flame rooms proceed out from this center room. In these flame rooms, the brothers in white attend other flames of the one hundred and forty-four. The flame of liberty, the fleur-de-lis of pink, blue and gold, blazes from one of these outer courts. The aura of the retreat is saturated with the golden flame of illumination, and as the Château de Liberté in France (also a focus of the threefold flame of

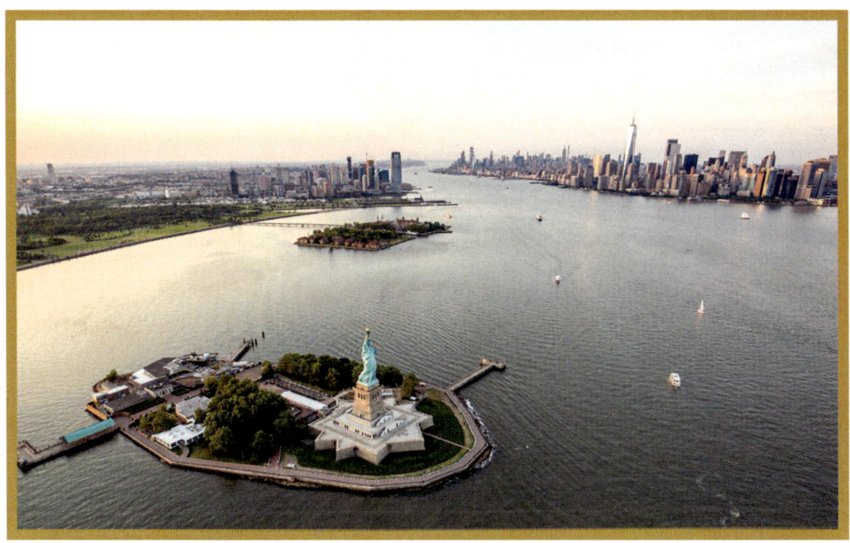

New Jersey (top left), Manhattan (top right), and Liberty Island

liberty) emits a pink aura, so we find that the twin flames of Helios and Vesta are represented in perfect balance in these two retreats dedicated to the liberation of all mankind. The gold and the pink reflect the wisdom and the love of our Sun God and Goddess.

The Goddess of Liberty says, "Give me your tired, your poor, your huddled masses yearning to breathe free, the wretched refuse of your teeming shore. Send these, the homeless, tempest-tossed to me. I lift my lamp beside the golden door."[1] Her Temple of the Sun is the open door of America from Europe, opening the door to all facets of the consciousness of humanity through the twelve aspects of the twelve solar hierarchies. The many millions who have come from Europe and Asia are the people who are destined to become a part of the mandala, or pattern, of the golden age.

The flame of this retreat inspired the creation of the Statue of Liberty. The book she holds is the Book of the Law that is destined to come forth in America, the teachings of the great masters of wisdom, the teachings of the ascended masters.

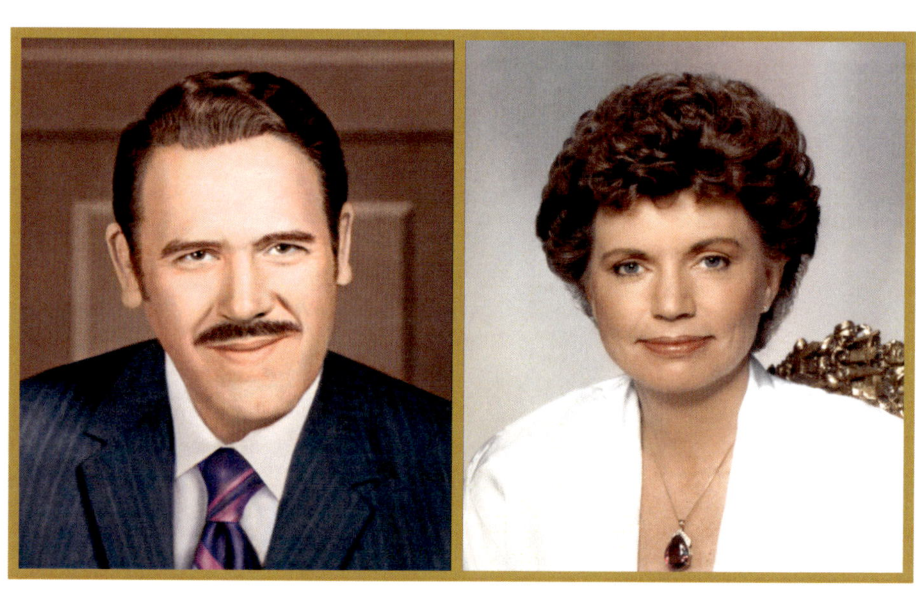

Who Are Mark L. Prophet and Elizabeth Clare Prophet?

For over fifty years, Mark L. Prophet and Elizabeth Clare Prophet served as authors, teachers, and messengers, whose calling was to be prophets of God—one who delivers the Word of God. In this role as messengers, Mark and Elizabeth communed with heavenly beings through the power of the Holy Spirit. Just as in the days of the prophets and apostles, one experiences an element of sacred fire in the messages they delivered to the world.

As you listen to or read the words of these messages, called "dictations," you may well experience a transfer of light that quickens and educates your soul.

Through these two messengers, profound teachings, messages, and prophecies have been released, which present a path and a teaching whereby every individual on earth can find his or her way back to God. As messengers, Mark and Elizabeth saw themselves only as the instruments of God and as the servants of the light to all students on the spiritual path and in all people.

During their mission and ministry, Mark and Elizabeth taught on a wide variety of spiritual subjects: karma and reincarnation, healing and wholeness, soul mates, twin flames and relationships, and practical spirituality, to name just a few. Their books and writings are intended to give everyone the opportunity to know the truth that can set them free. Their great desire has always been to share a path that will take true seekers, in the tradition of the masters of the Far East, as far as they can go and need to go in order to meet their true teachers—the ascended masters and their own Higher Self face-to-face.

As you read about the ascended master Paul the Venetian, you will understand that the purpose of these spiritual teachings and path are to lead the soul to the ascension—the reuniting of the soul into the Presence of the I AM THAT I AM, also called the I AM Presence. There are many souls who have reached this goal and who are therefore called ascended masters.

Mark L. Prophet and Elizabeth Clare Prophet fulfilled their mission as messengers and took their leave from this physical octave in the process of the ascension, leaving behind teachings such as those in this book. There is a banquet of teachings that have been published and are yet to be published, as the mission of the messengers carries on.

Notes*

Foreword

1. I Cor. 12:4–11.

CHAPTER 1: The Art of Loving God Is in the Art of Loving Man

1. I Cor. 13:9, 10.
2. This too shall pass. In a dictation given by the ascended master Daniel Rayborn on October 14, 1963, he explained how we can use the mantra, "This too shall pass!" in times of trial. He said, "Many of you who are at times afflicted by elements of doubt and shadow must recognize the constancy of the sun of your being that shines behind each cloud. You have heard it said that every cloud has a silver lining. But at times these words seem poor consolation to those going through their moments of trial. Men must recognize the need to not necessarily make decisions during moments of trial but to wait until the clouds have rolled away and the cycle has passed. The words 'This too shall pass!' are a fiat of authority that Saint Germain taught me as a mantram. When correctly understood and applied to life, this fiat tends to act as an eraser to wipe the slate of life clean and to remove unwanted pictures from the consciousness. 'This too shall pass!' stated three times and followed by 'The light of God never fails!' three times creates a mantram of Christ consciousness to clean the consciousness of unwanted conditions and to bring forth a positive victory over negative elements that may at times be projected into one's consciousness."

   On April 14, 1995, Elizabeth Clare Prophet gave a lecture on this dictation by Daniel Rayborn, in which she suggested that this mantra be given as follows:

   This too shall pass!
   This too shall pass!
   This too shall pass!

   The Light of God never fails!
   The Light of God never fails!
   The Light of God never fails!

   And the Beloved mighty I AM Presence is that Light!

*N.B. Books listed here are published by Summit University Press unless otherwise noted; available at Store.SummitLighthouse.org. For more information about *Pearls of Wisdom*, see SummitLighthouse.org/Pearls-of-Wisdom-Morya. For more information about the masters in these notes, see *The Masters and Their Retreats;* available at Store.SummitLighthouse.org

3. The ***Master of Paris*** is Chief of the Council of France. He is described as a tall gentleman with courtly grace who made his ascension more than 500 years ago.
4. The recent student unrest. An article in *Encyclopedia Britannica* explains that a student revolt at a Paris suburb campus was soon "joined by a general strike eventually involving some 10 million workers. During much of May 1968, Paris was engulfed in the worst rioting since the Popular Front era in the 1930s, and the rest of France was at a standstill. So serious was the revolt that in late May the French president, Charles de Gaulle, met secretly in Baden-Baden, West Germany, with General Jacques Massu, commander of the French occupation forces, to ensure Massu's support in the event that his troops were needed to retake Paris from the revolutionaries." The mass sit-ins, violent confrontations with police, and strikes across the nation brought hundreds of arrests and hospitalizations. The students and workers had been seeking social change, not a political one. The revolution indeed brought greater freedom of expression and opened the French society to many lasting changes. ("Events of May 1968," by Richard Wolin, at Britannica.com)
5. "We are behind the student revolts." In general, Communist philosophy seeks to undermine capitalism and its societies. In the 1968 revolt in France, the Communists were allied with and in fact were leaders in the workers' unions. Although the revolt began with students, more than 10 million workers joined the protests. When union leaders began to fear what was happening, they pushed the workers to return to work, thereby bringing the workers' strikes to an end.
6. Matt. 24:38; Luke 17:27.
7. Luke 17:26; Matt. 24:39.
8. John 15:1.
9. Gen. 1:26, 27.
10. Prov. 23:7.
11. Rom. 7:19.
12. II Sam. 7:5.
13. Rev. 21:4.

CHAPTER 2: **The Dangers of Astral Allurement**

1. John 10:34.
2. Gen. 1:27.
3. Ps. 17:15.

CHAPTER 3: **The Increase of the Sense of the Beautiful**

1. Luke 19:40.
2. Thomas à Kempis, "For man proposeth, but God disposeth," *The Imitation of Christ,* Book 1, chapter 19. See also Prov. 16:9.

CHAPTER 4: The Matrix of Universal Love

1. I Cor. 13:1, 2, 4.
2. Phil. 2:5.
3. Phil. 2:5.
4. Phil. 2:6–11.
5. John 3:16.
6. John 8:12.
7. Isa. 9:6.
8. Rom. 8:17.
9. Matt. 25:32.
10. Col. 2:9.
11. Heb. 11:3.
12. John 1:14.
13. John 1:14.

CHAPTER 5: The Symmetry of the Christ Mind

1. Heb. 9:23.
2. I Pet. 1:13.
3. I Cor. 3:13–15.
4. Heb. 11:3.
5. Beauty is in the eye of the beholder. Margaret Wolfe Hungerford, *Molly Bawn.*
6. Matt. 19:28.
7. Phil. 3:13, 14.
8. Exod. 13:21.
9. Brihadaranyaka Upanishad.
10. John 8:58.
11. Acts 17:24.

CHAPTER 6: The Mighty Magnet of Universal Love

1. I Chron. 16:34, 41; II Chron. 5:13; 7:3, 6; 20:21; Ezra 3:11; Pss. 118:1–4; 136.
2. Slings of outrageous fortune. William Shakespeare, *Hamlet,* act 3, sc. 1, line 58.
3. Luke 15:11–32.

CHAPTER 7: The Divine Artist Within

1. Matt. 25:14–30.
2. Luke 15:11–32.
3. Heb. 12:1.
4. William Shakespeare, "Each one has his exits and his entrances." *As You Like It,* act 2, sc. 7: "All the world's a stage, / And all the men and women merely players; / They have their exits and their entrances, / And one man in his time plays many parts, / His acts being seven ages."
5. Matt. 27:51.
6. James 1:8.

CHAPTER 8: The Greatest Valentine of All

1. II Cor. 3:18.
2. I Cor. 13:13.

CHAPTER 9: A Dispensation from the Lords of Karma: To Call the Children of God to the Heart of the Mother

1. Dan. 10:19.
2. ***Serapis Bey.*** Chohan of the fourth ray (the white ray) of purity, Serapis Bey is the ascended master who prepares and trains candidates for the ascension. He is the hierarch of the Ascension Temple at Luxor on the Nile River in Egypt. The Temple is part of the etheric retreat at Luxor, which is superimposed upon a physical retreat.
3. Ps. 24:1.
4. The messenger Mark L. Prophet made his ascension on February 26, 1973, and is now called the ascended master Lanello.
5. John 21:6.
6. ***Lord Maitreya.*** An ascended master who holds the office of Cosmic Christ and Planetary Buddha, serving in cosmic hierarchy under Gautama Buddha. He demonstrates the cosmic consciousness of the Christ in all areas of endeavor. Lord Maitreya was the Guru and Initiator of Jesus Christ, and was the one referred to in the Bible as the LORD God in Eden. From ascended levels, he continues to initiate souls on the spiritual path. In the East, Lord Maitreya is known as the Coming Buddha.
7. I Thess. 4:17.
8. Rev. 11:3.

CHAPTER 10: The Beauty of the Cosmic Christ

1. This time of transition refers to the transition between two ages. On July 29, 1973, the messenger Elizabeth Clare Prophet explained, "And so we are

living in a very momentous time, in an hour when the transfer of energies from Pisces to Aquarius has taken place, specifically on February 18, 1973—the passing of the torch from Jesus, the master of the Piscean age, to Saint Germain, the master of the Aquarian age." On this date and within a half hour of each other, Saint Germain delivered a dictation through Mark L. Prophet at the Motherhouse in Santa Barbara, California (which was the final dictation given through Mark), and Jesus delivered a dictation through Elizabeth Clare Prophet at La Tourelle in Colorado Springs, Colorado. In his dictation, Jesus said, "I come, then, and my legions come with me. And I, Jesus the Christ, stand before you to acknowledge this hour that mankind stand at the pinnacle of opportunity, that *open portal to* the divine *unity* that shall come to them by the hand of freedom, by the hand of wisdom, by the hand of service, loving service rendered—by the angels, by the Elohim, by the masters, and by people to people. Precious hearts, ride the crest, the golden wave of light that comes crashing upon the earth with the incoming of Pisces, the mighty hierarchy of water. And so the waters of light, the waters of fire, the golden liquid light floods the earth, washing man clean, scrubbing the pores of his consciousness, of his mind, preparing the way for the fires of freedom. Hierarchies of Aquarius and Pisces rejoice in this alchemical union this day. For at each change of the solar signs there occur the fusions of the mighty hierarchies as air becomes water, as water becomes fire, as fire becomes earth, as earth becomes air, and as air becomes water. And so the cycle goes around the cosmic clock. The torch is passed. And when the hands of the hierarchies grasp the torch, at that moment when both are holding the same torch, there is that fusion, there is that transmutation, there is that alchemy of the marriage of Cana."

After the ascension of Mark Prophet on February 26, 1973, the organization experienced many internal and external changes and challenges, including a great increase in attendees at conferences, the possibility of cataclysm and economic debacle, and preparations for an additional community in the wilderness for the physical and spiritual survival of the teachings. Preparations for the wilderness community were not completed until the purchase of the Royal Teton Ranch in 1981.

2. ***Lord Himalaya*** is the Manu of the fourth root race and the hierarch of the Retreat of the Blue Lotus in the Himalayan mountains, guardian of the ray of the masculine aspect of the Godhead focused directly from the heart of Alpha.
3. ***Vaivasvata Manu*** and his consort are the Manus of the fifth root race. They hold the archetypal pattern for that root race and sponsor the Christic path for all souls of that evolution. He maintains a focus in the Himalayas.
4. On July 1, 1973, at the *Freedom 1973* conference, Helios delivered a dictation in which he entered the atmosphere and said, "I AM Helios! And I have chosen to enter the atmosphere of Earth this day to quicken the

Electronic Presence and the vital power of the atom within every soul evolving upon the planetary body. I am calling Home the atom! I am calling Home the children of the Sun! And I stand forth for the realignment of your bodies in conjunction with the release of Cosmos' secret rays. I come to align the bodies of man and the body of the planet Earth. . . . I AM the God of the Sun, and the Sun is the Christ light. And the emanation of that light from my Presence is great enough to absorb the entire planetary body into the ascension currents. And thus my energies are stepped down this day, that you might receive that just portion which the Lords of Karma have meted out to you, each one. The Woman clothed with the Sun stands before you, and the Manchild is appearing high in the atmosphere as the great cosmic light that descends into the heart of the Mother to be released at the appointed hour for the blessing of all mankind. Vesta is the light of the Mother for this solar system, and together we release the golden pink glow-ray that comes from the very center of the great Cosmic Egg. And as these spirals are now anchored in the planetary body, there shall occur a rejuvenation in hearts of the appreciation of the Woman and her seed. For the archetype of the Divine Mother and of the Christ must appear again and again and again, and thus we impress this pattern upon your very souls as the magnet of her appearing to all life, in all life for the conclusion and the victory of the age."

5. ***Lady Master Venus*** is the twin flame of Sanat Kumara. As Sanat Kumara had kept the flame for earth, she has come to "tarry for a time on terra" to "dedicate anew the fires of the Mother." See chapter 20, p. 275, n. 9.
6. I Cor. 15:52.

CHAPTER 11: **The Art of Living Love**

1. Elizabeth Clare Prophet held the spiritual office of "The Mother of the Flame," which is held by one who is dedicated to the World Mother and who pledges to serve the sons and daughters of the flame wherever they are throughout the world. The Mother of the Flame is an honorary title and an office in hierarchy held successively by unascended feminine devotees appointed by the Great White Brotherhood to nourish, or mother, the flame of life in all mankind. In 1977, the ascended master Padma Sambhava bestowed upon Mrs. Prophet the mantle of Guru and the name "Guru Ma," meaning the teacher who gives adoration to the Divine Mother. Mrs. Prophet is also a mother, not only to her own five children but to thousands throughout the world who call her "Mother" as a term of endearment.
2. Gen. 14:18.
3. ***Mighty Victory*** is a Venusian master whose devotion to the flame of victory for more than a hundred thousand years has given him the authority over that flame through vast reaches of the cosmos. Mighty Victory was one of

the cosmic beings who responded to Saint Germain's call for cosmic assistance to the earth in the 1930s. He has twelve cosmic masters serving with him in addition to legions of angels and ascended beings who focus the consciousness of God's victory and the victorious sense to every soul evolving in the planes of Matter.

CHAPTER 12: The Revolution of Love

1. John 1:5.
2. "The great divorce" may refer to C. S. Lewis's novel by the same name, in which the narrator details his dream vision of both hell and heaven. Mrs. Prophet, on October 10, 1975, used the phrase "the great divorce" in her teaching. She said, "I speak of the great divorce because the souls of mankind, over tens of thousands of years, have been divorced from the inner identity, from nature, hence from the Holy Spirit—from the communion with life in the fiery core of the atom, of the mountains, the hills, the streams, and the waters. . . . We have lost our spiritual senses, our soul senses; they have atrophied. And so our contact is almost nil. And yet, in the first glimmerings of a golden age and in the light of Aquarius, we sense a new soul awareness because the hierarchy of Aquarius and their representative, Saint Germain, governs the chakra of the soul—the seat-of-the-soul chakra—where these sensitivities are developed."
3. That image and that painting. See chapter 11, this volume, pp. 89–90.
4. Colorado Springs refers to The Summit Lighthouse's headquarters in 1975, called La Tourelle, in Colorado Springs, Colorado, which has since been sold.

CHAPTER 13: The Beauty and Truth of Love

1. ***Cyclopea*** is the Elohim of the fifth ray (the emerald-green ray) of science, truth, healing, vision, and abundance. Also known as the Great Silent Watcher, Cyclopea uses the power of the All-Seeing Eye of God to hold the immaculate concept for every individual on this planet and for the entire spiritual-material creation. With his divine counterpart, Virginia, Cyclopea helps mankind and the elementals bring the abundance of God into physical form.
2. See *The Living Flame of Love* in *The Collected Works of St. John of the Cross,* trans. Kieran Kavanaugh and Otilio Rodriguez (Washington, D.C.: ICS Publications, 1973), pp. 569–649.
3. ***Purity and Astrea*** are the Elohim of the fourth ray (the white ray) of purity, perfection, hope and wholeness. It is the flame of the Mother and the flame of the ascension—the desire to know and be God through purity of body, mind, and soul through the consciousness of the Divine Mother, which embraces the natural laws governing all manifestation in the earth plane.

CHAPTER 14: The Face of the Son of Man

1. Rom. 13:8–10.
2. *Dieu et mon droit,* "God and my right." Richard I of England, surnamed *Coeur de Lion* "the Lion Hearted," at the Battle of Gisors in 1198, chose this phrase as his parole, or battle word, meaning that he was not the vassal of France but owed his royalty to God alone. He won a great victory, in honor of which the phrase was instated as the motto of the Royal Arms of England. The motto has also been attributed to Louis XIV of France, the Sun King, who in 1661 broke with tradition and assumed absolute monarchical power. Louis upheld the divine right of kings. He viewed rulership as "a totally divine function" and himself as God's representative on earth.
3. Isa. 66:1.
4. Matt. 20:25–28.
5. Matt. 2:1–18.
6. Matt. 1:18–25.
7. John 8:1–11.
8. John 3:17.
9. ***Gautama Buddha.*** Buddha means "the Enlightened One." Gautama attained the enlightenment of the Buddha in his final incarnation as Siddhartha Gautama (c. 563–483 B.C.). For forty-five years he preached his doctrine of the Four Noble Truths, the Eightfold Path and the Middle Way, which led to the founding of Buddhism. Gautama Buddha presently holds the office of Lord of the World and is the hierarch of Shamballa, an etheric retreat over the Gobi Desert.

   The thoughtform of the year. Each New Year's Eve, the thoughtform for the year is released from the Silent Watcher of this solar system to the Lord of the World, Gautama Buddha, who in turn releases it to earth's unascended evolutions from the Royal Teton Retreat. The thoughtform contains the keys to the outpicturing of the will of God for the planet for the coming twelve-month cycle. The pattern is a nucleus of light, a forcefield of energy that is deemed necessary for the next step of progress, the next level of initiation and release of light to the earth. On December 31, 1979, Gautama gave a dictation for the release of the thoughtform for the year 1980, in which he said, "Out of the inner spheres, out of the Great Central Sun, O my beloved, there comes the sealed light of the thoughtform for the year, as it is accounted in the earth, 1980. Out of the great heart of Sanat Kumara, whose heart is the chalice of Solar Logoi, whose hearts raise up the chalice unto the God of very gods, so there descends the thoughtform that delineates the matrix in the mind of God of that which is to be a year and a decade of integration. The great symbol of life begetting life that I give to your upraised chalices from our dear Lord now appears before us as a mighty, fiery figure eight. And, my beloved, it is a piercing light. And in the inner dimensions of cosmos, it is in all dimensions so spherical. And the movement of light illustrates even the very secrets of the movement of cosmos. Suspended, then, in the upper sphere is the Madonna of the Universal Mother. She is beautiful to behold—God as Mother—and her flowing garments and her light and the cherubim who surround her, and the billowing garments extend gently. And in the lower figure there appears the image of the Manchild, and that Manchild is the Person of the Cosmic Christ. And lo, the fulfillment of the Almighty in this year and the symbol of life is the coming of the Mother and the Child."

10. "Drink Me While I AM Drinking Thee." On November 25, 1979, Sanat Kumara delivered a dictation in which he explained the meaning of these words. He said, "In the inner chamber, called the Upper Room, there is an inscription that is written: 'Drink Me While I AM Drinking Thee.' Those who are received of the Lord on the path of the ruby ray to be partakers of his body and his blood are taught the meaning of this command of the Great Initiator [Lord Maitreya], which has become the mantra of Mother and Maitreya singing in the hearts of the saints. . . . This is the sign of the receiving and the giving of the waters of the Word—the true teachings of Christ."
11. I Cor. 11:3; Eph. 5:22–24, 33.
12. Isa. 54:5.
13. Matt. 20:1–16; 21:33–44.
14. ***Ramakrishna*** (1836–1886) was a nineteenth-century Hindu saint and mystic who is now an ascended master.
15. The ***Maha Kali,*** the Universal Mother, manifests herself in ascended lady masters and cosmic beings and in the sons of light who adore her flame.
16. ***Ishwara*** [Sanskrit for "Lord of the universe" or "Lord"]. In Hinduism, Ishwara is seen as the "immediate personal aspect of the supreme impersonal Godhead." The most widely disseminated form of Ishwara in Hindu thought is that trimurti, the Trinity of Brahma, Vishnu, and Shiva.
17. Rev. 12:5.
18. Acts 2:3.
19. John 15:16.
20. Matt. 25:1–13.

CHAPTER 15: **Message of the Chohan of the Third Ray**

1. Another anthem of the free. During the service preceding this dictation, the messenger read "The Garden of Your Heart," a *Pearl of Wisdom* by Paul the Venetian published in volume 1 of *The Art of Divinity,* chapter 17. Paul the Venetian invites the reader: "Come with me, then, to the garden of your heart. . . . In this garden come apart; / In this garden find your heart; /

In this garden is liberty; / Hear the anthem of the free!" His entire poem has been set to music and is found in the Church Universal and Triumphant's *Book of Hymns and Songs,* song 216, "A Ballad from Beloved Paul the Venetian." In preparation for the dictation, the congregation sang this song.

2. ***Lord Lanto*** is the chohan of the second ray. He volunteered with Sanat Kumara, the Ancient of Days, to come to earth long ago for the rescue of the planet and her evolutions. Lord Lanto embodied in ancient China as the Duke of Chou, also known as the Yellow Emperor (twelfth century B.C.). The Duke of Chou is regarded as one of the greatest statesmen in Chinese history and is considered to be the architect of the Chou dynasty and the true founder of the Confucian tradition. Confucius looked to the Duke as his model and believed it was his mission to reestablish the principles and culture of the early Chou era, which was thought to have been a golden age.
3. Mark 2:22.
4. Montana, here I come. At the time of this dictation, the headquarters of The Summit Lighthouse was in the process of moving to Montana from its previous location in the Santa Monica Mountains, near Malibu, California. This move occurred largely between 1981 and 1987, which included the relocation of many staff and community members.
5. Study groups and teaching centers are outposts of the teachings of the ascended masters in cities throughout the world. For further information see SummitLighthouse.org/about-us/contact-us/.
6. The very first steps of application. Serapis Bey recounted the story of Jesus coming to Serapis' retreat at Luxor as a young man. He said, "I recall full well when the Master Jesus came to Luxor as a very young man that he knelt in holy innocence before the hierophant, refusing all honors that were offered him and asking to be initiated into the first grade of spiritual law and spiritual mystery. No sense of pride marred his visage—no sense of preeminence or false expectation, albeit he could have well expected the highest honors. He chose to take the low road of humility, knowing that it was reserved unto the joy of God to raise him up."
7. Confucius delivered a dictation on August 26, 1982, during the *Retreat of the Seven Chohans of the Rays* at the Inner Retreat titled "Let Us Start." He said, "The Place of Great Encounters is truly the open door where heaven and earth meet and souls define a path of victory in every ray of the sun and every illumination light that is the key now to your heart. Now, in deciding what must be done, one by one, let us take those things that are essential and most important. Let us begin at the beginning. Let us build the school, the Motherhouse, the dormitories and offices whereby we, through you, may conduct our affairs here. It is very obvious, when you see the open land, the immediate limitation by an absence of defining of space for the work at hand. Let us understand that the time is past when

we must gather merely four times a year to know this joy of communion. We would know this communion every day of every year of all of our life and our becoming! Why should we be separated anymore? The land is plenteous, and you may surely determine how you may perform your dharma under the canopy of the Buddha's Shamballa, how you may come and therefore interact and attract the light that shall be for the liberation of souls."

8. The ascended lady master ***Magda*** is the twin flame of Jesus. She serves from the Temple of the Resurrection Flame with Jesus and Mary. Magda was embodied as Mary Magdalene, out of whom Jesus cast seven demons.
9. Teachings of the Mother on habit. See Magda and Jesus, "Believability: A Message to the American Woman," 1982 *Pearls of Wisdom,* vol. 25, no. 24.
10. A two-day seminar, *On the Mother,* was held November 27–28, 1981. The messenger lectured on Jesus and Kuthumi's teachings on "Habit" from *Corona Class Lessons* during this seminar. The contents of the original album is available at AscendedMasterLibrary.org. To stream or create a playlist, search albums for *On the Mother 1.* Events span from November 26, 1981, to December 7, 1981.
11. John 2:1–11.
12. ***Pallas Athena,*** the Goddess of Truth, is a tremendous being of light who ensouls the cosmic consciousness of Truth. The flame of truth is an intense bright emerald green. It combines the flaming blue power of God's will and the brilliant golden illumination of the intelligence of God. Her presence in the universe is the exaltation of the flame of living Truth. This truth she holds on behalf of the evolutions of earth as a member of the Karmic Board, where she serves as the representative on the fifth ray of truth, healing, supply, and precipitation.

CHAPTER 16: **The Art of Love**

1. I John 4:18.
2. Luke 21:26.
3. As you have been discussing this evening. Prior to this dictation, the messenger delivered a lecture on terrorism in the United States, which included videoclips and news reports as well as a discussion on the lack of awareness in government representatives concerning astral forces of absolute Evil working through international terrorists. For a more thorough discussion of absolute Evil in the forces of Antichrist and the fallen angels, see Archangel Gabriel, *Mysteries of the Holy Grail,* and Elizabeth Clare Prophet, *Fallen Angels and the Origins of Evil;* both available at Store.SummitLighthouse.org.
4. Norman Rockwell was an American painter and illustrator (1894–1978).
5. The poem that is "lovely as a tree." Poet Joyce Kilmer (1886–1918) wrote the poem "Trees" in 1913, which reads:

I think that I shall never see
A poem lovely as a tree.
A tree whose hungry mouth is prest
Against the earth's sweet flowing breast;
A tree that looks at God all day,
And lifts her leafy arms to pray;
A tree that may in summer wear
A nest of robins in her hair;
Upon whose bosom snow has lain;
Who intimately lives with rain.
Poems are made by fools like me,
But only God can make a tree.

6. John 13:34; 15:12.
7. Dictations by the seven chohans. Elizabeth Clare Prophet said, "A chela must understand that he is earning God-mastery on each of the seven rays. Just one of these rays will not suffice. We have to have the balance of the seven rays to move on. We have to have friendship, love, interaction, and a figure-eight flow with the lords of the seven rays. They each embody a specific ray and the law of that ray. They initiate us in our chakras." See Prophet, *Lords of the Seven Rays.*
8. ***Krishna*** is a divine being, an incarnation of the Godhead, an avatar, and he is one of the most celebrated Indian heroes of all time. Krishna is known as the eighth incarnation of Vishnu, the Second Person of the Hindu Triad. His story is told in the Bhagavad Gita, the most popular religious work of India, composed between the fifth and second centuries B.C. and part of the great Indian epic, the Mahabharata.
9. "I have decided to save the earth." On July 4, 1976, the Goddess of Liberty gave a dictation titled "A Report from the Lords of Karma," in which she said, "I adore liberty, I live in liberty, and I send forth liberty to all. . . . Suffice it to be that God has decided to save the earth. And when you ask how and why and where and who, the answer is: 'Through you!' My love to you. My wisdom to you. And all of my power, yours to command. Let us see now what the Lords of Karma can do to draw you into that starry light, that focus of the Son of God. Let us see what the Lords of Karma will do as we see once again what you will do when you go forth in the flame of victory."
10. The ***Keeper of the Scrolls*** is a cosmic being in charge of the akashic records of this galaxy, the impressions of all that has ever transpired in the planes of Matter. He has said, "I am here to tell you that there is not one jot nor one tittle of energy that passes through any of your lifestreams that is not recorded on the eternal scrolls. Fortunately, by the power of the sacred fire and the love of beloved Saint Germain, there has been established a special

qualification of the cosmic law whereby those who use the violet fire faithfully have an erasing action that takes place on the scrolls. And through the action of the violet flame, their karma is removed almost as soon as it is created."

11. Heb. 13:2.
12. The threefold flame anchored in the Washington Monument. In a dictation given in Washington, D.C., September 30, 1962, the ascended master K-17 announced: "There has been held a beautiful and wonderful session at Chananda's retreat in India... and a decision was made on the part of beloved Paul the Venetian whereby there was transferred from his retreat in France this day, at the hour of eleven o'clock your time, the full pulsation of the great liberty flame. This flame was permanently placed within the forcefield of the Washington Monument. And the pulsations of the liberty flame are intended to grace the heart of America as a gift from the Brotherhood and from the heart of beloved Paul the Venetian.... It is given as a treasure from the heart of France, from the spiritual government of France to the spiritual government of America.... The liberty flame is a gift of greater magnitude than the former gift of France, the Statue of Liberty, as a tribute to that great being, the Goddess of Liberty. It is incomparable, for the flame itself shall penetrate the structure of the monument, rising high into the atmosphere above it, and all who visit there shall become, even without knowing it, infused by the pulsations of the liberty flame within the heart of America."
13. In the heart of Helios. On July 4, 1984, during the Freedom conference, *The Flame of Freedom Speaks,* beloved Helios gave a dictation titled "Our Refuge and Our Strength." This conference was held from June 29 to July 9, 1984, in the Heart of the Inner Retreat at the Royal Teton Ranch, Park County, Montana. See 1984 *Pearls of Wisdom,* vol. 27, no. 48B.

CHAPTER 17: The Seven Chakras Must Blossom

Love's Mystery

1. Matt. 5:6.
2. The call to be mediators. In a dictation given on May 28, 1987, Jesus said, "Recognize, then, that the call to be the divine Mediator must be answered ere the earth changes that must come about take their toll in a cataclysmic way or perhaps in war, even that war prophesied by my Mother at Fátima."
3. He called me. See Acts 9:3–16. For further teaching on the embodiments of the ascended master Hilarion, see Prophet, *Lords of the Seven Rays,* Book One, chapter 5.
4. Eph. 5:14.
5. The path of the ascension. On May 28, 1987, Jesus said, "You have

descended from the All that is Real. Now *defend* the All that is Real. For this place, North America, is a land promised to you long ago, which through my heart, called the Sacred Heart by certain of the Christian devotees, has been consecrated unto the path of the ascension."

6. Ps. 2:1; Acts 4:25.
7. The last time. In a dictation given on December 31, 1986, Gautama Buddha said, "People of Earth, it is the last time. This master of light [Saint Germain] therefore comes in a final intercession in a final hour. May the children of the Sun run to greet him with Portia standing in the seventh ray waiting to take you each one by the hand." See I John 2:18.

CHAPTER 18: The Initiation of Hearts

1. Eph. 5:26.
2. Heb. 13:2.
3. Mu, or Lemuria, was the lost continent of the Pacific, which, according to the findings of James Churchward, archaeologist and author of *The Lost Continent of Mu,* extended from north of Hawaii three thousand miles, south to Easter Island and the Fijis, and was made up of three areas of land stretching more than five thousand miles from east to west. For more information, see "Lemuria, or Mu" in the Glossary, p. 286.
4. The Tablets of *Mem.* The etheric, or memory, body contains the Tablets of *Mem* (memory), the electronic, computerized recordings of all vibrations and energy impulses ever sent forth through the soul and its higher and lower vehicles. This life record (the L-field) is written on innumerable discs of light that comprise the changing, evolving identity pattern of the soul merging with the Spirit. It determines the patterns that will be outpictured in the three lower vehicles—the mental body, the desire body, and the physical body. Only the violet flame can permanently alter the effect by thoroughly transmuting the cause. For further teaching, see Serapis Bey, *Dossier on the Ascension,* pp. 87–88; also Mark L. Prophet and Elizabeth Clare Prophet, *Climb the Highest Mountain,* pp. 350–51.
5. Transferring the flames of the temples. See Prophet, *Lords of the Seven Rays: Seven Masters: Their Past Lives and Keys to Our Future;* (paperback) pp. 77, 117, 119, 139, 492; (trade size) pp. 59, 87–88, 90, 103, 383.
6. Pss. 6:3; 79:5; Rev. 6:10.
7. Gen. 14:18; Ps. 110:4; Heb. 5:5–10; 6:20; 7.
8. James 1:21.

CHAPTER 19: An Appreciation of the Heart

1. II Pet. 3:10, 12.
2. The being called the ***Buddha of the Ruby Ray*** has the buddhic mastery of the

ruby ray, an intense action of divine love. He was sent long ago by Sanat Kumara and Gautama Buddha to abide in the secret chamber of God in the heart of the earth. In 1989, Cuzco announced that the Buddha of the Ruby Ray, in answer to the call of the Keepers of the Flame, had literally walked step-by-step from the center of the earth to be present and to assist us in dealing with the negative forces at hand. This Buddha has angels of fiery intensity who maintain a cave of ruby light in the heart of the earth beneath the Royal Teton Ranch. His angels are available at all times to cut away and purge the density brought about by improper diet, poor choices in music, improper consciousness, and the saturation of the mind with entities.

3. The ***Five Dhyani Buddhas*** are celestial Buddhas visualized during meditation. The word *dhyani* is derived from the Sanskrit *dhyana,* meaning "meditation." The Dhyani Buddhas are considered to be great healers of the mind and soul. They are not historical figures like Gautama Buddha, but transcendent beings who symbolize universal divine principles or forces. Each Dhyani Buddha is associated with certain attributes and symbols. Each one embodies one of the five wisdoms, which antidote the five deadly poisons that are of ultimate danger to man's spiritual progress and keep him tied to worldly existence.
4. ***Padma Sambhava*** (fl. A.D. 8th century), whose name means "born of the lotus," is revered as the Great Guru of Tibetan Buddhism. According to a manuscript written by one of his feminine disciples, Ye-she-Tsho-gyal (lit., "victorious one of the ocean of wisdom"), the coming of Padma Sambhava was foretold by Gautama Buddha at his passing: "Twelve years after my departure, from a lotus blossom on the Dhanakosha Lake, in the northwestern corner of the country of Urgyan, there will be born one who will be much wiser and more spiritually powerful than myself. He will be called Padma Sambhava, and by him the Esoteric Doctrine will be established." (Mystery has surrounded his birth and death; some accounts record that the Great Guru lived for over 3,000 years.) Although much of the life and work of Padma Sambhava is obscured in legend, he was famed for his mystical powers and mastery of the occult sciences. In 746–47, by invitation of the Tibetan king Thi-Srong-Detsan, he traveled from India to Tibet, where he founded the Nyingmapa school of Buddhism. Under royal patronage, he converted the country to Tantric Buddhism, elevating the people from barbarism to spirituality. According to tradition, Padma Sambhava taught that his "Golden Mantra," OM AH HUM VAJRA GURU PADMA SIDDHI HUM, was to be used in a coming time of troubles, during which warfare, disease, and poverty would increase, as an antidote to the confusion and frustration of that dark age. Each word of the mantra is given with a different mudra. See Elizabeth Clare Prophet, *The Lost Teachings of Jesus and Maitreya on Your Divine Reality,* February 14, 1988; available at AscendedMasterLibrary.org; search albums.

5. The messenger has explained that the Five Dhyani Buddhas correspond to the five secret rays, which are placed on the cosmic clock on the axes of the half hours, from 7:30 through 11:30.

CHAPTER 20: **Love: The Age-Old Solution**

1. The focus of the threefold flame in the obelisk in Washington, D.C. See chapter 16, p. 271, n. 12.
2. The Temple of the Sun is the retreat of the Goddess of Liberty on the etheric plane over Manhattan Island, New York. It is one of the most important retreats on the planet. The Goddess of Liberty focuses the flame of liberty, the fleur-de-lis of pink, blue, and gold (also known as the threefold flame), on the central altar, which is surrounded by twelve shrines dedicated to the twelve hierarchies of the Sun. For more information, see "An Invitation to Visit Paul the Venetian's Etheric Retreats," pp. 249–55 of this volume.
3. The decrees of divine love are printed in the pink section of *Prayers, Meditations and Dynamic Decrees for Personal and World Transformation* and is available at Store.SummitLighthouse.org.
4. "Sacred Ritual for Transport and Holy Work" is Ashram Ritual 5 in *Ashram Notes,* a series of letters from El Morya to his students worldwide, which assists the soul in performing world service while out of the body during the hours of rest. *Ashram Notes* and the companion *Ashram Rituals* booklet or CD are available at Store.SummitLighthouse.org.
5. Ashram rituals are spoken meditations from El Morya designed to simultaneously "link hearts worldwide for the union of consciousness." Mark L. Prophet writes, "The Ashram of Morya El is one answer to the call of unascended lifestreams who desire to reduce world suffering and serve the cause of world awakening."
6. Opportunity for elementals to earn a threefold flame. In a dictation on June 30, 1988, the Elohim Heros and Amora promised the elementals that they could earn a threefold flame by assisting the sons and daughters of God. Addressing the elementals, Heros and Amora said, "Those whom you . . . serve who do attain the ascension . . . shall in turn endow you with a threefold flame. . . . For all of your giving and all of your service, the hour draws nigh when those to whom you have given so much may turn and give to you what they have long desired to give."
7. Jesus' gift of the resurrection flame to elemental life. In a dictation given March 29, 1964, Jesus Christ announced that he was endowing elemental life with the flame of his momentum of the resurrection and that from that day forward, the elementals would "never again have the sense of death." Jesus said, "They shall feel my flame always. A portion of that flame resting in them shall remove for all time immemorial all that fear that they have outpictured."

8. The conclusion of the year 2002. In this period of transition from the Piscean to the Aquarian age, the Great Law requires that the evolutions of planet Earth deal directly with the momentums of personal and planetary karma set aside for centuries by the grace of God through his Sons incarnate (i.e., Jesus Christ and other avatars). In the face of the same propensity for darkness prevalent before the Flood, when "the wickedness of man was great in the earth" and "every imagination of the thoughts of his heart was only evil continually," (Gen. 6:5) the Lords of Karma decreed this action in order to deter an even greater abuse of life's opportunity and to forestall that cataclysm which may be the ultimate consequence of the rising tide of world sin. On August 20, 1969, the messengers explained that "the coming of the Dark Cycle simply means that the hand of mercy that for centuries has stood between mankind and their own dark deeds has been withdrawn. The law of God will bring swift and compelling judgment to those who have thought they could flaunt the Law." Be not deceived; God is not mocked: for whatsoever a man soweth, that shall he also reap. (Gal. 6:7) The Dark Cycle began on April 23, 1969, and concluded on April 22, 2002.
9. ***Sanat Kumara*** (the Ancient of Days in Daniel 7:9, 13, 22), accompanied by 144,000 lightbearers, volunteered to come to earth and keep the threefold flame of life on behalf of earth's evolutions in an hour when the ignoring of the God flame within their hearts and their failure to fulfill their reason for being had caused the Cosmic Council to decree the dissolution of earth. On January 1, 1956, Sanat Kumara returned to his home star, Venus, and on May 25, 1975, Lady Master Venus announced that she had come to "tarry for a time on Terra" to "dedicate anew the fires of the Mother" while Sanat Kumara keeps the flame on Venus.
10. Matt. 21:44; Luke 20:18.
11. James 1:17.
12. Descend the spiral staircase for thirty-three consecutive nights. On New Year's Eve, December 31, 1992, prior to this dictation by Paul the Venetian, Lanello gave a dictation in which he said, "The Holy Spirit *is* the Great Multiplier, beloved. Therefore understand that when your heart is a well of living fire, the multiplication of that fire is also infinite. But if there be lurking somewhere in the folds of the garment of the unconscious indeed a force of anti-love neglected, left there long ago, which you have since sought to transmute but you have not—if this be the case, beloved, there is also a multiplication, by your tie to the Great White Brotherhood, of that substance. . . . Be the deep-sea diver! Go down to those levels and ask to be taken this night not to retreats but to the caverns and canyons of your own subconscious and astral body and the unconscious, beloved. For this is the place that you must now revisit. . . . I wish to quicken the memory, and I wish you to offer the prayer and use this call, beloved. And this is the way it goes:"

Call to Lanello to Descend the Spiral Staircase

I call now to my beloved Lanello, my mentor of the Spirit. I call to El Morya, Archangel Michael, and the Lords of Karma, my own Holy Christ Self and I AM Presence and all who assist me on my way.

Take me now, O holy ones of God, down the spiral staircase into the depths of the subconscious, the electronic belt, the astral plane, and the unconscious. Take me there, O God! With covering cherubim guide my feet, guide my heart and mind.

Therefore I ask for the armour of seraphim and of Archangel Michael and for the helmet and shield of the Lord and the sword of blue flame. And I ask to be guided by the Maha Chohan as to what I may be delivered of, and I would perform that exorcism under the living Christ Jesus, my Lord.

I call, then, that day by day for thirty-three days I shall achieve the undoing of those substances that dwell within me and that will not speed me on my way to the glorious God-freedom that I seek but will only hold me back.

And therefore, O God, I surrender that portion of myself that helps neither you nor me. And I ask that I might be cut free from all individuals that I have ever been a part of where the will of God dictates that I ought to be cut free. And I ask to help those whom I may help and to remain tied to those with whom I should remain tied to, according to the will of God. And I call for the balancing of all karma by the violet flame.

It is my deep desire, O mighty I AM Presence, that I might be delivered of excess baggage now, that I might become a better servant of the Lord Sanat Kumara, and that I might be free to help others—free of the schisms in my own psyche, free of all encumbrances of the human consciousness so that I need not withhold the perfect gift to anyone, friend or foe or stranger, who does knock at my door.

I commend this prayer to the heart of God for adjudication. And I pray for the dividing of the way of the Real and the unreal within myself, that Victory might have his day through me.

As a humble pilgrim on life's way, I seal my prayer this day, O God.

God, help me! God, help me! God, help me!

13. The retreat of the Divine Mother is in the etheric octave in the Rocky Mountains on the northern border of Yellowstone National Park. The physical focus of the retreat is the Royal Teton Ranch, a property secured by students of the masters under their guidance as an outer focus of the Great White Brotherhood.

14. That which you have written about to the Lords of Karma. The Lords of Karma meet at the Royal Teton Retreat biannually, at the turn of the year and at summer solstice, to review petitions from unascended devotees and to grant dispensations for their assistance. Traditionally, students of the ascended masters write personal petitions to the Karmic Board on New Year's Eve and the Fourth of July, requesting dispensations and sponsorship for constructive purposes. In handwritten, sealed letters that are consecrated at the altar and then burned, students offer their service upon the altar of God and ask for divine intercession in their personal lives, the community of the Holy Spirit, the nation, and the world. The letters are delivered to the Royal Teton Retreat on the etheric plane, where they are read and acted upon by the Lords of Karma.

CHAPTER 21: The Love of God Is the Divine Solution

1. Freedom 1993: *Healing the Earth* was a conference held from June 25 to July 4, 1993, at the Royal Teton Ranch, Park County, Montana.
2. Exod. 2:11, 12.

CHAPTER 22: Love Is the Great Challenge

1. Isa. 40:1.

CHAPTER 23: Walk in the Flame of Divine Love

1. *Love Meditations.* Originally a cassette album of prayers, affirmations, and music for the healing of the heart, these devotions are available on a CD album, *Decrees and Songs of the Third Ray,* at Store.SummitLighthouse.org, or as a download at AscendedMasterLibrary.org.
2. I Pet. 5:8.
3. Matt. 25:21, 23.
4. The Lords of Karma have given a dispensation whereby the ascension can be achieved by balancing 51 percent or more of one's karma while in embodiment, with the remaining 49 percent balanced after one's ascension.
5. Matt. 10:6–8.
6. Choosing three chohans to apprentice under. On April 16, 1995, El Morya said, "Before you can become a direct disciple of the Holy Spirit under the Maha Chohan, you must submit yourself to the paths of the seven chohans, and master at least three of those paths, one of which must be the path of the first ray under me. The chohans who preside over the other two paths of your choosing may accept you, whether as a preferred chela or a beginning student, or they may tell you to diligently follow the path taught by the messengers until you may be invited to be directly under the tutelage of one or both of these chohans. I exercise the same discretion."

7. A remembering of responsibilities. On June 26, 1995, prior to this dictation by Paul the Venetian, the Maha Chohan said, "If the would-be chela cannot remember for a moment or a day a promise that he has made to God or a promise that God has made to him, then I say, what a pity!"
8. The flower remedies. See the teachings of Edward Bach, M.D., and F. J. Wheeler, M.D., in *The Bach Flower Remedies* (New Canaan, Conn.: Keats Publishing, 1979). See also Mechthild Scheffer, *Bach Flower Therapy: Theory and Practice,* trans. A. R. Meuss (Rochester, Vt.: Healing Arts Press, 1988).

CHAPTER 24: **Gain the Immortality of Your Soul**

1. Ruth Hawkins, the twin flame of Paul the Venetian and a long-standing Keeper of the Flame, made her ascension in October 1995 at the age of eighty-eight. Her maiden dictation immediately followed this dictation by Paul the Venetian.
2. *Rex and Nada, Bob and Pearl* are ascended master youth who lived in the twentieth century in the United States. They received the initiations for the ascension under the auspices of the Great Divine Director, Saint Germain, Lady Master Leto, and the messengers Godfre and Lotus in the 1930s. For more on Rex and Nada, Bob and Pearl, see Godfré Ray King, *The Magic Presence* (Chicago: Saint Germain Press, 1935).
3. The messenger Elizabeth Clare Prophet conducted guided soul retrieval meditations at quarterly conferences between the years 1995 and 1998. Currently the ritual of soul retrieval is conducted at each quarterly conference using the messenger's videotaped meditations. Archangel Michael has explained the need for the ritual of soul retrieval, saying, "Inevitably, during the centuries of human history, you have engaged in many wars and battles. In the course of these confrontations, you have literally lost fragments of your soul, the result being that today your soul is not whole and therefore she must be restored to wholeness through the exercise of the spoken Word. By invoking the Great Central Sun Magnet, the messenger magnetizes back to the lawful owner soul particles that have been lost or stolen. However, it then becomes the soul's responsibility to hold on to the retrieved particles. But if for want of sufficient momentum of the sacred fire, the soul does not have the necessary magnetism to hold the particles in her orbit, she may lose the very particles she was able to salvage through the messenger's invoking the Great Central Sun Magnet."
4. Maldek, once a planet in our solar system, was destroyed when its lifewaves waged a war ending in nuclear annihilation.
5. For further teaching on the laggard civilizations, see Prophet, *Climb the Highest Mountain,* "The Coming of the Laggards"; the Great Divine Director, 1965 *Pearls of Wisdom,* vol. 8, nos. 3–26, "The Mechanization Concept";

and the Great Divine Director, 1974 *Pearls of Wisdom,* vol. 17, nos. 5–6, "The Future of a Planet Read from the Scroll of Cosmic History."

CHAPTER 26: The Call of Serapis

1. The seven temples of the seven Holy Kumaras. San Francisco is sometimes referred to as being built on seven hills, which are usually listed as Telegraph Hill, Nob Hill, Russian Hill, Rincon Hill, Twin Peaks, Mount Davidson, and either Lone Mountain or Mount Sutro. In July 1979, the messenger taught, "Every time you look out at the Pacific Ocean you're really looking at the place where the lost continent of Lemuria was, where the Mother was. San Francisco was a great city of light, and the seven hills of San Francisco in the days of Lemuria held focuses of the seven Holy Kumaras."
2. The ***Goddess of Purity*** focuses the flame of Cosmic Christ purity in her service to the evolutions of earth. From her retreat over Madagascar, where the flame of purity has been sustained for thousands of years, angels of purity carry light rays to the four corners of the earth. The Goddess of Purity also holds the focus of one of the ancient temples of Lemuria that was located in the city of the seven hills, where San Francisco now is. This is a magnificent etheric retreat, and the intensity of the flame of purity that is focused there is beyond what man can imagine. This retreat was established hundreds of thousands of years ago. It is a focus of the Mother flame of Mu as well as a focus of the ascension flame.
3. The recent earthquake. On August 6, 1979, a magnitude 5.7 earthquake occurred on the Calaveras Fault near Coyote Lake, in Santa Clara County, California. Although the shock was felt in the San Francisco Bay area, the damage was limited to the nearby towns of Gilroy and Hollister, and no deaths were reported.
4. Matt. 10:38; 16:24; Mark 8:34; 10:21; Luke 9:23; 14:27.
5. Matt. 11:30.
6. The political and economic theories of Karl Marx and Friedrich Engels were later developed by their followers to form the basis for the theory and practice of Communism.
7. John 21:16, 17.
8. The path of the ruby ray is being revealed by Sanat Kumara. These teachings are published in *The Opening of the Seventh Seal: Sanat Kumara on the Path of the Ruby Ray* by Elizabeth Clare Prophet. Available at Store.Summit Lighthouse.org.
9. Camelot was the name of the community founded by the ascended masters in California's Santa Monica Mountains near Malibu. It was a unique experiment in community life, where parents, children, and people of all ages could come together to share in the joys and challenges of the spiritual path.

Camelot served as international headquarters for The Summit Lighthouse and Church Universal and Triumphant beginning in 1978. In 1986 the community of Camelot moved to the organization's new headquarters, the Royal Teton Ranch, in southwest Montana.

10. The leaves of the judgment book unfold. Paul the Venetian quotes from "Bedouin Song" by American-born poet Bayard Taylor (1825–1878).

An Invitation to Visit Paul the Venetian's Etheric Retreats

1. Words by Emma Lazarus, from "The New Colossus."

Glossary

Art of Divinity

Akashic records. All that transpires in an individual's world is recorded in a substance and dimension known as *akasha.* These records can be read by adepts or those whose soul faculties are developed. An ascended master or an unascended adept can look at a record just the way an archaeologist would look through layers of the earth. They can look through layers of records and pinpoint any age or time since the earth was created and read the record of what happened at that particular point in time and space, both personal and planetary.

Ascension. The ascension is the culmination of the soul's God-victorious sojourn in time and space, often through many lifetimes, and is the ritual whereby the soul reunites with the Spirit of the living God, the I AM Presence. The path of the ascension is a spiritual acceleration of consciousness and a process that follows the natural course of spiritual evolution. All of the thoughts, feelings, and deeds from the present and past lives count toward or against the ascension. In taking progressive steps on the spiritual path, the Christed one ultimately finds his way back to the heart of God and enters eternal life.

Astral plane. The astral plane, or astral realm, is the frequency of time and space immediately above physical matter, yet below the mental plane and corresponding to the emotional body of man and the collective unconscious of the race. It is the repository of mankind's thoughts and feelings, conscious and unconscious. Because the astral plane has been muddied by impure thought and feeling, the term *astral* is often used in a negative context to refer to that which is impure or psychic.

Atlantis. The island continent that existed where the Atlantic Ocean now is and that sank in cataclysm (the Flood of Noah) approximately 11,600 years ago, as calculated by James Churchward. Atlantis has been vividly depicted by Plato, "seen" and described by Edgar Cayce in his readings, recalled in scenes from Taylor Caldwell's *Romance of Atlantis,* and scientifically explored and authenticated by the late German scientist Otto Muck. The history of Atlantis is also told by W. Scott-Elliot in *The Story of Atlantis and the Lost Lemuria,* based on clairvoyant readings by students of Theosophy who were trained by the adepts Morya and Kuthumi, and anthropological discoveries.

Bodhisattva. A Sanskrit term meaning literally a being of *bodhi* (or enlightenment), a being destined for enlightenment, or one whose energy and power is directed toward enlightenment. A bodhisattva is one who is destined to become a Buddha but has foregone the bliss of nirvana with a vow to save all sentient beings on earth. In the Mahayana school of Buddhism, becoming a bodhisattva is the goal of the Path. The path of the bodhisattva is generally divided into ten stages, called *bhumis.* The bodhisattva strives to progress from one stage to the next until he obtains enlightenment.

Causal body. The causal body of man surrounds the I AM Presence as the chalice for all good that the individual has elected to qualify in word, thought, and deed since the moment of creation, when the blueprint of the soul's identity was sealed in the fiery core of the God Self. (For more information, see the Chart of Your Divine Self, volume 1, p. 245.)

Chakra. Sanskrit for "wheel," "disc," "circle"; a term used to denote the centers of light anchored in the etheric body and governing the flow of energy to the four lower bodies of man. There are seven major chakras corresponding to the seven rays, five minor chakras corresponding to the five secret rays, and a total of 144 light centers in the body of man.

Chohan. The Tibetan word *chohan* means "lord, master, chief." Each of the seven rays has a chohan who focuses the Christ consciousness of the ray, which is the law of the ray governing its righteous use in man. The seven rays are light emanations of the Godhead, i.e., the seven rays of the white light that emerge through the prism of the Christ consciousness. Each ray focuses a frequency, or color, and has specific qualities. The first ray (blue) focuses faith, will, power, perfection, protection. The second ray (yellow) focuses wisdom, understanding, enlightenment, illumination. The third ray (pink) focuses compassion, kindness, charity, love, beauty. The fourth ray (white) focuses purity, discipline, order, joy. The fifth ray (green) focuses truth, science, healing, music, abundance, vision. The sixth ray (purple and gold) focuses ministration, service, peace, brotherhood. The seventh ray (violet) focuses freedom, mercy, justice, transmutation, forgiveness.

Cosmic Council. A court of appeal beyond the Lords of Karma. They function in grander spheres or dimensions and work with the Four and Twenty Elders. The Cosmic Council is known as the council of the one hundred and forty-four.

Cosmic clock. The science of the cosmic clock is a means for the charting of the cycles of our lives. It is not traditional astrology. It is an inner astrology whereby we can chart the cycles of our karma and be the master of our fate, our cycles, and our destiny. It also allows us to chart the cycles of our dharma and to fulfill our reason for being. As the wheel of the cosmic clock turns day by day and we experience the cycles of our tests and initiations in life, an awareness of this science can help us pass these tests. For more detailed teaching on how to chart your own personal cycles on the cosmic clock, see Elizabeth Clare Prophet, *Predict Your Future: Understand the Cycles of the Cosmic Clock;* available at Store.Summitlighthouse.org.

Darjeeling Council. A council of the Great White Brotherhood with El Morya as its chief and headquartered at his etheric retreat in Darjeeling, India, consists of ascended masters and unascended chelas. Members include Mother Mary, Kuan Yin, Archangel Michael, the Great Divine Director, Serapis Bey, Kuthumi, Djwal Kul, and numerous others whose objective is to train souls for world service in God-government and the economy, through international relations and the establishment of the inner Christ as the foundation for religion, education, and a return to golden-age culture in music and the arts.

Deathless solar body. Known as the wedding garment (Matt. 22:11, 12) that the soul must wear if she is to enter into the alchemical marriage—the soul's permanent bonding to the Holy Christ Self—and the ritual of the ascension.

Divine blueprint. That which is etched upon one's soul as one's own unique identity, one's own fiery destiny.

Divine Image. See Real Image.

Eightfold Path. Also called the Middle Way; the message Gautama Buddha taught in his first sermon and that is still the cornerstone of Buddhism today, which includes the Four Noble Truths and the Eightfold Path. The Four Noble Truths are:

(1) that life is *dukkha,* "suffering"
(2) that the cause of this suffering is *tanha,* "desire" or "craving"
(3) that suffering will cease when the craving that causes it is forsaken and overcome
(4) that the way to this liberation is through living the noble Eightfold Path, which consists of:

Right Understanding or Views
Right Thought or Aspiration
Right Speech

Right Action or Conduct
Right Livelihood
Right Effort
Right Mindfulness
Right Concentration or Absorption

Gautama explained that by avoiding the extremes of self-indulgence and self-mortification, one gains knowledge of the "middle path," which leads to insight, wisdom, calmness, knowledge, enlightenment, and nirvana. He advocated the Middle Way because he had learned from his own experience that the two extremes of sensual indulgence and harsh asceticism do not lead to liberation.

Etheric. Of or relating to the highest plane of the Matter cosmos, i.e., the heaven-world. The etheric frequency and its correspondent plane of consciousness is the repository of the fiery blueprint of the entire physical universe.

Etheric cities and retreats. See Universities of the Spirit.

Five secret rays. The five secret rays represent a going within for the mastery of God consciousness, whereas the seven outer rays represent the coming out and the mastery of the environment. These cycles are a pattern of the going within and the coming out—the Eastern teachings, going within; the Western teachings, coming out.

Four and Twenty Elders. The Four and Twenty Elders are described in the Book of Revelation: "And round about the throne were four and twenty seats: and upon the seats I saw four and twenty elders sitting, clothed in white raiment; and they had on their heads crowns of gold." (Rev. 4:4. See also Rev. 4:10, 11; 5:5–14; 7:11–17; 11:15–18; 14:1–3; 19:4.) They are twelve pairs of twin flames representing the twelve hierarchies of the Sun in the masculine and feminine power/wisdom/love of Elohim. This council of cosmic beings presides with Sanat Kumara at the Court of the Sacred Fire on the God Star, Sirius (the seat of God-government in this sector of our galaxy), as instruments of the judgment of Almighty God. In approximately 2000 B.C., we entered the age of Aries. Two thousand years ago we entered the age of Pisces, and we have now entered the age of Aquarius. Passing through each of the twelve signs of the zodiac, there is a dispensation from the Great Central Sun whereby the Four and Twenty Elders and the Four Cosmic Forces impart to the evolutions of the planet a new awareness of self in relationship to a new awareness of God.

Four Cosmic Forces. The Four Cosmic Forces sustain the vision of the LORD God Almighty as universal awareness of the Creator within the creation. Full of eyes before and behind, the Four Cosmic Forces are perpetually stepping down the light of Solar Logoi, cosmic messengers of Alpha and Omega positioned in the flaming yods of the galaxies. Thus by their six wings, the three and three, and the three-times-three, they render the light, the energy of the Word, intelligible to electrons small and great in man and beast, vegetable and mineral. (See Prophet, *The Opening of the Seventh Seal,* chapter 4.)

Fourfold consciousness of man. The four sheaths consisting of four distinct frequencies that surround the soul—the physical, emotional, mental, and etheric—providing vehicles for the soul in her journey through time and space. The etheric sheath, highest in vibration, is the gateway to the three higher bodies, which are the Christ Self, the I AM Presence, and the causal body.

Great Central Sun. Also called the Great Hub; the center of cosmos; the point of integration of the Spirit-Matter cosmos; the point of origin of all physical-spiritual creation; the nucleus, or white-fire core, of the Cosmic Egg.

Great Karmic Board. Eight ascended beings who are responsible for dispensing justice to this system of worlds are known as the Lords of Karma. They adjudicate karma, mercy, and judgment for the lifestreams of earth, who must pass before the Karmic Board before and after each embodiment. The Karmic Board includes seven ascended beings who serve on the seven rays, plus the Dhyani Buddha Vairochana. The members of the Karmic Board are the Great Divine Director, the Goddess of Liberty, Lady Master Nada, the Elohim Cyclopea, Pallas Athena, Lady Master Portia, Kuan Yin, and Vairochana.

Great White Brotherhood. A spiritual order of Western saints and Eastern adepts who have reunited with the Spirit of the living God through the ritual of the ascension and who comprise the heavenly hosts. They have transcended the cycles of karma and rebirth and ascended into that higher Reality, which is the eternal abode of the soul. The word "white" refers not to race but to the aura of white light surrounding their forms. The ascended masters of the Great White Brotherhood, united for the highest purposes of the brotherhood of man under the Fatherhood of God, have risen in every age from every culture and religion to inspire creative achievement in education, the arts and sciences, God-government, and the abundant life through the economies of the nations. The Brotherhood also includes in its ranks certain unascended chelas of the ascended masters. Jesus Christ revealed this heavenly order of saints "robed in white" to his servant John in Revelation. (Rev. 3:4, 5; 6:11; 7:9, 13, 14; 19:14)

Karmic Board. See Great Karmic Board.

Keepers of the Flame. Members of the Keepers of the Flame Fraternity, founded in 1961 by Saint Germain. This is a nondenominational spiritual order of men and women of goodwill who pledge to keep the flame of life on behalf of themselves and earth's evolutions. The fraternity warmly welcomes spiritual seekers from all religions, and members are encouraged to practice their religion or faith as they see fit. Keepers of the Flame receive graded lessons in cosmic law dictated by the ascended masters to their messengers Mark L. Prophet and Elizabeth Clare Prophet. (See KeepersOfTheFlame.org.)

Lemuria, or Mu. The lost continent of the Pacific, which, according to the findings of James Churchward, archaeologist and author of *The Lost Continent of Mu,* extended from north of Hawaii three thousand miles, south to Easter Island and the Fijis, and was made up of three areas of land stretching more than five thousand miles from east to west. Churchward's history of the ancient Motherland is based on records inscribed on sacred tablets he claims to have discovered in India. With the help of the high priest of an Indian temple, he deciphered the tablets. During fifty years of research, he confirmed their contents in further writings, inscriptions, and legends he came upon in Southeast Asia, in the Yucatan, Central America, the Pacific islands, Mexico, North America, ancient Egypt, and other civilizations. He estimates that Mu was destroyed approximately twelve thousand years ago by the collapse of the gas chambers that upheld the continent. The history of Lemuria is also told by W. Scott-Elliot in *The Story of Atlantis and the Lost Lemuria,* based on clairvoyant readings by students of Theosophy who were trained by the adepts El Morya and Kuthumi, and anthropological discoveries.

Logos. The universal consciousness of God that went forth as the Word, which God used to fire the pattern of his divine identity in his sons and daughters and to write his laws in their inward parts. The individual Christ is the fulfillment of this Word, this Logos, in the individed duality.

Lords of Karma. See Great Karmic Board.

Martian perversions. The ascended masters teach that Mars in its true state is the planet that represents the Divine Mother and the base-of-the-spine chakra. Long ago, the evolutions of Mars took that pure white light of the Mother and perverted it in war and misuses of the sacred fire. Through the misuse of free will and the base-of-the-spine chakra, they perverted the Mother light in what we call the "Martian misqualifications." These misqualifications can manifest through any of the chakras but specifically relate to the misuse of the Mother light in the base-of-the-spine chakra. They include aggression, anger, arrogance, argumentation, accusation, agitation, apathy, atheism, annihilation, aggravation, aggressive mental suggestion, criticism, condemnation and judgment, malicious, ignorant, sympathetic and delicious animal magnetism, anti-Americanism, anti-Father, anti-Mother, anti-Christ and anti-Holy Spirit manifestations in the four quadrants of Matter.

Mother of the World. The highest representative of the feminine ray on earth is she who attains to the Office of Mother of the World, or the World Mother. The one selected by the Lords of Karma and the Lord of the World as the representative of the World Mother to the earth wears the crown of the World Mother—a crown of twelve stars—and holds her scepter of authority, keeping the flame of the immaculate concept on behalf of all evolving upon the earth. "And there appeared a great wonder in heaven; a woman clothed with the sun, and the moon under her feet, and upon her head a crown of twelve stars." (Rev. 12:1)

Real Image. The true image of God after which man (male and female) was made in the Beginning. (Gen. 1:26, 27) The Real Image is the likeness of God, the Christ, or light emanation of God. It is the blueprint of the true identity of the sons and daughters of God.

Ruby ray. The ruby ray is an intense and holy love that is developed through the path of sacrifice, surrender, selflessness, and service to uplift all sentient life. The ruby ray activates the first secret ray and ultimately all five secret rays. It is the ruby fire of ultimate love that annihilates ignorance and evil.

Sangha. The spiritual family and community of the Buddha, traditionally composed of four groups: monks, nuns, laymen, and laywomen. In Buddhism the Sangha is one of the Three Jewels in which the disciple takes refuge and turns to for protection and aid. The Three Jewels are the Buddha, the Dharma, and the Sangha. The Buddha is the Enlightened One, the Dharma is the teaching of the Buddha, and the Sangha is the community of disciples.

Solar Logoi. Cosmic beings who transmit the light emanations of the Godhead flowing from Alpha and Omega in the Great Central Sun to the planetary systems. They are also called Solar Lords. The Solar Logoi maintain the tone and the sound of the Logos, or Word, that sustains the creation. We are all a part the vastness of the Solar Logoi, and they are a part of us.

Spoken Word. Also referred to as the science of the spoken Word. The release of the energies of the Word, or the Logos, through the throat chakra by the children of God in confirmation of that lost Word. It is written, "By thy words thou shalt be justified, and by thy words thou shalt be condemned." (Matt. 12:37) When man and woman reconsecrate the throat chakra in the affirmation of the Word of God, they become the instruments of God's own commandments that fulfill the law of their re-creation after the image of the Son. Forms of the spoken Word are:

Affirmation

Assertion that something exists or is true; confirmation or ratification of the truth; solemn declaration. A positive statement, usually beginning with the name of God, "I AM," that affirms and strengthens the qualities of God within oneself, helping to bring those qualities into physical manifestation. Affirmations are fiats that may be of greater length and more specific detail. They affirm the action of Truth in man—in his being, consciousness, and world. They are used alternately with denials of the reality of evil in all of its forms. Likewise, they affirm the power of Truth that challenges the activities of the fallen ones.

Call

A demand, a claim, a request or command to come or be present; an instance of asking for something; the act of summoning the LORD, or the LORD's summoning of his offspring. "And the LORD God called unto Adam, and said unto him, Where art thou?" (Gen. 3:9) "Out of Egypt have I called my son!" (Matt. 2:15) To call: *vb.* to speak in a loud or distinct voice so as to be heard at a distance; to recall from death or the astral plane, e.g., "Lazarus, come forth!"; to utter in a loud or distinct voice; to announce or read loudly or authoritatively. The call is the most direct means of communication between man and God, and God and man, frequently used in an emergency; e.g., O God, help me! Archangel Michael, take command! The byword of the initiate is "The call compels the answer." "He shall call upon me, and I will answer him." (Ps. 91:15) "They called upon the LORD, and he answered them." (Ps. 99:6)

Chant

A short, simple melody, especially one characterized by single notes to which an indefinite number of syllables are intoned, used in singing the psalms, canticles, etc., in a church service. In both East and West, the name of God is chanted over and over again in the ritual of atonement whereby the soul of man becomes one with the Spirit of God by intonation of the sound of his name. This is given in Sanskrit as AUM or AUM TAT SAT AUM and in English as I AM THAT I AM. By sounding the name of God or that of a member of the heavenly hosts, the vibration of the being is simulated and thereby Being itself is drawn to the one chanting. Therefore chants, when properly used, magnetize the Presence, whether universal or individualized, of the Divine Consciousness.

Decree

The decree is the most powerful of all applications to the Godhead. It is the command of the son or daughter of God made in the name of the I AM Presence and the Christ for the will of the Almighty to come into manifestation as Above, so below. It is the means whereby the kingdom of God becomes a reality here and now through the power of the spoken Word. It may be short or long and usually is marked by a formal preamble and a closing, or acceptance.

Fiat

An authoritative decree, sanction, order; a pronouncement; a short dynamic invocation or decree usually using the name of God, I AM, as the first word of the fiat, e.g., I AM the Way! I AM the Truth! I AM the Resurrection and the Life! Fiats are always exclamations of Christ-power, Christ-wisdom, and Christ-love consciously affirmed and accepted in the here and now.

Invocation

A form of prayer invoking God's presence; any petitioning or supplication for help or protection said especially at the beginning of a public ceremony; a call to God or to beings who have become one with God to release power, wisdom, and love to mankind or to intercede in their behalf; supplication for the flow of light, energy, peace, and harmony to come into manifestation on earth as it is in heaven.

Mantra

A mystical formula, often in Sanskrit, to be recited or sung for the purpose of intensifying the action of the Spirit of God in man. A form of prayer consisting of a word or a group of words that is chanted over and over again to magnetize a particular aspect of the Deity or of a being who has actualized that aspect of the Deity.

Prayer

A devout petition to God; a spiritual communion with God as in supplication, thanksgiving, adoration, or confession; a formula or sequence of words used in or appointed for praying: the Lord's Prayer, the Hail Mary.

Suicide entity. An "entity" is defined as "an independent, separate, or self-contained existence." "Discarnate entities" (or disembodied spirits, as they are commonly referred to) are made up of the personality consciousness as it expresses through the astral, mental, or etheric bodies of lifestreams who have passed through the change called death. The name of the suicide entity is Annihla, a she-devil luring her victims by her lust for death and for the light essence of her victims released in death. This entity projects feelings of depression, worthlessness, hopelessness, and utter frustration with life into the subconscious minds of those whose consciousness is open to this type of suggestion. When these feelings surface to the mental and feeling bodies, they influence the victim to accept a philosophy of nihilism, of his own nonexistence. Intense calls must be made to bind the suicide entity that may be preying upon an individual.

Sun behind the sun. The spiritual cause behind the physical effect we see as our own physical sun and all other stars and star systems, seen or unseen, including the Great Central Sun. The Sun behind the sun of cosmos is perceived as the Cosmic Christ—the Word by whom the formless was endowed with form and spiritual worlds were draped with physicality. Likewise, the Sun behind the sun is the Son of God in the Christ Self, shining in all his splendor behind the soul and its interpenetrating sheaths of consciousness called the four lower bodies. It is the Son of man—the "Sun" of every manifestation of God. The Sun behind the sun is referred to as the "Sun of righteousness" (Mal. 4:2), which does heal the mind, illumine the soul, and light all her house and as "the glory of God," the light of the City Foursquare.

Threefold flame. The flame of the Christ that is the spark of life anchored within the heart of the sons and daughters of God. It is the sacred trinity of love, wisdom, and power that is literally a spark of sacred fire from God's own heart. It is the soul's point of contact with the supreme Source of all life. It is also referred to as the flame of liberty.

Twin flames. The origin of your identity is in the white sphere that is Almighty God. Out of this white sphere, twin flames are born. The whirling action of the mighty sphere of life produces the polarity that becomes the plus and the minus of twin flames. These two souls, each making up half of the whole, have the same electronic pattern or blueprint, which is not duplicated anywhere in cosmos. Twin flames are intended to be the totality of the Father-Mother God in expression. Soul mates on the other hand are complementary souls who are working out a polarity of manifestation in one of the planes of consciousness. Their tie is for a particular mastery in time and space, whereas the ultimate union is with one's twin flame. The energies that twin flames share are the energies of God, and when these energies are consecrated to the glorification of the Real Self and of Reality, we find that joy and bliss and expansion of consciousness and creativity follow them wherever they go.

Universities of the Spirit. Spiritual classes are held in the etheric retreats where souls receive instruction and guidance from members of the cosmic hierarchy. At the universities of the Spirit, students can visit each one of the seven chohans of the rays for fourteen consecutive days and then go on to study with the Maha Chohan, who is the director of the seven chohans of the rays. In this way, students receive step-by-step instruction on the rays, which enables them to increase their self-mastery. While studying at the retreats, souls also prepare to more efficiently balance their personal karma in daily life.

Violet flame. The seventh ray aspect of the Holy Spirit. The violet flame is the sacred fire that transmutes the cause, effect, record, and memory of sin, or negative karma. It is also called the flame of transmutation, of freedom, and of forgiveness. The violet flame is more than violet light. It is an invisible spiritual energy that appears violet to those who have developed their spiritual vision. In previous centuries, knowledge of the violet flame was given only to a chosen few who had proven themselves worthy. Saints and adepts of East and West have long used the violet flame to accelerate their spiritual development, but this once-secret knowledge was not revealed to the masses until the twentieth century. The violet flame has many purposes. It revitalizes and invigorates us. It can heal emotional and even physical problems, improve relationships, and make life easier. More importantly, the violet flame changes negative energy into positive energy, which makes it an effective tool for healing. Today we are learning more than ever before about how disease can be rooted in our mental, emotional, and spiritual states. By transforming negative thoughts and feelings, the violet flame provides a platform for our healing.

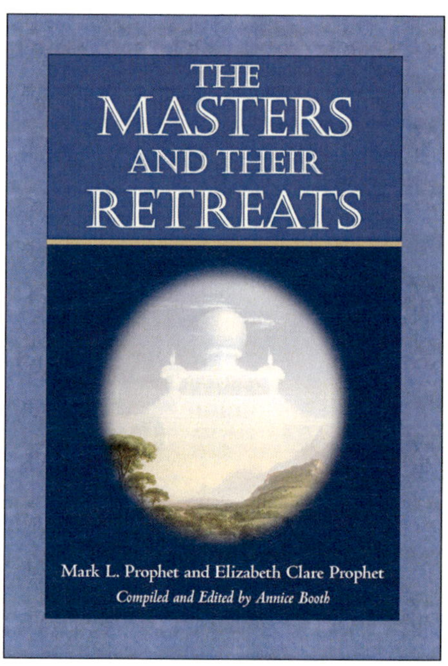

The Masters and Their Retreats

The great lights who have come out of all the world's spiritual traditions and graduated from earth's schoolroom have become widely known as Masters. They demonstrate to us that in the world of Spirit, there is no division of race, religion or philosophy—there is simply oneness, ineffable sweetness and love.

What is not so widely known is that these great Masters have retreats—temples and cities of light in the heaven world—where we can go in spiritual meditation and while our bodies sleep at night.

In this magnificent work, Mark and Elizabeth Prophet talk about these great Masters, the stories of their lives and their incredible spiritual retreats.

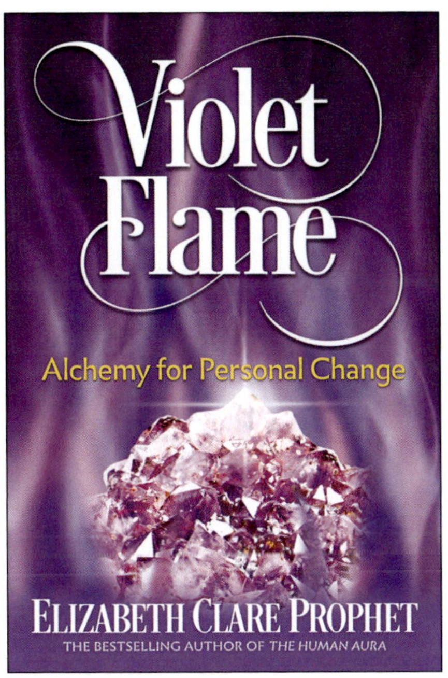

Violet Flame
Alchemy for Personal Change

For thousands of years the violet flame was a secret, experienced by mystics and known to spiritual teachers East and West who taught it only to their closest disciples. Now the violet flame is available to all!

The violet flame is a high-frequency light that you can use to change your life. It dissolves negative energy and restores it to positive energy. It is a missing key to vitality, health, and inner wholeness. This flame can transform and enrich your relationships. It can free the unlimited power that exists right within you.

World-renowned author Elizabeth Clare Prophet unlocks the mysteries of the violet flame. With penetrating insight and compassion, she explores how this flame works and gives practical techniques for using it to help resolve everyday problems. You can easily integrate the violet flame into any path you follow or simply try it by itself. The benefits and joy of the violet flame can change your life forever!

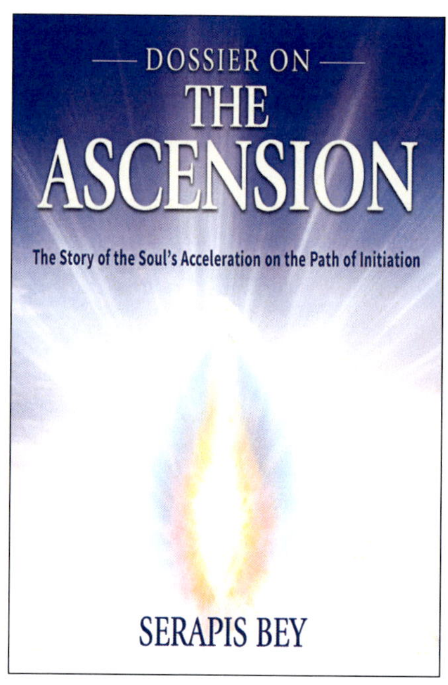

Dossier on the Ascension

The Story of the Soul's Acceleration on the Path of Initiation

Breaking the wheel of rebirth...
Union with God...
The ascension...

Throughout the ages, those of all faiths have sought to go beyond the limits of the mind, to attain immortality. History leaves the record of a few who reached that goal—Zarathustra, who ascended back to God in "the great flame"; Elijah, who was carried up into heaven in a "chariot of fire"; Jesus, who was taken up into a cloud from Bethany's hill.

Now, Serapis Bey and the Brotherhood of Luxor reveal inner secrets of the path to the ascension. They open the door to their mystery school, sharing keys to immortality. And they show how you can apply their spiritual techniques to find the answers to life's ultimate questions.

- Journey to the Central Sun through the meditations of the seraphim.
- Learn the meaning of the Deathless Solar Body as the vehicle of the soul beyond the veil.
- Find your ultimate freedom to be your Real Self.

The flame of the ascension is the key which unlocks the door to immortality for every man.
Serapis Bey

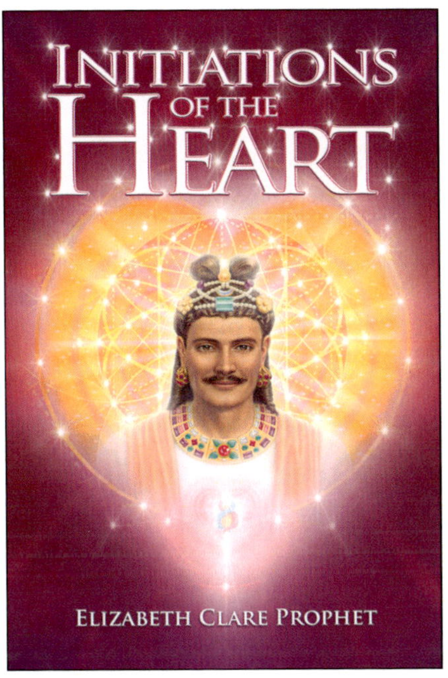

Initiations of the Heart

Teachings from the Mystery School

Did our hearts not *burn* within us . . .

The mystics have always known that the heart is the most important center of consciousness. We can gain visions through the third eye, enlightenment through the crown. But the true fount of cosmic consciousness is always the heart. How do we develop our heart—the chakra of Divine Love? How can we increase the fire of the heart? How can we expand the threefold flame, the very source of Life within us?

Within *Initiations of the Heart,* the ascended masters reveal the mysteries of the heart. Most importantly, as we enter into their Word, each one offers a transfer of light—a unique initiation of the heart.

The apostles felt the fire of the heart in their encounter with the risen Christ on the road to Emmaus. May you also experience that fire through your encounter with the masters in this age.

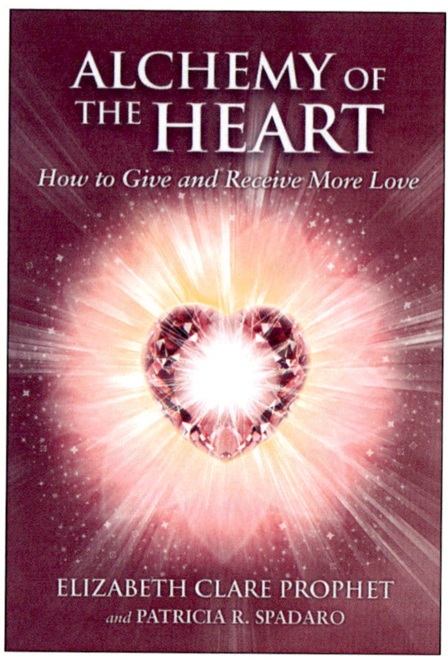

Alchemy of the Heart

How to Give and Receive More Love

Finding a higher love

These sensitive, profound and rare insights help us gain entrée into the most precious, and misunderstood, component of our being—the heart. They show us that while love can be compassionate and nurturing, it can also be powerful, dynamic and practical—a catalyst for spiritual growth.

You'll learn how the mature heart overcomes hidden blocks to giving and receiving more love. How you can soften and strengthen the heart to create more meaningful relationships in all areas of your life. And how even the most intense lessons of love, if we are willing to learn from them, can be the open door to a higher love—and a higher way of loving.

About The Summit Lighthouse

The Summit Lighthouse is an internationally recognized spiritual center for the advancement of inner awakening. Our international organization is a global family that is inspired, guided, and sponsored by those known as the ascended masters.

The ascended masters are the most beloved and trusted transcendent beings guiding our planet's material and spiritual evolution. Most of the world's religions are currently based on the revelations of one or more of these masters before their ascension. We openly embrace spiritual seekers from all paths of light including the mystical traditions of the world's religions.

The ascended masters and their messengers have given us over fifteen thousand hours of invaluable inner wisdom and insightful instruction, and they have provided the means for our direct initiation into higher consciousness.

For the ascended masters . . . no subject is off-limits! Their teachings contain amazing truths and awesome answers on spirituality, alchemy, astrology, sacred geometry, spiritual science, karma, reincarnation, ascension, archangels (and fallen angels), and even those issues that are considered taboo or "out of this world."

Primary Goals of the Teachings of the Ascended Masters

The ascended masters challenge us daily to be bold, to dare to be who we truly are, and to face adversity with courage, patience, perseverance, honesty, integrity, inner love, discipline, and discernment—all for a greater sense of inner peace, fearlessness, stillness and silence, harmony, self-mastery, compassion, and wisdom.

These teachings help our souls get back to the origin of their individualized inner source of True Self-Love—the Higher Self, or I AM Presence. Our point of contact with our Higher Self is the "Spark of Life" or "Sacred Fire of the Heart," the place where our consciousness expresses its true divine nature of unconditional love and happiness, universal oneness, and an authentic desire to serve others.

How Our Teachings Came into Being

Our teachings were all released through highly trained and trusted messengers, Mark L. Prophet and Elizabeth Clare Prophet. Mark was contacted by the ascended master El Morya at the age of eighteen and received training from him for many years before he was instructed to establish The Summit Lighthouse in 1958 in Washington, D.C.

With his ascension in 1973, Mark passed the torch for the mission to his gifted wife, Elizabeth Clare Prophet, who continued her service until her retirement in 1999.

The dictations of the ascended masters were regularly given in public. The ascended masters also inspired thousands of lectures delivered by the messengers. The content of the dictations are, by most human standards, beyond the mind's ability to construct in real time. They carry very powerful frequencies of light, awakening us to the highest truths we've ever experienced.

We leave it up to you to decide their value for yourself.

Moving toward Your Victory

No matter what path of light you are on, spiritual freedom is attained using tools that have been passed down in wisdom teachings through the millennia: meditation, selfless service, devotional music, prayer, mantra, and the science of the spoken Word. The masters bring an accelerated understanding of these principles, especially suited for the challenges of the modern world, including dynamic decree work and the use of the violet flame.

Next Steps

We are genuinely excited to meet you on the Path and hope you are too. We extend a warm welcome from everyone at The Summit Lighthouse, and we invite you to explore the teachings of the ascended masters at **SummitLighthouse.org.** Check out our free online lessons and hundreds of articles on a wide range of spiritual subjects. Browse through our online bookstore. And if you would rather talk to someone in person, please feel free to contact us today!

The Summit Lighthouse®
63 Summit Way, Gardiner, Montana 59030 USA

1-800-245-5445 / 406-848-9500
Se habla español.

info@SummitUniversityPress.com
SummitLighthouse.org